10925
11/11
Phil.

10.

Hypothesis and the Spiral of Reflection

SUNY Series in Systematic Philosophy
Robert Cummings Neville, Editor

Whether systematic philosophies are intended as true pictures of the world, as hypotheses, as the dialectic of history, or as heuristic devices for relating rationally to a multitude of things, they each constitute articulated ways by which experience can be ordered, and as such they are contributions to culture. One does not have to choose between Plato and Aristotle to appreciate that Western civilization is enriched by the Platonic as well as Aristotelian ways of seeing things.

The term "systematic philosophy" can be applied to any philosophical enterprise that functions with a perspective from which everything can be addressed. Sometimes this takes the form of an attempt to spell out the basic features of things in a system. Other times it means the examination of a limited subject from the many angles of a context formed by a systematic perspective. In either case systematic philosophy takes explicit or implicit responsibility for the assessment of its unifying perspective and for what is seen from it. The styles of philosophy according to which systematic philosophy can be practiced are as diverse as the achievements of the great philosophers in history, and doubtless new styles are needed for our time.

Yet systematic philosophy has not been a popular approach during this century of philosophical professionalism. It is the purpose of this series to stimulate and publish new systematic works employing the techniques and advances in philosophical reflection made during this century. The series is committed to no philosophical school or doctrine, nor to any limited style of systematic thinking. Whether the systematic achievements of previous centuries can be equalled in the 20th century depends on the emergence of forms of systematic philosophy appropriate to our times. The current resurgence of interest in the project deserves the cultivation it may receive from the SUNY Series in Systematic Philosophy.

Hypothesis and the Spiral of Reflection

David Weissman

State University of New York Press

Published by
State University of New York Press, Albany

For information, address State University of New York
Press, State University Plaza, Albany, N.Y., 12246

Library of Congress Cataloging-in-Publication Data

Weissman, David, 1936-
  Hypothesis and the spiral of reflection / David Weissman.
    p.   cm.–(SUNY series in systematic philosophy)
  Bibliography: p.
  Includes index.
  ISBN 0-7914-0130-8.–ISBN 0-7914-0131-6 (pbk.)
  1. Metaphysics. 2. Hypothesis. I. Title. II. Series.
  BD111.W38   1989   88-37049
  110–dc19   CIP

10 9 8 7 6 5 4 3 2 1

For Kathy

Contents

Contents

Acknowledgments

The Research Foundation of the City University of New York helped support me as I wrote this book. I am grateful to Marshall Spector for his careful reading of the manuscript, and to my family for their patience.

Occasional paragraphs and pages of this book are reprinted, with permission of the publishers, from several of my papers. They are: "Values and Intentions: Does Consciousness Matter?" in *Studies in the Philosophy of J. N. Findlay*, edited by R. Cohen, R. Martin and M. Westphal, Albany: State University of New York Press, 1985; "The Spiral of Reflection," in *New Essays in Metaphysics*, edited by R. Neville, Albany: State University of New York Press, 1986; "First Considerations," in *Creativity and Common Sense*, edited by T. Krettek, Albany: State University of New York Press, 1987; and "Metaphysics after Pragmatism," *Review of Metaphysics*, Vol. XLII, No. 3, March, 1989.

Introduction

Philosophy is always many things. There are its disparate subject matters or problems, and what seem to be various methods for investigating or solving them. I suggest that this appearance is deceiving, and that our choice of methods reduces to these two: We inspect the things set before us when they have been given to or constructed by our minds; or we use thoughts or words as signs, creating thereby the plans and hypotheses representing possible states of affairs. The first of these methods, called *intuitionism,* is described in the predecessor to this book, *Intuition and Ideality.*[1] This current book describes the alternative, hypothetical method, especially as it applies to metaphysics.

Metaphysics in our time is dominated by the prescriptivist style of intuitionist thinking.[2] Prescriptivism supposes that mind creates a thinkable given by projecting form onto phenomena of some kind, in the way that Kant described the schematizing of sensory data by the categories of understanding. The forms prescribed are alleged to be intelligible in themselves, as theories and the rules of ordinary language are entertained before being applied; or forms are uninspectable until used to differentiate and organize the matters at issue, thereby making them thinkable.

One program for metaphysics starts here, in the assumption that the world's categorial features are determined by the language used for thinking it. Notice the ambiguity: Is it the grammatical forms of a language or its existence claims that are decisive when we use the language for creating a thinkable world? The emphasis on language develops in both these ways.

On one side are prescriptivists who restrict themselves to the formal apparatus of language, including its grammatical forms, referring expressions, and quantifiers. As Quine writes of canonical form:

> The quest of a simplest, clearest overall pattern of canonical notation is not to be distinguished from a quest of ultimate categories, a limning of the most general traits of reality. Nor let it be retorted that such constructions are conventional affairs not dictated by reality; for may not the same be said of a physical theory? True, such is the nature of reality that one physical theory will get us around better than another; but similarly for canonical notation.[3]

Quine reminds us of the variability among languages. We might suppose that languages are grammatically similar at some deep level, so that every world rendered thinkable exhibits the same categorial, i.e., grammatical, features. We could as well say that categorial features differ among worlds as there are differences of canonical form in the languages used for thinking them. Either way, i.e., as Kantians making universal claims about every language and world, or as neo-Kantian relativists, we are to agree that thinkable form in the world originates in the grammatical forms of thought and discourse.

The other way of regarding language emphasizes our sense-making, meaning-bestowing interpretations of the world:

> Language is not just one of man's possessions in the world, but on it depends the fact that man has a world at all. For man the world exists as world in a way that no other being in the world experiences. But this world is linguistic in nature. . . . Not only is the world "world" only insofar as it comes into language, but language too, has its real being only in the fact that the world is re-presented within it. Thus the original humanity of language means at the same time the fundamental linguistic quality of man's being in the world.[4]

> [I]n language the world itself presents itself. The experience of the world in language is "absolute." It transcends all the relativities of the positing of being, because it embraces all being-in-itself, in whatever relationships (relativities) it appears. The linguistic quality of our experience of the world is prior, as contrasted with everything that is recognized and addressed as being. The fundamental relation of language and world does not, then, mean that the world becomes the object of language. Rather, the object of knowledge and of statements is already enclosed within the world horizon of language.[5]

The interpretations Gadamer describes are not so much the representations of a separate place as they are the matrices wherein these "worlds" are constituted. The "structure of being" and the "structure of our experience" are, he says, founded in them.[6] Metaphysics has only to reflect upon these interpretations to know whatever categorial features are ingredient within the "worlds" they schematize.

Cultural prescriptivists are quick to seize upon language as a vehicle for creating a thinkable, teachable set of practices. Their point of reference is, however, somewhat different from that of prescriptivists captivated by language. They suppose that metaphysics is, or should be, a reflection upon the categorial assumptions distinguishing an epoch or culture. Every culture does inevitably have metaphysical assumptions, as a theocratic society makes some large claims about the character of knowledge and being. Hegel supposes that we create both reality and our place there by acting upon these general but substantive ideas:

> The spiritless formal universality which characterizes the sphere of right takes up every natural form of character as well as of existence, and sanctions and establishes them. . . . The means, then, whereby an individual gets objective validity and concrete actuality here is the formative process of culture.[7]

> That which, in reference to the single individual, appears as his culture, is the essential moment of spiritual substance as such, *viz.*: the direct transition of its ideal, thought-constituted, universality into actual reality; or otherwise put, culture is the single soul of this substance, in virtue of which the essentially inherent becomes something explicitly acknowledged, and assumes definitive objective existence.[8]

We may grant Hegel's prescriptivist claim that thought has constituted a "world," but what shall we say upon discovering that different cultures create different "worlds," so that categorial features distinguishing one of them have no currency in the others? Anthropologists might be satisfied by the information that cultures organize and understand themselves in diverse ways. Metaphysicians are not. We want to know the world's categorial form. Our inquiry is frustrated by the news that these sets of categorial features are contraries: Their claims could not all be true, though all of them could be false. Prescriptivists answer that there is no "objective" world against which to measure these views as true or false. There are only the "worlds" created by the many cultures. Still, the metaphysician persists. He wonders if all these cultures misrepresent the world.

Why does it happen that prescriptivists settle for self-justifying distortions, or worse? The answer I suggest is that prescriptivism, like intuitionisms of every sort, is both a method for acquiring knowledge and a theory of reality. As method, prescriptivist intuitionism is a reaction to the skeptical fear that reality may be inaccessible to us. There might be no possible knowledge of it. We may be lost in a world we cannot know. These intuitionists respond by demanding that mind secure its position within a "world," first by creating its own intelligibilities in language or culture, then by using them to create a thinkable experience. Our access to reality is then guaranteed, for reality is mind's own product. We make it by projecting thinkable form onto sensory data, or by using forms as rules to organize the personal and communal practices of everyday life.

What should be our starting point for learning of the world if language and culture are not the necessary points of reference? We have a firm beginning in everyday practice and the problem-solving behaviors which secure us in the world. Each of us has no choice but that of acting in circumstances we have not made. Problem-solving practice is our accommodating but controlling response to the world. Nothing else teaches us so much about our situations and ourselves. Language and culture are vital for communicating about the maps and plans directing these behaviors, though we learn to distinguish their projections and prescriptions from the matters at hand. We gladly alter these maps and plans as circumstances and our interests require.

There is nothing in these reality-testing behaviors to justify our saying that language or culture is the sufficient ground for everything rendered thinkable within experience. Those who do say it worry that our knowledge of the world is precarious unless we bridge the gap between mind and the world by displacing all of thinkable form from the world into mind. This is panic turned grandiose, though the world does not require that we create it, or even that we make it thinkable, if there are differentiations and relations, i.e., a form, intrinsic to the world. Nor do we require an *a priori* illumination of that form, by way of language or culture, if we can formulate and test hypotheses about the world. There may be only these two choices: a world having an intrinsic but discoverable form of its own; or a "world," better called "experience," which mind creates as we direct behavior, or project thinkable form onto sensory data. Language and culture are our starting points only if we believe, as I do not, that the second alternative is defensible.

The hypothetical method I favor might be generally approved; though usually with the remark that philosophers have been making hypotheses about a world independent of mind since the pre-Socratics. This estimation is partly true; but mostly false. Philosophic uses of the hypothetical method are much more rare than might be assumed. That is so, because hypotheses are fallible, though intuitionist philosophers have required that knowledge claims be certain. Hypothesis, for them is usually no more than a supplementary method, one that suggests conclusions unsuitable for knowledge until they are confirmed in the standard intuitionist way, i.e., by inspection. Phenomenalists, for example, might speculate about a dragon's scales, always assuming that anything said about them would reduce to claims about sensory differences. That emphasis is changed when hypothesis has displaced intuition, for then we suppose that seeing the scales as green is only one of the many possible natural signs of the thing perceived. There is likely to be other evidence of its character, as inferences founded in the spectroscopic analysis of fossilized dragon scales might teach us as much about dragons as seeing them would do. Here is a case where hypothesis exceeds the perceived differences on the way to speculating about their causes or grounds. We understand that hypotheses about these conditions are fallible, but we prefer these revisable inferences to the intuitionist certainties about whatever data are alleged to be inspectable. For never mind that we cannot put aside the mediating inferences and evidence so that we might have direct unmediated access to the things themselves. Hypotheses carefully formulated and tested do supply information, indeed the only detailed and reliable information, that we may have of the things inferred.

Someone who is firm in his regard for our predecessors might insist that the hypothetical method is already celebrated in these very terms by philosophers such as Whitehead. No one is more insistent that we speculate beyond the immediacies of experience on the way to telling a comprehensive story about all of reality. Whitehead is, however, a speculator with restricted aims. His hypotheses are generalized descriptions.[9] They move from a characterization of human experience to the claim that everything is a "drop of experience,"[10] or the aggregate of these drops. The speculative style I favor is explanatory and abductive, not merely descriptive. Having inferred from smoke to fire, we also use abduction to speculate about the conditions for effects of a larger scale, then to test these hypotheses by looking for the sensory evidence that would be available if the matters specified by our hypotheses did obtain. Metaphysical hypotheses, like the ones of practice and science, must be testable, because it is only these verifications that anchor our speculations, making them responsible.

Some metaphysicians reject the demand for empirical testability. Isn't this a call for the verificationism used against metaphysics fifty years ago? Why should anyone suppose that metaphysics might be renewed by a practice meant to subvert it? One good answer is that testability is the measure of applicability, hence of truth. There were, however, various considerations justifying our suspicion of verificationism. Six of them are relevant here.

First was a confusion resulting when verification was not distinguished from the demand for empirical meaning. Is talk of God problematic because claims about God may be false; or rather because of our failure to define the terms used descriptively when speaking of God by way of the sensory affects that would occur in us if there were a God? Is God reducible to these sensory data, as the truth of "There goes Spot" might require that Spot be identified with his effects upon us? Should the conditions for meaning and truth be separated so that matters of fact do not reduce to their sensory effects? Verificationists were not always careful to distinguish the requirements for meaning and truth, with the result that testability often seemed to be the expression of a dogmatic phenomenalism.

Second was an incommensurability between the units of empirical meaning and the ones of material truth. If individual terms are the units of meaning, but sentences are the units of truth, we may have sentences making claims that are not testable (we don't know what empirical difference their truth would make), though some or all their terms are empirically meaningful, e.g., "Life is a dream."

Third was the inability to formulate a verificationist rule not subject to trivialization, as every claim is testable empirically if we allow that it be extended by one or many disjuncts, e.g., "The Absolute is lazy . . . or grass is green." Why take verificationism seriously if it cannot be formulated in a way that is not easily evaded?

A fourth disincentive were those classical theories generally acknowledged as the zenith of philosophic speculation. If Plato's myths are not empirically testable, then all the worse for the demand that every passable theory be verifiable.

A *fifth* consideration emphasized the futility of compromising the authority of metaphysical ideas by making them testable. Why risk the tests that might show a theory to be false, when we can avert a decisive test while affirming the theory for some other reason, e.g., it coheres with our beliefs and values? If scientists don't mind conceding that there is no ether because of having alternative theories, we metaphysicians are not equally resourceful. Surrendering a theory refuted by the evidence may leave us with no theory at all.

The *sixth* point was relevant here. Verificationism was rejected in preference for the claim that theories are justified as we use them for making consistent sense of the world; i.e., verificationism was superseded by prescriptivism. We stopped asking for the empirical evidence testing hypotheses when prescriptivists denied that the world stands apart from theory as a control upon our speculations. "Worlds," they supposed, are the products of our thinking. They are created when the differences and relations founded within theories are projected onto sensory data, or used to organize our behaviors. The experiences thereby created could only have the character determined by these interpretations. There is no way of setting created "worlds" apart from our experience-schematizing theories, and no way of using sensory data as evidence for or against the truth of claims about a world whose character and existence are independent of theory. This realist idea had been the leading principle for inquiry. Prescriptivism made it defunct.

My emphasis upon the testability of metaphysical hypotheses is a reversion to this objectivist standard. Metaphysical claims, like the ones of practice and science, characterize or explain some aspect of the world. The states of affairs represented by hypotheses are usually distinct from their empirical affects in us, though these affects are the only evidence we have of the things represented when *a priori* illumination is discounted. Practice and science require these sensory data as the evidence for and against their hypotheses. Metaphysics appeals to the same affects as we test the accuracy of its claims. There is no domain of "special" evidence available to us. Our characterizations of the world are sometimes very general and abstract, but the data on which we rely are the same ones available to everyone else.

I shall be saying that this emphasis upon testability is appropriate to every inquiry devoted to formulating true claims about the world. There is, however, a certain embarrassment, even aversion, to the idea that metaphysics might be held to the requirements for making true statements about the world. Prescriptivism itself justifies this response; it has transformed the notion of ideas "about" something to the one of rules used for creating a product, i.e., experiences, cultures and worlds. An architect's instructions to bricklayers and carpenters are directives for building, not the representations of a house already made. A theory used prescriptively, like the drawings used by these builders, does come to be true of its product, but only because of prefiguring those differences and relations that the theory or drawings are used to create. The truth of philosophic theories has come to be understood in this revised way: not as the truth of theories representing a world that stands apart from mind, but rather as conceptualizations anticipating those "worlds" they are used to make.

There is also this other reason for doubting my view that philosophic claims might be "true of the world." Is that a plausible claim when each of the competing metaphysical theories justifies a notion of truth appropriate to itself? Where is there an idea of truth that every theory must satisfy?

Some philosophers resolve this question in an unexpected way.[11] Rather than choose among the various theories, they withdraw from first-order theorizing about the world in order to regard the many theories. Marveling at this diversity, they use a taxonomy to catalogue them. "True of the world" is, from this standpoint, the naive slogan of someone promoting his own theory without regard for alternative notions of truth. The meta-philosopher squelches this bit of vanity, first by assigning each theory its place within his classificatory system, then by affirming that there are these many "legitimate" ways of thinking metaphysically, each of them "true to the world" in its own terms. First-order thinkers testing their claims against one another and the world may believe that opposed theories should be set against one another until one of them identifies the errors of its competitors while incorporating whatever is valid in them. The meta-philosopher ignores this instinct for dialectic, or he denies that we might formulate a single theory capable of resolving the incommensurabilities of the many others. He affirms that each of the many theories is one or another expression of pure conceptual types, as Plato, Aristotle, and Democritus might be the paradigms for three distinctive sets of theories. Each of these exemplars is secure against dialectical assault and revision as it holds its place within the periodic table of metaphysical doctrines.

This meta-philosophic stance encourages us to think metaphysically without the risk of having to formulate or defend any single metaphysical claim. It is sufficient that we read and compare other people's texts, though we might wonder about the security of second-order inquiry. Perhaps the disparities among competing theories are the expression of their merely partial or badly formed ideas, as some notions of truth are not viable or even plausible. Perhaps the dialectic of opposed theories can generate a new theory, one incorporating their virtues while being applicable and adequate to all of being. Meta-philosophers also assume the possibility of this comprehensive, and finally unchallengeable, representation, e.g., as they compare Aristotle to Plato, or Spinoza to Hume. Always affirming the accuracy of their textual claims, they presuppose a correspondence notion of truth. First-order thinkers must always compete, though we are to believe that second-order observers describe the texts as they are while discovering the one rubric that fits all of them because of accurately representing their essential structures and differences. These first-order theories are, presumably, part of the larger world. A single true representation of them implies that there might be a single, applicable, and adequate representation for all the world. Or should we suppose that meta-philosophy must dissolve into contention as meta-philosophers disagree about the elementary forms of the first-order theories before them?

Second-order thinkers do not usually acknowledge that their claims are vulnerable to alternative, mutually exclusive formulations. There is instead the intimation that we escape this quandry by moving from first-order theorizing to second-order transcendental reflection. That standpoint is thought to guarantee an unobstructed, undistorted view of first-order styles of thinking. Why should second-order reflection be exempt from the disagreements of first-order thinking? For a reason implicit in Descartes' claim that nothing is better known to mind than mind itself.[12]

Consider the gap between mind and the world, and the implication that minds using theory to address the world cannot confirm that any particular theory is true of it. We eliminate the distance between speculating mind and the world by saying that theories are used prescriptively so that any "world" is only the product created when the differences and relations within a theory are projected onto sensory data. We solve the problem of knowing a remote and alien world by creating, within mind, an experience and "world" that are immediately accessible.

There are, however, the incommensurable theories and anomalous "worlds." Do we pay for solving the one problem by creating a Babel of theories, and a diversity of "worlds" inaccessible to anyone not using the proper theory for schematizing it? No, we merely rise to the second-order perspective, for there, still within mind, we survey the many theories as they stand directly before the thinking mind's eye. There is nothing here to duplicate the speculative quality of theories addressed to a world unavailable for inspection. Theories are the mind's own products. They may be arrayed before us and accurately perceived. Discerning their essential structures and the differences among them, we may organize the many theories in ways that exhibit these distinguishing features. We are reminded of Carnap's fascination with conceptual frameworks. Questions about a "world," he says, are "internal" to a framework. Questions about the world-in-itself, as distinct from questions about the theory used for thinking it, are meaningless.[13] Where theories are formulas for prescriptivist world-making, we are to savor the catalogue of possible theories as we might read a book of recipes.

There is no reason for submitting to meta-philosophy and its skepticism about our knowledge of the world if we can support these other claims: (1) that metaphysical theories may engage one another dialectically to the point where criticisms lodged from the perspective of any one force revisions in its competitors; (2) that revision may enable one theory to incorporate the strengths of its competitors, as a theory of matter may provide for considerations once thought to be unassimilable when theories about static matter were opposed to theories about ephemeral events; (3) that every creditable theory be tested empirically for the sensible differences that would be available if the matters of fact alleged by the theory did obtain. Second-order comparison and taxonomy are, I suggest, an intuitionist substitute for the first-order activity of formulating, testing, revising, and defending a theory that is applicable and adequate to the world. Comparing texts has its uses and pleasures, but this is no substitute for making and testing hypotheses about a world whose existence and character are independent of our claims about it.

The naivete of my realism may also be challenged in this other way. I suppose that metaphysics, like science, wants the best explanation for the matter at issue. Arguing abductively, we infer from something observed or implied by theory to its conditions. These conditions may include a thing's constituents, its causes, or constraining laws. "Best" explanations cohere with accepted hypotheses while specifying alleged conditions in ways more economical, systematic, or fruitful than those of competitors. Even these "best" explanations are revised under the pressure of new evidence and the revisions of previously accepted hypotheses. Never settling for this relative "best," we formulate successive proposals intending that each one should approximate more accurately to the real character of things. Progress is irregular. We come to be preoccupied by expressive style rather than truth, or truth is our aim, but we are captivated by distorted or mistaken hypotheses. We recover, because of having dialectic and experiment to correct these errors. Knowledge, in the form of hypotheses correctly representing the world and our place there, is the likely result.

Now the objection: Why claim that metaphysical hypotheses might be testable and "true of the world" to some approximation when this idea of truth is rejected by many philosophers of science? How could metaphysical hypotheses satisfy this standard if scientific ones never do?

Two converging assumptions justify this objection. One is the prescriptivist notion of theory: Theories, it says, are rules for interpreting, i.e., schematizing, sensory data. The other assumption concerns the idea of experiment. The familiar view is that experiments are procedures for interfering with an already formed nature in ways calculated to produce effects in us. We turn on lights in dark closets to see the things stored there. Those things were present already, fully formed. Light enables us to see, without changing them. Their primary properties were established before we turned the switch. The effects in us are their secondary properties. This realist notion of perception is challenged by experiments supporting quantum theory. We interpret them as evidence for saying that this part of nature does not have an already established character, one revealed to us by way of the secondary properties occurring as we interact with it. Instead, nature at this scale seems to be a determinable flux where determinate properties are generated as participant observers engage it. This revised notion of experiment is anticipated in the *Theatetus*. No thing, says Plato, "has any being just by itself" but only in its interaction with a perceiver, so that "all arise in all their variety as a result of their motion."[14] Plato was writing of the whiteness produced in the "thing" perceived and in the eye as motions originating separately in these two are mutually engaged, then diverted back to their origins. We may want to embellish this account, saying that all of nature's properties are undecided until mind is joined to nature, in thought or perception. Their character would be determined by the features for which we test, and by the manner of our testing.

This notion of experiment subverts the assumption that nature has a character of its own irrespective of our relations to it. We also have this convergence: Scientific experiment is said to engage nature in ways creating determinate properties or states of affairs, while scientific theory creates "worlds" by schematizing sensory data. We may combine these claims, saying that experiment creates the differences anticipated by theory. This explanation does fall short of saying that theory and experiment create whatever states of affairs are desired for personal or social reasons, but only this additional claim would be more generous testimony to mind's powers for world-making. It should no longer be plausible, or even respectable, to insist (as I believe) that the existence and character of things are independent of our thinking, talking, and acting. Before, practice and experiment were thought to be ways of circumventing idealist strictures: We could turn on lights to see things as they are, or (at worst) as they appear under this condition. Now that route to information about an independent world is to be denied us. Doing, as much as thinking, is to be a kind of making. Experiment, like theory, is to be the exercise of idealist world-making.

How shall we appraise this result? There are several points to consider. *First,* this altered notion of experiment is incomplete. It ignores the fact that experiment does not create things in a void. Nature must have some established features before we can mount the experiments producing determinate effects in determinable contexts. Plato agreed. He denied that the flux might have no decided character. He wrote of every coupling of percept and thing perceived, saying that they are "things that would never have come into existence if either of the two had approached anything else."[15] There is, he implies, some established if determinable feature of nature conditioning whatever effect is generated when experiment engages us within nature. Theory may specify that determinable feature without regard to any particular determination, as we might suppose that time has properties which are determinable and undetermined, whenever it is unobserved. We could experiment for evidence of this property, but always at the cost of giving it some particular determinate expression. *Second,* this notion of experiment is applicable, principally, to quanta. It does have some other applications, as testing children is often a way of teaching them, so that testing is a way of giving more determinate expression to a determinable capacity.

11

However, most of the properties for which we test are not altered by our tests, as there are no paired ways of looking that precipitate determinability into a silk purse or a sow's ear. Reality is one, the other or neither. *Third,* we uncouple this radical notion of experiment from the prescriptivist claim that theories are rules used for schematizing experience. The prescriptivist view is rejected for its intuitionist origins and idealist motives, even as we agree that nature's character may be uncertain within some domains: In them, nature may be a flux constrained by specific but determinable properties, or it may be fully formed, i.e., determinate, in every respect. Hypotheses, in practice, science and metaphysics, may represent states of affairs independent of themselves whether we regard nature in one way or the other. The experiments used to test these hypotheses do not usually create determinations in otherwise determinable contexts (as testing the claim that mind is the activity of a physical system does not create this state of affairs). Other times, the scale and dynamics of our intervention may precipitate the determinate expression of some determinable (as might happen if we were to test a hypothesis about space by interpreting a quantum physicist's experiments for evidence that space is continuous or corpuscular). The experiment might create one effect or the other, and we might use this result as evidence for our claims about the conditioning, determinable character of space. Experiments of both sorts may provide evidence for hypotheses about some aspect of nature that we have not made, not in theory or experiment. We are not compelled to be idealists. There is an alternative to the prospect of reality-creating experiments coupled to world-creating theories.

This book is an argument for using hypothetical method to discover the categorial aspects of a world we do not make. This appeal to method does not imply that there might be a set of rules applied mechanically as we generate one or a succession of particular hypotheses, in practice, science, or metaphysics. Hypothetical method is satisfied if we formulate, test, revise, and defend our claims, irrespective of their particular content. All of the claims made here should be testable in this way. There is, however, this difference among the substantive claims of the book. Some of them, especially in the first chapter, are examples only. I believe that these claims are true, but that is incidental to the contexts where the examples are used. Other examples would have done as well. Metaphysical claims of the other sort explicate the hypothetical method as it serves the interests of practice and knowledge. These other hypotheses are essential to my claims about method. Hypotheses introduced as examples are amplified and defended to the degree required by their context. Metaphysical claims decisive for hypothetical method are elaborated to whatever degree is required for defending them.

This assortment of examples and claims is not, and is not meant to be, a comprehensive metaphysical theory. This is a book about method and its metaphysical applications. It also proposes a set of tasks for metaphysics, and an orienting metaphor to suggest their order and relations. There is, however, no systematic theory present and argued here. I believe that our world is the instantiation of one among the many possible worlds, and that its principal components are the nested, overlapping, and sometimes independent homeostatic systems I call *stabilities*. This is the skeleton of a comprehensive theory, not that whole story. I sometimes appeal to these ideas for essential support as regards the conditions for inquiry. It is metaphysical inquiry, however, not a particular systematic theory, that concerns me here.

My emphasis upon inquiry is meant to encourage one long-term effect: Metaphysical practice needs redirection. Metaphysicians who study the structures and presuppositions of conceptual systems, or the "transcendental" character of mind and its activities should imitate practice and science as they learn about nature and our place within it. These philosophers have despaired too soon about the prospects for metaphysical inquiry. Retreating into prescriptivism, or the role of underlaborer, we ignore Peirce's directives for inquiry. He distinguished four ways of fixing belief: tenacity, authority, *a priori* illumination, and hypothesis (especially abduction).[16] Philosophy, he suggested, too often devotes itself to merely "logical," conceptual data, because of its concerns for certainty, clarity, and order. Too many of us exemplify his point: We dwell endlessly upon the structure and details of conceptual systems, while having nothing to say of the world itself. A priorists reply in the familiar prescriptivist way: There is no world apart from the one or many created when theories are used to schematize sensory data or for organizing behavior. Rejecting this idealist claim exposes us to all the errors of partial and mistaken hypotheses. We cannot avoid these risks. We might as well embrace them. Doing that joins us to the other inquirers, in practice and science, who describe or explain some things not created by their representations.

This is the progression from certainty about the matters standing before our minds to risk and error about all the things known by way of signs, including the natural signs of perception and the conventional ones of language. Peirce encouraged this leap. My book amplifies his claim. It surveys the tasks to be performed as we relinquish the preoccupation with mind and its products for testable characterizations of nature and our place within it.

13

What are the metaphysical topics provoking inquiry? Here is a short list of concerns for which we provide hypotheses. First is the task of discovering nature's categorial form. We want to know the elementary, because generic, properties of the things comprising our world. There should also be, complementary to this inventory of least differences, a blueprint of nature. Like the architect's drawing, this blueprint should represent the aggregated or configured shape of things. This first task for metaphysics requires that we look beyond ourselves while asking about nature's pervasive features. The second task directs us the other way, to our singularity and circumstances. What is our character, and place within nature? Is there a special significance, a "meaning", to what we are and do? The third task for metaphysics requires that we look beyond ourselves, and all the rest of nature too. We need to tell whether nature is self-sufficient or conditioned. Does some aspect of nature, or nature altogether, presuppose a condition or conditions distinct from nature, e.g., as possible worlds are alleged to be conditions distinct from it? Fourth and last is this consideration. With representative claims about nature and its conditions before us, we ask of being in itself. Is there a single way to be, or are there several, complementary modes of being? This fourth task is elusive, for how shall we specify the being common to everything, or common to all the instances of one mode, when we usually ignore being in itself in order to differentiate the things having it, e.g., dogs from cats.

Elucidating these four questions while describing the method to be used for answering them is the motive for all of this book. The demise of intuitionism, with its grandiose but crippled psychocentric ontology,[17] clears the way for a different notion of reality. With hypothesis as our method, we extend our testable claims about the world to all the domains closed to us when we suppose that nothing can be real if it is not inspectable.

This book, as the sequel to *Intuition and Ideality*, is sometimes dominated by the need for sharpening the differences between the hypothetical and intuitionist methods. The degree of that concern varies among the chapters. Chapter 1 introduces the program for metaphysical inquiry. Chapter 2 is a précis of intuitionist claims about method and reality. Chapters 3 and 4 describe hypothetical method, with special regard for its metaphysical applications and aims. Chapters 5 and 6 describe, respectively, hypothetical method's ontological and psychological presuppositions. Chapter 7 compares the hypothetical method to intuitionism, marking its advantages. It also affirms that there is no third method superior to these two: We must choose between them. Chapter 8 recapitulates the first pages of Chapter 1. It reaffirms my claim that the values and interests provoking inquiry may be set apart from claims about matters of fact. This book is, through all these proposals and arguments, a wager that minds locked away in bony skulls can use mediating signs on the way to knowing the world and themselves.

My frequent references to the themes of *Intuition and Ideality* are matched, sometimes, by the use of ideas about ontology, meaning and truth drawn from another book, my *Eternal Possibilities*.[18] Those ideas are sometimes obscure without the support of that book's arguments, though most of their applications here are detailed to whatever extent is useful in the context of this book. No one requires familiarity with those preceding books as a condition for following the arguments here.

There are three points still to mention: one substantive, another organizational, and the third semantic.

The material question concerns the purity of my own anti-intuitionist views. I propose that we reject the image of mind as a theater, and the method requiring that we scan the things set before us on stage or screen. Reality is not reducible to these things inspected, so that knowledge of the world could never result merely from surveying them. No one ever inspects anything in this way, all our experience looking at books, sunsets and paintings notwithstanding. There is no mind's eye, while eyes and ears do not see and hear merely by entertaining the data presented within our "phenomenal fields." Compare these assumptions to my claim that knowledge is acquired as we formulate and test hypotheses. Knowledge of the world is mediated by the thoughts and sentences construed as representations, and used hypothetically. These thoughts and sentences are, I allege, conventional signs of the things they represent. Shouldn't I admit that the signs themselves stand before our inspecting minds?

This way of formulating the question implies its own limitation: We are to suppose that signs cannot be used if they are not inspected. That is plainly false to many occasions when signs are used. We talk quickly and long, never once "entertaining" any one of the words or sentences we utter. Most of our unverbalized thinking, including the deepest thinking, carries on without the benefit of pictures or even chance fragments of visual imagery. These two examples are ample justification for saying that mediating signs do not commit us to the intuitionist metaphor of mind as a theater.

Perception is the one conspicuous reason for loyalty to this metaphor. We do look at pictures, faces, and pages, seeming to scan things located within the visual field. The words we read seem to be present here within this field. Let us concede that people do regularly inspect one another and their surroundings. We do read books. It is the metaphor of mind as a theater, and the complementary one of things inspectable there which I reject. How shall we explain the contrary appearance that we do have inspectable contents "within (or before) our minds." I cannot explain it, though several points qualify this admission. First, no one else can explain it. Second, no brain can behave in the way that intuitionists require of our minds. Third, we do have some preliminary ideas about the hierarchical organization of neural activity, and the fact that some neural activities are monitored by concurrent neural activities. Information of this sort may suggest an explanation for the experience, which so dominates our interpretations of mental life. Intuitionism could not be dislodged when the idea of mind as a theater seemed unproblematic to the point of self-evidence, while no other interpretation was forthcoming. The mere fact of having information and ideas for a different explanation liberates us from having to affirm that mind is the luminous ampitheater where ideas and percepts are presented and seen. The many uses of signs requiring no concession to this model, e.g., talking and thinking, are reason enough for saying that the use of signs does not commit us in any way to this intuitionist story.

Organization of the sections and subsections within the chapters below is indicated by number and letter headings, and section titles. This style may seem unnecessarily didactic. I use it, because these headings are a way of indicating the order and importance of the various claims; and because readers unconvinced by one or another section can appraise its value for the argument at large from the heading.

One semantic ambiguity is significant for the claims I shall be making. *Hypothesis* may be used as a noun or as a verb. I use the word, as a noun, to signify a well-formed thought or sentence as it represents a possible state of affairs. As an act, hypothesis is the inference, i.e., the speculation, that some possibility does obtain. I am especially concerned that we acknowledge this overreaching aspect of our thinking. *Hypothesis* is used more often here as a noun. Where the verb is required, I shall more often write *hypothesize* or *speculate*. Speculation is the power and freedom we recover when thought abjures the false security of thinking that any "world" captured by inspecting mind could be big enough to threaten or secure us. Poetry, fiction, and art may sometimes seem to justify the narrowing of aesthetic attention, and this metaphorical notion of "world." Practice, science, and metaphysics never do. Each of them requires that understanding should surpass sensibility on the way to locating us within a world that stands clear of our every way of representing it. Hypotheses are the signs with which we speculate about the world's character and our own.

16

1

The Spiral of Reflection

Many philosophers describe themselves as "metaphysicians," but what is that word meant to signify? Can we identify tasks and a method that might be accepted all around as metaphysical? This first chapter speaks to that unsettled question. It makes some provisional but firm declarations about the character and pursuit of metaphysical inquiry.

I suppose that thought moves in a spiral, turning from the plans and projects of everyday life through scientific hypotheses and theories to the speculations of metaphysics. Why describe this motion as a spiral? Because our focus is steady as thought turns upon the specificities of each thinker's life, advancing from immediacy and contingency to constraining universals, from his or her singularity to all of being. Describing this spiral, and our progress back and forth along it, is meant to justify my claim that metaphysics is a reasoned extension of that speculative attitude which directs all of our thinking. For everyone, whatever his time or circumstances, may look beyond the practical urgencies of his life to ask these questions: what is our place in nature; what are nature's categorial form and conditions; what is being throughout the range of these diverse expressions?

This chapter provides for these questions by marking out successive places for them along thought's spiral. When discussion of them is done, I shall consider two neglected points: first, the intuitionist assumption that metaphysics is first, not late or last, in the order of inquiry; second, the import of philosophical history on current metaphysics.

1. Maps, Plans, and Interpretations

Consider the man set down in an unfamiliar but spacious house. He will need to pass through several rooms, looking out the windows and climbing the stairs if he is to have even a partial idea of the house's design. The metaphysician's situation is like that: he cannot hope to discover the world's character or his place there, until he has moved through and studied some parts of it. Only as we know particulars and some intermediate generalities can we speculate successfully about nature's most general differentiations and constraints.

Reflection begins as we make the plans that direct behavior. Each plan has these four aspects: (1) A succession of behaviors is prescribed; (2) A map represents the terrain where the plan is to be enacted; (3) An evaluation affirms the utility of this plan within a hierarchy of values and ends; (4) A conceptualization situates these behaviors, values, and terrain within a more or less integrated account of the world and our place there. A rain dance prescribes a sequence of behaviors. Dancers have a more or less explicit and detailed map of the stage where the dance is to be performed, together with their convictions regarding its value. They also have a theory, more or less explicit and coherent, about the relation of dancers and dancing to the God who makes rain. These four considerations are mutually enforcing. Prescribed behaviors invoke the map of the region where a plan directs us, while success in using a plan is evidence for the accuracy of the map. Values and theory help to determine the sequence of behaviors, as success in action confirms both of them.

These four aspects converge as thought-directed action engages us within the world. We act in order to live. We are successful, because our behaviors are mediated by sense-giving interpretations, by aims and regulative values, and by the maps representing those places in the world where plans are enacted. That success is misrepresented—we ignore its conditions— if we distort our account of these engagements by emphasizing one or several of these four aspects while trivializing or neglecting the rest. This distortion regularly occurs, especially as we ignore the maps required for using plans in favor of the conceptualizations used for situating us within a "meaningful" world. There are, for example, the meanings provided by talk of a holy war. Boys are urged to swarm over mine-fields without maps or other protection as evidence of their dedication to this larger view of things. Their mutilation or death is then redescribed in the terms appropriate to the idea inspiring them. We are to call it "martyrdom," thereby disguising the wounds and pain. This disregard for maps in preference to meaning-giving conceptualizations is not usually so blatant, though there

18

are many small examples of it, as when fashion is the excuse for shoes too tight for comfort. A world-view overcomes us, prescribing its values while blotting out whatever portion of reality is accurately represented by our maps.

There are, of course, some nearly irresistible motives for ignoring maps in favor of the other three considerations. We may, for example, desire a world that is everywhere familiar and congenial, a world of the sort provided by a sense-making interpretation. This assumes that our access to the world is guaranteed where all the differences and relations ascribable to the world have been prefigured within our interpretation. Though we risk an off-setting danger, when the urge for having an accessible, recognizable world makes us oblivious to evidence that the world is more alien than we imagine. Who is to say that the world does have a character and existence independent of us if we can ignore the evidence of whatever things resist our interpretation just because that evidence is unthinkable in its terms?

A second reason for ignoring maps is the force of will and conviction in someone who accepts no direction but the one fixed by his personal values. No matter then if the world resists us. We shall dominate it, seeing our values realized just because we carry on thinking and acting in ways that are sanctioned by our interpretation. Maps representing those features of the world that we have not made and cannot change are, on this telling, merely the embarrassing evidence for a lack of resolve. A third consideration is the impression made by a plan successfully executed: We have anticipated all of the obstacles, moving easily through the world on the way to achieving our aim. Perhaps, we come to think, there were no obstacles, all of them having been eradicated by a clever plan joined to our resolve in using it. Someone who always or usually succeeds in his plans might come to believe that the world is altogether malleable, taking whatever shape a well-considered plan might dictate.

Imagine now a culture affirming that strong will is a principal virtue, where anyone having it can alter circumstances in ways required by a world-view. Maps should have no separate authority. They are reduced to being the projections of desire coupled to those meaning-giving interpretations that make us intelligible to ourselves.

The view just outlined is extreme. We often resist it when the interpretations used for making life coherent have an acknowledged basis in facts that are independent of our thinking or willing. Truth is a value for us, one requiring that we interpret many of our inquiries, the practical and scientific ones especially, as procedures for testing hypotheses about the world. There are, however, as many or more occasions when vaguely specified claims about the world are joined to fantasies that express other values and desires while securing our self-esteem or advantage. It is often these myths, not the well-tested factual claims, that appease and sustain us. More often, actions performed without regard for our circumstances get us into trouble, so that successful action requires at least the complementarity of accurate maps and cultural biases. Needing shelter, we look for warm houses, not for tepees or caves. Wanting love, we think about it in the ways encouraged by romantic or puritanical fantasies. These two things, accurate maps and cogent interpretations, are the intellectual context for our choice of behaviors. They direct or contrain us as we choose among the several possible solutions for the tasks before us. The one bespeaks our place within nature, and the fact that we cannot operate effectively there if our representations are faulty. The other expresses the sense we make of ourselves and our place in nature. That interpretation is usually more than a personal statement. It is likely to express the values shared by all or many of a culture's members. It is likely, too, that an effective culture has wanted to suppress the evidence of possible conflicts between maps and interpretations by incorporating within its interpretation whatever maps are required for acting on the values it prescribes. Where pilgrimages, to Mecca, Rome, or Jerusalem, are required of the faithful, there are useful maps for getting there.

There is, nevertheless, a permanent and ineliminable conflict between maps, and value-giving, sense-making interpretations. That is so because interpretations usually overshoot the mark: they overdescribe whatever reality is represented in our well-tested maps in order to justify the values recommended. One interpretation declares that automobiles are the mark of freedom and vitality. Our maps are edited accordingly: We ignore information about the effects of carbon monoxide and automobile accidents. There is often a tension within us as we first acknowledge the real character of things, and then the interpretation requiring that we suppress this information out of respect for the values espoused by the interpretation. This conflict would be resolved, if the only values we require could be gleaned from our well-tested maps, or if there were interpretations that did not misrepresent nature, or encourage our violations of it. Neither possibility obtains. Nature tolerates a diversity of behaviors and cultures without preferring one of them. Interpretations are inevitably selective in their accounts of nature, because they distort our representations of it for the purposes of the values espoused. We rarely bring these two into perfect alignment, so that interpretations supplement, without distorting, our well-tested maps. We can enjoy a sunrise without altering it; but we cannot tell stories about the sun-god without compromising the maps of our astrophysics.

The reason for this conflict might seem to be the role of value: Interpretations are usually explicit in recommending certain values, while maps, we might think, are value-free. This cannot be right, for maps often do represent real values in nature. There are, for example, the maps of ecological systems. They may distinguish the things having value in sustaining a system from those which destroy it. The map is not a partisan for one value or the other, but it does represent them. Suppose that this point is acknowledged, for then the discrepancy between maps and interpretations might only express a conflict in the values represented or espoused, e.g., as smokers may feel the tension between opposing values when drawing a cigarette while reading the warning on its pack. Neither explanation is trivial; but neither do they suggest a still more fundamental reason for the conflict of maps and interpretations.

That issue is truth. Maps are worthless if they are not accurate to the scale desired, as equally, plans are effective because of truly representing certain of the instrumental relations obtaining in nature. Truth of this literal sort may be irrelevant, however, to the justification for affirming some interpretation. We often ask a different question of them: do they exalt us or otherwise secure us in the persuasion that we are valuable? Are we, perhaps, made "in God's image"? We may be powerfully affected by believing that this claim is true, though we may have no evidence for it. Indeed, we hardly know what this metaphor signifies when we have negative theology affirming that God is unthinkably different from us. Here is an example where the truth ascribed to an interpretation is best understood in the terms of William James's "Will to Believe," where the truth of an opinion reduces to the persuasion that a favorable difference is made to our conduct or feelings when we believe it.

It is truth of the sort appropriate to maps, not wish-fulfillment, that animates the spiral of reflection. The spiral begins as we formulate the strategies that may secure us in the world. With learning and planning to substitute for instinct within us, we pay for our adaptability by having to make and test the maps and plans that direct us. Reflection moves a turn beyond this starting point as we mark the difference between these two notions of truth. One is truth as correspondence, meaning the satisfaction of a thought or sentential sign by that state of affairs which embodies whatever differences and relations are ascribed to it by the thought or sentence. The other is truth as a persuasion rooted in feeling or belief, as "our truth" may be identified with the particular moral or aesthetic discipline enjoined by a set of practices or beliefs. The life or lives expressing these virtues are, on this account, the apotheosis of truth: We create a life and "world" by organizing behavior and experience so as to realize the values prescribed.

Notice the effect of this second notion of truth on metaphysics. It becomes autobiography, or the natural history of disparate value systems.

21

It is the one as we reflect upon the articulation of our own values, and their role in shaping our lives and "worlds." It is the other as we describe and classify the many value-bestowing interpretations and the "worlds" they prefigure. Is it enough that metaphysics should restrict itself to the projects launched by the individuals or communities determined to create their congenial "life-worlds?" Everyone who schematizes his or her experience in the way prescribed by an interpretation may communicate easily with those other people who organize their experience in this way, but is this a sufficient test of our understanding, as regards the world or ourselves? I don't believe that it is, when "world-making" is a pretense inherited from the intuitionism I reject. Everyone deploring intuitionism and especially this prescriptivist version of it denies that reality might reduce to mind and the "life-worlds" it creates when sensory data or behaviors are organized by value-bestowing interpretations. We stop telling ourselves this epistemological creation story in order to locate ourselves within a world we have not made.

The metaphysics of a different sort starts here. We commit ourselves to that notion of truth appropriate to maps and plans, as we ask the questions listed before: What is our place in nature; what are nature's categorial form and conditions; what is being throughout the range of its expressions? It is our maps and plans, not the hopes and fantasies expressed in our meaning-giving interpretations that provide the sound beginning for these inquiries. Extending these maps, by enlarging the domain of their applicability and raising the level of their generality, is the direction to go as reflection moves beyond practice to science and metaphysics.

2. What is Missing in a Phenomenology of Experience

We are easily deterred from wanting to extend these maps beyond the circle of our practical interests. Why look beyond the immediacy of our circumstances when each of the activities supporting life and all the concrete details of it are centered here? Shouldn't philosophy begin and end in a reflection upon our circumstances, with special emphasis upon the world as we value and observe it while being engaged within it? There is, for example, the view of those phenomenologists who locate us within the *lived world*. They imagine the engineer in his locomotive, describing him as he accommodates himself to levers and gauges, isolation, power, and speed. This man is "thrown."[1] He is quixotically here in his cab, not there behind a merchant's counter or sitting at a desk. He may remark this accident of fate, but he is all the while joined in action to the furnishings of his situation, all of them "ready-to-hand" and appropriate to the task.[2] The engineer in-

22

terprets his situation by using a conceptual scheme to integrate his various perceptions, responses and persuasions. Using the interpretation helps to articulate this man's place in the world: his connections to it are all the firmer because of his clarity in discerning these joints.

Notice, however, that this emphasis upon the perceived utilities of things, and our feelings about them is a distortion of experience. Recognition of the things ready-to-hand and appreciation for their look is still, whatever Heidegger's intention, too much the expression of a slightly removed, aesthetic sensibility, one that is more committed to observing its "world" than to acting within its circumstances. Why say this? Because Heidegger ignores that sort of understanding which is indispensable to action, though it is less conspicuous when observation is detached and passive, and also when thought merely integrates the things observed. Understanding of this other kind secures an agent's control of himself and other things in situations where he works to achieve some effect. The engineer's circumstances are paradigmatic. Like most car drivers, he might know nothing of the design and mechanics of his machine. More likely, he runs it well because of having one or more hypotheses about the material variables significant for making it go. He runs it best when his understanding of the controls at hand extends to testable claims about their linkage to engine and wheels, for then he can modulate his behavior in ways appropriate to the changes he wants to make.

This man's principal objective is a successful performance, where success depends upon the machinery at hand and the plan directing its use. The phenomenologist who observes him, perhaps encouraging the engineer to observe himself, cares too much for the aesthetic appreciation of things existing "alongside" us and "ready-to-hand."[3] I am assuming that things ready-to-hand are encountered in circumstances where their efficacy is decisive for achieving some intended result: these are not the items displayed in the design collection of a museum. Heidegger, like phenomenologists in general, shows too little regard for the mediating, directing activities required of mind as we use these things. The engineer, for example, has a number of hypotheses, confirmed to the point of habit, regarding the instruments about him. These hypotheses are, in the first instance, symbolic structures representing both the effects desired, and the conditions required for achieving them. Every phenomenological proposal distracting the agent from the sequence of thought-directed behaviors by reminding him, or us, of noise, smell, the look and feel of things, exhilaration, or boredom is merely aesthetic and precious. Worse, it emphasizes the mere presentation and recognition of these meaning-suffused things, e.g., they are ready-to-hand; though the actual task of thought is the one of sequencing our use of these instruments on the way to achieving some desired result. No amount of contempt for this adaptive, directing use of intelligence reduces its power and value wherever we humans make a place for ourselves within the world. We may also reflect upon and enjoy the manner of our engagement in nature, but that more contemplative, appreciative attitude is less important to the success of our accommodations than the maps and plans tested in action.

Phenomenologists often deplore this notion of intelligence. They dislike both its instrumentalism and the mediating role claimed for those signs which represent some aspect of the world while directing action. These phenomenologists identify understanding with the contemplation of things, or at most with mind's value-directed integration of the things contemplated. They reject the contrary notion that understanding is representational (because of using signs for things which may not be currently observed or observable), and explanatory (because of inferring from something desired to its conditions). This instrumentalist notion of thought is, for them, the expression of our pathological concern for manipulating the things about us. These phenomenologists appeal, more or less explicitly, to the intuitionist notion that mind acts most authentically when it reflects upon the matters set before it, e.g., as *nous* perceives the Forms. This contemplative norm is, however, false to our circumstances where thought-directed action, not contemplation, is first demanded of us. This consideration, together with the absence of innate ideas, impels the formulation of those hypotheses used as maps and plans. These hypotheses are the signs with which we represent, explain, and then control, the circumstances where action serves the purposes of life. We test these hypotheses, thereby achieving that control, by acting upon them. Sitting in the engineer's seat, wearing his hat while feeling the levers and reading the gauges, is not a test. Running the train while concentrating only upon the look and feel of it is incidental to the test, because of ignoring the maps and plans that make the driving possible. It is these mediating, directing representations which phenomenologists too often neglect. They ignore the truth of our representations, and the conditions for truth, because of an exaggerated regard for presence, feeling, and familiarity. They are intuitionists, concerned that nothing of reality be concealed to inspecting mind. There is little or nothing in them to acknowledge that we operate successfully within a world where everything is "concealed" because nothing is inspectable. We rely instead upon the natural signs of perception and the conventional ones of language as we signify the world's aspects or parts, all the while testing our claims by searching for those observable differences which should obtain if our hypotheses are true.

Some phenomenologists may want to appropriate these hypothesis-testing behaviors for their own purposes. Isn't behavior just "practice," where practice serves the Kantian aim of schematizing, then presenting for inspection a differentiated and ordered, hence thinkable, experience? Where a conceptual system used for making experience is formulated in ways determined by the values it serves, we are not surprised that the experience created by using the system is itself suffused by these values. But then it follows that practice is just the activity of infusing experience with value, either because we use a value-bestowing conceptual system to schematize sensory data, or because we use the system for directing behavior. These two ways of understanding our practice have this one effect: Action locates us within a familiar and congenial "world" by creating it. Interpretations do require testing, but the only test required by these prescriptivist phenomenologists is the demand that the experience and "world" created by our schematization should be coherent in itself, and consistent with the values directing us.

This way of construing our hypothesis-testing behaviors is one-sided. It fails to distinguish behaviors directed by sense-making, value-espousing interpretations (as we create and confirm the reciprocal expectations of people engaged within the activity that binds them); from the behaviors required for testing those maps and plans which direct our accommodations to a physical and social world we have not made (as we use a road-map). Creating a significant experience, performing a rain dance for example, is not the same as testing the accuracy of a representation, however much we emphasize the "lived-experience" of the two behaviors. It will not matter that our views about the world and the behaviors affirming them are culturally sanctioned and much beloved, if these views get us into trouble because of misrepresenting the world, and our place within it.

3. Thought is Speculative

Our focus is truth, not presence or sense-making interpretations, as we reflect upon the conditions for successful practice. The maps and plans qualifying as good representations express these two features of our thinking: first, the thought formulating them is always speculative; second, thought must prove its responsibility by showing that its representations do have application. Hypotheses must be testable.

Thought is speculative because minds lacking innate ideas can direct our behaviors only as they repeatedly make and revise their representations of our circumstances. Intuitionism promises an immediate, confirming inspection of the realities themselves, but intuitionism is repudiated. We are

25

left having to know the world by way of signs, including the natural signs of perception and the conventional ones of language. Our problem is the one of organizing and construing signs as the representations of possible states of affairs, then the one of confirming that the possibilities signified do obtain.

Thought is speculative in several ways. Most conspicuous is the fact that we make and act upon our plans without being able to guarantee their outcome. The behaviors sequenced by a plan may accurately represent the instrumental relations which have previously obtained, but this is a world we cannot altogether anticipate or control. Speculation of this first sort is the estimate that a plan will work. The test of its truth requires that we have the conviction and power for seeing the plan fulfilled. Only then do we say that the plan was a true representation of what could be done, where the evidence for saying this is our success in doing the thing intended.

I mention this first consideration in order to discount it. Will and power are incidental to those aspects of speculation which are important here. There are four of them.

1) Thought is speculative as it uses words and ideas. For thought does more than construct or entertain the ideas, sentences and theories that are set before our minds and inspected. Descartes could emphasize these two kinds of thinking, because he relied upon God to secure the objective reference of clear and distinct ideas. Most of us no longer suppose that God is the guarantor of our ideas. We need to explain the relation of words and ideas to the things they signify.

We say that words and thoughts are construed as the signs of possible properties or possible states of affairs. Construal is speculative, because it regards a sentence, word, or thought as sign of its object, though the object might be possible only, not actual. A sentence or thought is meaningful because it signifies a possible state of affairs, while satisfying syntactic rules. It is speculative because of raising this other question: Is the representation true, because the possibility signified is actual? There might be a plan for hunting where the map embodied by the plan has an entry for centaurs. But are there any centaurs? Thought using the map speculates that there are. Thought is speculative wherever we construe the sign for some possibility without also confirming in the course of this act that the possibility is actual. We recognize this conclusion as one lesson from Descartes: Every truth-claim, apart from the one affirming one's own existence, is speculative because of being fallible.

2) Thought is speculative because of the overdetermination of evidence by theory: Our claims about the world have implications that exceed all possible evidence for them. There might be several or many theories ac-

counting for all of the data, where there are no *a priori* ideas or criteria enabling us to decide among them. Where each of the theories is economical, consistent, coherent, and fruitful, choice is confounded. Calling something an apple, we are unable to confirm this ascription (though repeated true predictions do justify it) so long as there are other interpretations for all the pertinent data. Our characterization of this or any thing is, therefore, unalterably speculative and fallible.

3) Thought is speculative when it generalizes from things of a kind observed previously to any next instance or to all the instances of that kind. If there were always necessary and sufficient conditions for some effect, as being a right triangle is necessary and sufficient for the applicability of the Pythagorean theorem, we could predict, when knowing those conditions, what property or properties a thing would have. There are, however, three considerations making our generalizations fallible: first, we do not usually know the necessary and sufficient conditions for some property; second, we do not know what other factors, independent of these necessary and sufficient conditions, might prevent a thing's having this property when those conditions are fulfilled; third, we have no universally applicable reason for supposing that every difference, relation, and existent does have necessary and sufficient conditions. These several considerations make us cautious in predicting that a next individual having some of a kind's properties shall have all of them. The next crow might not be black, as there might be no more crows.

4) Thought is speculative when we infer from something thought or observed to its conditions, e.g., its constituents or causes. Seeing smoke, we think of fire. Considering mind's various ways of behaving, we ask if these might be the activities of an exclusively physical system. Both inferences exceed the things thought or observed on the way to explaining them. Usually, there are competing explanations as "smoke" might be the steam rising from dry ice. These abductive inferences[4] are the familiar style of all our practical thinking, as we infer from a result desired to the sequence of behaviors required for achieving it. These are also the leveraged inferences familiar to science, as we argue from something thought or observed to its conditions.

Intuitionism admonishes us never to use abduction for philosophic purposes. Hume, for example, argues that we have no power for making inferences beyond the one of inferring to one of a pair of observed conjuncts when the other term is perceived or remembered. Hume would reduce all of our thinking, practical, scientific, and philosophic, to the recording of things set before our inspecting minds. Practice and science, this implies, are errantly speculative, when the only reliable knowledge claims

27

are the ones confirmed by inspection. Yet intuitionism is, I suppose, rejected: Reality does not reduce to the things inspected, and mind is not restricted to learning about matters of fact by inspecting the phenomena given to mind, or constructed by it. We need to consider the possibility that philosophy, as much as practice and science, may use abduction for extending thought past the things observed to their conditions.

Consider now the four kinds of speculation, and their effect. These four together show thought reaching beyond sensory data as we estimate what the world is, and can be made to be. This is thought as it dissolves the isolating membrane of individual or social consciousness. Denunciations of speculation are usually a not-so-veiled defense of this isolation. They express the intuitionist demand that nothing be said of the world unless inspecting mind has immediate access to the matters signified, i.e., evidence sufficient for making our claims incontrovertible. Too bad that intuitionism ignores the circumstances where animals of every sort satisfy their individual and social needs by accommodating themselves to the larger world about them. Speculation is the ineliminable risk that falls to thought as it directs the behaviors securing us within the world. Refusing to believe, refusing to act short of the evidence that would make a belief certain, we settle for tautologies and wait for death.

Speculation is a bad word only as we forget that this overreaching side of thought is joined to its confirming, experimental side. We often say more than we can prove, though we regularly act upon our hypotheses in ways confirming a fair part of what is said and planned. Action and experiment, in pursuit of an aim or defense of a hypothesis, are the essential but ordinary complements to speculation. They supply the evidence confirming that our speculations do have application. Is anything green? Can anyone catch fish with a straw hat? These are hypotheses expressed as questions. Neither of them flaps loosely in the speculative breeze, because each one signifies a possibility. There will be a factual difference confirmed by experiment if one or another of these possibilities does obtain, so that it is not speculation, but only untestable, undecidable hypotheses which are at issue. Thought is correctly and irretrievably speculative. Our problem is confirmation, i.e., the formulation of meaningful and testable hypotheses.

Confirmation is urgent where reflection begins, because thought makes plans which satisfy or relieve some need or desire. Errant speculation is quickly exposed: The instrumental relations specified by a plan do not obtain; or we are frustrated, wet, and hungry when the map for applying it misdirects us. Behavior is successful only as our maps and plans look beyond personal and social concerns to things in themselves. It is the truth of these maps and plans, and not only our needs and convictions, whether

28

personally or socially founded, that explains the success of our thought-directed actions.

4. The Maps of Practice as Extended and Tested Within Science

The truths confirmed in practice liberate thought from narrowly practical objectives. They carry us, in the midst of our most intense self-concern, beyond ourselves. The earliest of our maps and plans have a focus that is specific and particular. They contain very little that is general, as the infant knows the shape of his or her crib without generalizing to all rectangles. The child does eventually generalize, and then maps that were based upon his partial survey of a particular place or thing begin to incorporate various orders of generality. He generalizes about kinds and relations, e.g., any dog, every circle, and also about the constancy of things, the connectedness of regions or moments in space and time, and the regularity of changes occurring about him. He knows his own efficacy, and also that causality which is apparently a universal feature of the world. His maps represent these several kinds of generality, with the result that his plans are more accurate and flexible, his behaviors more successful.

This regard for objectivity may become our premier interest. Rather than map some part of the world for the purposes of need or desire, we may represent it in the more neutral interests of science. We speculate now about the entities and relations within various domains, some (like astronomy) which extend well beyond us, others (like biology) which include us. We test these hypotheses by acting upon them, though action now serves as a test of thought in contrast to the times before when thought and action were the instruments of desire. This objectivist bent does enhance social and self-interest by providing more accurate maps and greater control of nature; human action and experience do, consequently, fill a larger part of the world. Still, this regard for objectivity never reduces to merely utilitarian value. The practice of science becomes a right: We wish to know about things in themselves, with nothing beyond that desire to justify the practice. We demand only that scientific speculation be responsible. Granting that hypotheses imply more than experiment can ever confirm, we insist that hypotheses be testable, i.e., that there be some empirical criterion for choosing among the various claims about nature. The overdetermination of evidence by theory does embarrass us when two or more quite different theories are certified by the same evidence, as all the data confirming Newton's theory of gravity also confirm the one of Einstein. But this irresolution only delays the choice of theories without forever thwarting it.

Two considerations facilitate our choices: first, there are very few competing theories, because of the difficulty of formulating a theory adequate to all the significant theoretical and empirical considerations; second, we do inevitably, so far, discover phenomena which are unexplained by one or another of the competing theories. The choice among theories is plain, though not always final, when the theory confirmed by some critical datum is also the one that explains the largest array of phenomena while best cohering with the theories already accepted.

The product of theory and experiment is a complex network of more or less integrated theories, each of them confirmed to some least acceptable strength within its domain. Some of the hypotheses and theories are weak because of being merely descriptive, as psychoanalysis may be more adept at describing pathology than explaining it. Other hypotheses are stronger because of identifying those variables which generate the observed behaviors. Still others, quantum physics is an example, are troubled by anomalies requiring that we revise either the theory or our assumptions about certain categorial features of nature. Unevenly and still problematically, we resolve our uncertainties about nature, as thought achieves a good, if still partial, representation of nature's constitutive and organizing features.

5. The Beginnings of Metaphysics in Practice and Science

Metaphysics gets its first impulse as the need for securing ourselves within the world requires that we understand some fundamental things about its operation and design. Our ideas of space and time, causality, thinghood, reciprocity, potentiality, and actuality, indeed most of the distinctions affirmed by Aristotle's metaphysics are plausible hypotheses about the world formulated as we accommodate ourselves to it. Scientific inquiry is alternately advanced and hindered as it extends the maps inherited from these practical engagements, and from our later, more disinterested reflections upon them. Science eventually alters our ideas of these things, as we come to believe that space is curved, and that space and time are distinguishable but not separable. Where life and mind had seemed distinctive, and perhaps immaterial, science discovers their sufficient material conditions; or it designs physical systems that mimic these behaviors.

The scientists who revise these practical views of the world would likely deny that their hypotheses and experiments serve a metaphysical purpose. But they do. That is plainer if we recall that no tasks are more fundamental to our metaphysical aims than the ones of describing the world's most general features and our place there. It is altogether appropriate, therefore, that reflection has turned metaphysical within science itself, just as practice was the source of metaphysical ideas.

Calling these reflections metaphysical is not a way of implying that responsible thought suddenly gives way to fantasy. It is rather that thought's claims about the world have achieved the generality of *categorial form*. Maps that have represented the details of our locale and some of its pervasive features, then the properties and relations important to the particular sciences, have been elaborated to the point of representing nature's most general features. These hypotheses, our maps, are general in either or both of these two ways: they represent the world with the economy of an architect's blueprint, signifying thereby the design of the whole; or they specify those least properties and relations that are constitutive of any possible entity or region in the world. Practice and our reflections upon it have suggested some of the notions science refines and tests. But it is science, and only science, that supplies reliable content for our ideas about these two aspects of categorial form. Space and time are obvious enough to everyone who moves about in any way; but then physicists speculate about that geometrized space-time which constrains the distribution of matter in our world. This is science as it identifies those entities and relations which may be constitutive of every state of affairs.

Philosophers sometimes shiver with embarrassment when recalling the old characterization of scientists as "natural philosophers"; but that title is exactly right. Metaphysics promises to describe the generic, features of reality, though nothing surpasses or even competes with science as an authority about that part of reality which is nature. Where practice in defense of our interests engages us full-time within nature, science enhances practice by enabling us to control some of the factors important to our aims. But then science also carries reflection beyond these interests and behaviors, to a detached account of nature's constituents and organizing forms. These are the categorial features represented by its most general hypotheses.

The design of the whole with a specification of nature's elementary but pervasive features is a considerable part of categorial form; but there is more. Practice and science have formulated their plans and hypotheses under the direction of certain regulative principles, including the assumptions that events have causes, that nature endures, and that positions in space and time are connected. Now, with the greater part of categorial form articulated by scientific theory, there is still the obligation for telling what these principles signify, and what evidence we have for their truth. These too are claims about nature. How shall we confirm that the factors they name are embedded somehow within it?

One response will be that these regulative principles have no significance beyond their utility as leading principles, as though principles that organize and direct inquiry need have no application to the character and relation of things in nature. But is that so? Is causality, for example, nothing more than a rubric for organizing experience and our thoughts about some relations within nature? Causality prescribes that we look for causes sufficient to produce whatever effects do occur, as we often discover particular causes, and kinds of causes, for typical effects. Mumps are causes, as Picasso and Monet are the makers of the paintings they signed. Intuitionists have tried to eliminate interaction and productive activity from our inventory of reality's categorial features, because of being unable to inspect these dynamic relations in the data set before their inspecting minds. Though no one but these Humeans supposes that the reciprocal action among a set of causes is properly described as the contiguity of atomized sensory data. Does anyone standing in a drenching rain believe that this effect is merely subsequent to, not consequent upon, its antecedents? Hume did claim that this is so, but he only dared say that after reducing all of reality to sensory data having no external relations other than their spatial and temporal ones. No one who rejects this intuitionist notion of reality, no one acknowledging the reality of motion and change, is the least tempted by Hume's idea of cause. The natural basis of the causal principle, and the range of its application is, at the same time, more assured and more problematic than he imagined. Quantum physics, for example, seems to limit the generality of the causal principle; though its restrictions are all the more reason for determining where and why the principle applies. The status of the other regulative principles is similar to that of causality: They seem applicable universally, or applicable to a limit that is so far inexplicable, as we may ascertain a continuous path connecting any two position in space and time, down to but possibly not including elementary quanta. Still, the question of ontological status is unresolved, when the confirmations and even the limiting disconfirmations leave us pondering the basis in nature for these principles. No wonder that we prefer the easier solution of describing them as leading principles for inquiry.

Is there, perhaps, an indirect way of determining the natural footing for these principles? Consider the evidence that justifies their use, i.e., we test the principles by applying them, as finding the cause for some effect is evidence for the truth of saying that every difference or relation has a cause. Finding this one additional, confirming instance of the principle does not add much to its confirmation, when there are an infinity of cases still to go. It happens, nevertheless, that careful attention to the particular examples confirming a leading principle teaches us something of the natural basis for its application.

One instance of this search for origins goes as follows. We start with the regulative principle affirming that actuality presupposes potentiality. This example may seem pathetic. Why bother to argue about the alleged basis in nature for an antique and discredited principle? One reason for doing that is our use of the principle in practice and science: We don't ask one-legged men to run the 100-yard dash, though we do trace the potentiality for some genetic trait to the genes that condition our having it. Another reason is my hope of resurrecting a useful and well-founded principle: We often infer from some actuality to its conditioning potency.

Justifying this inference begins with the purging of some incidental assumptions. First among them is the view that potencies are subsistent rumblings or incipient but undetectable activations. We do better by saying that this regulative principle is a modal expression of sufficient reason, hence the complement of that principle's other expression, the requirement that every event have a cause. It is causes, we infer, that have potencies, as an infant with the proper gene can have red hair. Though now the principle seems all the more obscure, for how can we locate potencies within the material configuration of an actual body? The answer is that potencies, some of them at least, are relational properties founded in the geometrical-structural properties of things.[5] There are, for example, lock and key. The key's potential for opening the lock derives from the complementarity of their shapes. More exactly, lock and key qualify for certain geometrical but dynamic relationships because of their geometrical-structural properties. The potencies are just these qualifications for relatedness.

Here is a case where the example falling under a regulative principle shows us the natural basis for the principle's application. Though my way of accounting for the principle may not be a universal solution. There are too many moral and other potencies for which there does not seem to be either a conditioning geometrical property or some geometrical relationship for which things having the property would qualify. The example is, nevertheless, an instructive solution, because it justifies our saying that regulative principles do sometimes, at least, originate as materially founded constraints within nature. It is reasonable enough that inquiry should locate the expressions of these constraints, and reasonable too that scientific discoveries about categorial form should be supplemented by hypotheses specifying the generic constraints internal to nature.

6. Assigning Responsibility for a Comprehensive Account of Categorial Form

Let us suppose that philosophers have successfully identified the material basis for some of the regulative principles used in science and practice. Thought's spiral has moved beyond science as the responsibility for categorial form passes from scientists to metaphysicians. This transition is all the plainer when metaphysicians supply the comprehensive representation of categorial form. These might be scientists thinking as philosophers; nevertheless, the task belongs to metaphysics. Why should this be so? Trivially, because scientists are usually too busy with their special interests to care about the whole. More to the point, because scientists are uneasy with, and not especially adept at, some of the considerations pertinent to categorial form.

Suppose, for example, that physicists have identified those variables and relations constitutive of all phenomena, so that laws representing the relationships of these variables have application throughout nature. The theory coordinating these laws should be, we infer, the most exhaustive and best possible representation of nature and its categorial form.

The reason for making metaphysics, not science, responsible for the comprehensive representation of categorial form is illustrated here in the treatment of natural laws. Consider the status of these laws: Are they merely the sentences of our theories; or might they be intrinsic constraints upon change? Suppose that natural laws are merely sentences, for then nature itself would be lawless. What result should we predict if that were true? Only that chaos where anything may randomly succeed the occurrence of anything else. There is, of course, the statistical chance that events might be orderly even to eternity, as an honest coin might always come up heads. But this is an outcome having minuscule probability. Notice too that citing the Humean account of change—where anything may succeed anything else—deprives us of an explanation for the regularities observed. They do just happen that way, Hume argues; they occur by chance. Yet, chance is not a cause, and references to it are not any sort of explanation. Appealing to chance is rather a way of saying that regularities persist in the absence of a generating, sustaining condition. Hume has argued that the regularities are inexplicable. He has no explanation for them. We are left to marvel that regularities endure in the absence of sufficient generating conditions. Can we do better than Hume? Can we supply a hypothesis that cites conditions sufficient for the observed regularities? Yes, we can. We say that laws intrinsic to nature are one of the conditions for regularity. This is, of course, a merely partial solution until we have identified these normative constraints upon change. What could they be, and how are they located within nature? One basis for them is the geometry intrinsic to space, hence to every material thing. Other things being equal, locks do invariably open to keys of the complementary shape.

Notice the effect of this argument: It precludes our saying that the law sentences of our most comprehensive and well-confirmed theory or theories could be, in themselves, a complete specification of categorial form. These law sentences will not have specified the basis within nature for the regulative force of the laws they represent. Nature's categorial form is established as much by the structures that condition its regularities as it is by the stable or recurring features of the things changing. A theory that predicts, describes, and explains every change while ignoring any one of the categorial factors conditioning these regularities is less than we require of a theory adequate to categorial form.

Every dispute about the responsibility or right for proposing this comprehensive theory is jurisdictional only. That is plain where science and metaphysics are two overlapping moments in the spiral of generalizing thought. Assigning this responsibility is, nevertheless, important if we are emphasizing that thought moves beyond scientific concern for the various kinds of regularity to those categorial features science exploits without explaining. These features include its laws, dispositions, causal relations, probabilities, modalities, and hierarchical structures. One or more of these considerations may have no place within nature, with thought or language being the only basis for whatever claims we make about it. We require that someone distinguish among these claimants for a place within nature. That someone is a metaphysician. What is implied, he or she must ask, if any one of these factors is located exclusively within thought or language, having been drawn as Hume draws matter, cause, law, motion and necessity from nature? Where argument confirms that nature might not, or would not, be as we observe it in the absence of these conditions, we speculate about their regulative force and foundation within nature. Our various proposals may be tentative, *ad hoc* and superficial, as 'dormative power' is the place-marker for something more important. Nevertheless, we demur when told that some ideal scientific theory might be applicable and adequate to all of nature. We grant that such a theory would identify the constitutive features and generating conditions for every natural phenomena, including every perceived difference. Still, this theory would be deficient as a representation of categorial form, because of its silence regarding those factors presupposed, as immanent laws are presupposed, by the regularities we observe. Humeans would have us ignore these laws, settling instead for the regularities observed, and the law sentences correctly representing and predicting them. Theories of categorial form answer to an additional demand: we want the best explanation that might be proposed for the things observed. Where regularities are observed, but chance is no explanation for them, we want their conditions specified. Our hypotheses about categorial form are extended to provide for these conditions.

7. A Theory of Categorial Form

Are there examples of categorial schemas supplementing our scientific hypotheses about nature? The one best known is still Aristotle's metaphysics. His views about substance and the four causes were for centuries the favored account of those categorial features exhibited everywhere in the phenomena important to practice and science. Several considerations, most of them factual, but one dialectical, justified this belief.

The factual evidence included the apparent character of our perceivings. They seem to reveal a world of things qualified by their properties, while retaining identity as their properties change. There was also the grammar of ordinary language. It divided the things represented into subjects and predicates, thereby confirming that characterization of substances and attributes based upon the things known to perception.

The dialectical argument supported this result. It was motivated by the desire to save Plato's Forms from reification. Matter was to be the instrument for doing this, because matters are particular and stable. A form instantiated, meaning a form enmattered, could be designated, perceived, and relied upon to hold its form. Form, reconstrued in this way, became a principle for organizing matter. This might be matter of the sort common to physical things, or matter of the kind ascribed to minds. Either way, it provided a ready explanation for the immanent constraining force of law: we could say that things of the same kind, meaning matters organized in the same way, can only behave as their organizing form enables them to do. Substances, this implies, have the integrity of internally organized material things. Each thing is, to some degree, cause of itself.

This emphasis upon the independence of freestanding material agents is no longer defensible in a theory of categorial form. Nothing in this world is independent of every other one for all of its character and existence. Accordingly, we replace Aristotle's theory, for the purpose of illustrating a theory of categorial form, with this other schematization. Rejecting his view that nature is an aggregate of freestanding substances with Earth at its center, we speak of a protean, uncentered space-time, one having an immanent geometry and dynamics, where matter derives from the combination of motion and form. This space-time is the One. It has four powers:

36

1. The One is self-differentiating, in three aspects:
    a) It is self-diversifying, resulting in the generation of myriad properties.
    b) It is self-dividing, resulting in a diversity of particulars.
    c) It is self-stratifying, using configuration and aggregation to produce systems dominant or subordinate to one another.
2. Space-time achieves self-differentiation; i.e., it is self-transforming, because its dynamics are causal. Further properties, particulars, and stratifications are produced by the reciprocal effects of differences already current there. We acknowledge that space-time must already be differentiated in order that it may transform itself.
3. This complex is self-coordinating, implying that each differentiation is consequential, i.e., has value, for some others. The patterns of these values, whether positive or negative (favorable or unfavorable, good or bad), may pervade a region, connected regions, or all of space-time.
4. This differentiated space-time is self-perpetuating, though only in the manner determined by its internal dynamics.

These four powers have a product: Nature, as the self-differentiating, geometrized, hence enmattered space-time is comprised of overlapping and nested *stabilities*. Each stability is a system of properties having persistent organization and cohesion. It has some degree of resistance to external, intrusive forces, and a measure of self-regulation; i.e., it has an outside and an inside. Each stability is faced, metaphorically, with a permeable membrane: viz., it extracts energy or information from its environment while sustaining its own organization and processes. This resistant perimeter, with its powers for self-regulation, qualifies the stability for a degree of internality. It can behave as a monad, developing in ways determined by its internal constituents and organization. A human being is a stability, but so is a rainstorm, a solar system, a government, and a spade. The persistence and organization of stabilities, their resistance to external influences, and their self-regulation explain their relative autonomy. Every stability may have a developmental history exempt from changes within other, possibly contiguous, but independent or overlapping stabilities. Nevertheless, stabilities are coordinated and subordinated to one another; none is perfectly autonomous because each is generated within, and is nourished by those others which comprise its environment. These dependencies are confirmed whenever radical changes in one stability affect other ones. The one, fully autonomous stability is the whole, though the evidence for a single, all-embracing stability is inconclusive. It is equally likely that the many separate, overlapping and stratified stabilities cohere with one another in a way that is imperfectly harmonious, with only space-time and the laws deriving from its geometry to unify the whole.

This sample schema provides for categorial factors by locating them within the structures just described, as the laws of motion are founded in the geometry of space-time. We speculate, though without sufficient evidence, that other laws also derive from its geometry. That would happen as successive orders of aggregated or configured phenomena are constrained by the geometry of their context and constituents. This might, of course, supply only a necessary, not a sufficient, basis for these laws, as we might be unable to derive the force laws, i.e., those laws applying to various restricted domains, from only the geometry of space-time. Then too, it would seem that still other laws, e.g., the one correlating guilt to sin, are not constrained in any way by the geometry of space-time. This categorial blueprint is, therefore, incomplete.

That same inadequacy is apparent as we provide within this schema for causality. We start by reformulating Aristotle's four causes. Formal cause is the geometry of space-time, hence of every system embodying that geometry. Material cause derives from motion and form. Efficient cause is the motion that produces and then impels matter in space-time. Every stable system persists; it achieves, if only for a while, a sustainable equilibrium within itself. Final causes are the least energy principles sustaining these systems, in only mechanical ways, as they evolve. Final cause, this implies, is like the other three causes: This cause, too, is grounded in the space-time geometry as that geometry limits the magnitude and direction of motion. Still, this notion of causality, like the one of law, is incomplete, because these causes are suitable to the dynamics of physical systems but inadequate or irrelevant to the fact that an increase in lending rates causes inflation. Here, too, this schematic account is too spare for the representation of all categorial form.

An example does not have to be a finished theory, and this one, a generalized description of self-sustaining and equilibriating thermodynamical systems, is not. This account is, however, more plausible and more powerful than Aristotle's schema; and it does illustrate the schematic representations with which metaphysics is to integrate and interpret the combination of scientific theories and regulative principles. This is moreover, a viable schema, one that proves its universal applicability when any next domain of problematic entities is shown to be comprised of these stable systems.

This hypothesis, like every practical and scientific one, is provisional and fallible. Notice, however, that there is nothing in our fallibility to imply that there is no categorial form, or that categorial form is too complex ever to be represented. That might have been true: we might have discovered ourselves to be living in a world that is endlessly complex, or in one whose categorial features are indiscernible amidst the anomalies that plague our theories about it. Quantum theory might seem to be a theory of that confounding sort, though we have no reason apart from the irresolution within this still transitional theory, to conclude either that there is some limit to our capacity for testing an adequate theory of categorial form, or for conceding the idealist claim that nature has no coherent form apart from the one that we use when thinking about our interactions with it.

8. Confirming that a Theory of Categorial Form Applies to Human Beings

The schematic rendering of categorial form is a well-marked place in thought's spiral. This is not, however, the end of the spiral, the place to which thought should rise, then rest. Reflection has three more tasks, each of them metaphysical. On the one side, we advance from our theory of categorial form to speculate about nature's conditions, then to characterize all of being. On the other side, we retrace our steps, descending the spiral in order to describe ourselves and our place in nature.

Suppose, for example, that nature has the categorial form described above. It is comprised of systems which are stabilized in two ways: their parts are reciprocally related, while each system is nourished by its relations to the other systems of its environment. We might say any one of three things about this hypothesis as it bears upon us human beings and our behaviors. One claim is that we humans are, like inkwells, oceans, and city governments, nothing but stable systems of the sort described above: We are complex, self-sustaining physical systems of reciprocally related parts. Like other stabilities, we overlap and are nested within the larger-scale systems that limit our freedom while supporting us. A second claim to be tested avers that this hypothesis is applicable but not adequate to us: We are stabilities of the sort described; but we are also different from, because more than that. The third claim is that we are not, in any respect, examples of these stable systems: The hypothesis is not adequate or even applicable.

This third alternative seems plainly mistaken: We humans are stable systems in all the respects pertinent to our physical and biological nature. Dispute centers only upon the other two alternatives: Is everything that is distinctive of us explicable in the terms of these systems? The answer may be currently undecidable, but three peculiarly human concerns, value, intentionality, and knowledge, do fall to this explanation. Where these three

39

are explicable in its terms, there is good reason for thinking that this hypothesis about categorial form is applicable and adequate to us.

8A. Value

We start with value. No topic is more resistant to physicalist accounts of human nature, though the principal obstacles to understanding it disappear when we start from the assumption that human beings are stable systems reciprocally engaged with many others in a flux where stabilities are regularly made and dissolved. There are two things to consider: the values within nature, and the attitudes we strike when using these first values to achieve some desired result.

The values within nature are relational. They are, more exactly, the consequential relations among complex systems, as water is consequential for plants. Having enough of it, they thrive; having too much, they drown. Value, this implies, is founded in causal relations, though its basis there is obscured by the shadow of Hume's analysis. There is, he supposed, no reason in nature why an event need have an antecedent or successor.[6] Anything might happen without conditions, for Hume supposes that cause and effect are both distinguishable and separable. Imagining either one without the other, we have established that each can exist in the absence of the other. Neither one is, therefore, the condition or cause of the other; neither one is consequential for the other. These several claims will surely mislead us if we want to argue that consequential relations are the sustaining or transforming relations within and among stable systems. Water and plant, for example, are interacting complex systems, where the effect resulting from their interaction is a change in one or both of them. The causes survive their relationship, where survival-in-modification is transformation. This is the basis for saying that causal relationships are consequential for the things affected and, more generally, that anything modifying some other one has value for it.

Every stable system is formed in the broth of these objective values. But then some stabilities are organized so that they may initiate behavior, not merely react to the other things affecting them. These systems sometimes control the various consequential relations to their own advantage. We humans are systems of this kind. Here, in the power for directing ourselves, is the locus for values of the other sort, i.e., for valuing. Valuing begins as the act of choosing among consequential relations accordingly as one cares to achieve, perpetuate, or terminate their effects. It extends to the power for representing circumstances that are unachieved, then for sequencing behaviors until that desired effect is achieved, or the objective is revised.

40

Valuing is, accordingly, the activity of a system that must pick and choose among the values provided by its environment on the way to securing and satisfying itself. Other stable systems needn't make these choices when impulse alone is sufficient for securing them within the world. We do not have that advantage, having been liberated to make our way in a diversity of environments, and in ways so idiosyncratic that each of us may baffle the others.

We might have hoped that the acknowledgement of objective values would confirm the intrinsic worth of some things we value, especially ourselves and some of the things we make. There is, however, nothing to support this claim in the consequential relations of reciprocally engaged stable systems. Nothing in those relations entails that any of the things related is valuable in itself. Still, we are able to value ourselves, our products, and the consequential relations that secure us while supporting our productive activity. We defend these interests by using rules and laws to regulate ourselves. Many of our expectations, opportunities, and responsibilities are founded in them. One might think that the power for making these rules is evidence against the claim that we humans are only stable systems, for how could a tulip or table come to regulate itself? Self-regulation and mutual regulation are, however, characteristic of every sustainable stable system, and of every complex of systems. We are different only because of representing a form of relatedness, i.e., a rule, before learning to use the rule to regulate ourselves.

Declaring that these rules, procedures, and consequences are goods, we aver our own worth, though we cannot forever evade the fact that these conventions, and even our own lives, may be valued without being goods in themselves. We can declare and act upon the presumption of our value, but this is not by any means sufficient to demonstrate that we are intrinsically valuable. Nothing within the soup of these self-stabilizing but ephemeral systems is a value of that ultimate sort.

How shall we proceed when there are no fixed navigating lights, no intrinsic goods within the flux? We resort to the two kinds of value described above: consequential relations and our power for valuing the things that sustain and secure us. We begin by discovering our situation in the tide of consequential values, but then we also represent, and choose some particular way to be from among the several or many possibilities. We are restricted in making these choices by our individual experience and culture, and also by having to acknowledge that each of the possible choices has its price. We choose among the alternative ways of securing ourselves, while being more or less able to identify these benefits and costs. For there is no exemption from consequential relations. They will have an effect upon us, hence a value for us, whatever our valuing. We may especially value ourselves and our collectivity. Granting that life is sustainable in a variety of ways, we may revere our own solutions, as every tribe does, while being intolerant of everything that subverts us.

There are, this implies, no authentic "final" values, but only consequential values and our own valuings. Could it be true, however, that we have merely displaced the mystery? That might seem to be our predicament when all the burden of valuing falls upon those mental activities covered by the word *intention*. Where is there a place within the idea of self-regulating systems for the fact of intentionality, as expressed, for example, in our valuing?

8B. Intentionality

A stable system may be "intentional" in one or more of four ways.

1) The system intends its own persistence, though this intending is not usually conscious. Stones and the chassis of old cars are intentional in this way, because of a least energy principle: viz., things persist because the energy required for altering them is greater than the energy sustaining them. The "intention" to persist reduces to the fact that things do persist for this reason.

2) Another kind of intentionality, one still relevant to the conditions for survival, is exhibited in a system's behaviors as it adjusts to its environment. Chesapeake Bay is tidal but not as salty as the Atlantic Ocean, nor as sweet as the freshwater rivers that empty into it: The bay accommodates to them while having a sustainable integrity of its own. Someone who is set in his ways but threatened by a new boss acts in a parallel way; he alters his behavior just enough to satisfy the revised expectations. Common sense denies that there is anything intentional in the behaviors of the bay, while agreeing that the man's behavior is intentional. Yet both are intentional in this respect: Each one accommodates to its circumstances in ways that concede some least alteration of its own behaviors, organization, or constituents while sustaining its integrity as a stable system. Both are homeostatic systems.

3) A different sort of intentionality also promotes a system's ability for sustaining itself. This time, the objective is utilization or incorporation, i.e., the system extracts information or energy from its environment, information, so that it may act more effectively upon its surroundings and within itself, energy, so that it may be nourished. Behaviors of this sort often satisfy our commonsense notions of intentionality, as someone going to school or the grocer is acting purposively. Still, that consciousness of one's purpose may be lacking, as sharks and hurricanes do something comparable when they take a part of the world about them in order to sustain themselves.

4) Only this last kind of intentionality is distinctively human, as we use signs to represent some remote or prospective state of affairs. No matter then if the medical student is not yet a doctor. He or she can symbolize that outcome, directing himself or herself for years at a time under the regulative force of this objective. Intentionality of this fourth kind is the use of mediating thoughts or words. We construe them as signs, thereby intending and sometimes desiring their objects. This last sentence is the difficult one, because it marks out construal and desire as the two intentional notions requiring elaboration. Neither one is problematic. Construal is association, as words or thoughts are associated with other words and thoughts, and sometimes with those behaviors that give us perceptual access to the things intended. Desire is often expressed as strong feeling accompanied by representations of its object. These are, however, only the frequent symptoms of desire, especially of desires frustrated. Desire is more often expressed as goal-directed behavior, where intention is the sequencing of behaviors appropriate to an aim. Successful behavior continues or not, depending on the character of its object, e.g., a momentary hunger satisfied or long-term health.

Each of these four kinds of intentionality may be understood as a behavior of self-regulating systems. The self-regulating system has a repertoire of these learned but modifiable behaviors. It uses them for securing and satisfying itself, and also for accommodating itself to impinging circumstances. The stability monitors these circumstances and itself, taking its own pulse while acting in ways appropriate to its circumstances and interests. Valuings are the assessments of relevance and worth presupposed by each stability's directives to itself. Nothing in them justifies our saying that the things valued are good in themselves. Even the work of Bach or Mozart does not have to be good in this intrinsic way in order to be sought and prized for having qualities that affect us.

8C. Knowledge

The stabilities using signs, hence capable of intentionality, have knowledge. But every stability "knows" something of its environment and itself when its responses to external and internal stimuli are properly inflected, i.e., appropriate and effective, however gross and unconsidered. Human knowledge is different from these lesser adaptations in several ways: (1) Symbols mediate between the facts represented and whatever changes we may cause because of our ways of acting upon them. (2) These symbols are compounded by a grammar, so that they are well-formed or not. (3) The symbols allow for various degrees of precision and complexity in representing

43

the matters at issue. (4) The symbols are general, as *red* applies to many different red things, and to things that differ in the shade of their redness. (5) The symbols "freeze" the impelling circumstances by representing them, thereby enabling us to defer action while considering alternative behaviors and their likely results. (6) We demand justifying reasons for affirming that some part of the world has the character signified by our thoughts or words, and reasons for choosing among alternative plans of action. Reasons of this second kind may be interests or desires; but reasons of the first sort are factual claims about the world. With knowledge as our objective, these factual allegations are testable claims about matters of fact. They are falsified or confirmed as we turn into the world, looking for the empirical differences that would be perceived if these factual claims were the accurate representations of things present there.

These six points together imply that knowledge comprises well-formed signs connected to the world by the behaviors appropriate for testing them and, more remotely, by the dispositions for these behaviors. We may often mean (i.e., signify) and know more than these tests verify, where evidence is overdetermined by theory. Still, it is only these behaviors that confirm the relation between knowledge claims and their objects. Why should a stability have knowledge? Out of the practical necessity that a system under-endowed with instincts should be able to formulate, then act upon plans that are appropriate and effective.

Knowledge, we assume, is a peculiarly human achievement; but even this truth needs shading as we locate ourselves within the world of recipro-cally related stabilities. Granted that we are different from many other sta-bilities in our use of signs, it is true nevertheless that this sort of inten-tionality is present in systems not capable of anything so elaborate as human thought and language. Indeed, there are instances of sign-like behavior wherever the relation between a system's behaviors and its internal condi-tion is mediated by some third thing. These mediators are percepts in the case of lower animals. They may also be uninspectable electrochemical changes, as happens when the body's immune system "interprets" particu-lar changes within it by acting to suppress some response of its own, or by acting to eliminate an alien presence. These various examples, like our use of conceptual or linguistic signs, exhibit this generic similarity: Each one is the instance of a mediator serving as the link in a causal sequence. Each of the mediators is, in turn, variable in two ways: The link has more or less autonomy within the causal chain; and the linkage may be loose to the point of being unreliable as a basis for inferences about the character of the things connected by the mediator, (e.g., as the perceived color of an apple is only an effect occurring in us, not the property of the apple itself). There is more of this autonomy and unreliability as we move beyond the tightly causal mediation of instinctual or impulsive behaviors to the mediating role of conventional signs and the learned inhibition of voluntary behaviors. Protozoa may have little or none of our freedom for withholding a reaction to mediating signs while considering the likely effects of our behavior. Nor can they invent the words that need construing, words whose own properties are little or no clue to the character of their referents. These differences among stabilities are real; but they are less important here than the striking fact that human, as against every other sort of intentionality, is only a specific difference. Many stabilities relate to a third one by way of a mediating second. We are unique, because of our power for creating and construing that middle term.

8D. Self-regulation

Bringing value, intentionality, and knowledge under some candidate theory of categorial form is a vital step on the way to proving that the tested hypothesis is adequate to human nature. There is, however, more to do in showing the theory to be adequate, and a different way of doing it. Rather than analyze particular activities for the evidence that they are instances of the entities and relations described by the theory, we may consider the theory as a prescription. We ask what it requires of human nature, then we look to see if there are examples of character and behavior satisfying the prescription. My hypothesis regarding interdependent stable systems encourages us to ask if we, ourselves, might be examples of these nested and overlapping stabilities. Is there evidence of accommodation, dominance, and dependency in our physical and social relations? Furthermore, can we use the idea of reciprocally engaged, nested and overlapping stable systems so as to alter, for our benefit, the plastic relations among us? Is there evidence that we are, by our nature, amenable to that self-regulation which this theory anticipates wherever reciprocal relations are determinable and plastic; and wherever our understanding of the pertinent consequential values together with desires and powers for directing ourselves enables us to achieve and sustain a particular manner of relatedness.

There is considerable evidence that we do behave as this theory prescribes. Suppose that social rules, legislation, constitutions, and even moral laws have this complex origin: They are formulated as we reflect upon our individual and social interests; and upon our character as stable systems where each of us has some autonomy while being nested within, or overlapping, other stabilities. Earlier on, when reflection was engaged altogether by the maps and plans used for solving our practical concerns, we responded more or less effectively to our circumstances without understanding their categorial features. We made traffic laws because of the practical urgency, not because of regarding ourselves as self- and mutually regulating stable systems. Now, as we return to these laws and behaviors with the hindsight of a hypothesis about categorial form, we understand somewhat better both the problem and the constraints upon solving it. Traffic laws are neither divine commandments nor the expressions of natural law. They are expedients addressed to our circumstances, hence solutions validated by their consequences. Ends, they remind us, do often justify their means.

Traffic laws were made and applied because we have wanted to use our cars while reducing bottlenecks and accidents. Now, as we consider the matter anew from the perspective of categorial form, we set this earlier understanding within a context that is generalized and more articulate. We remark that nature is constituted of stable systems, each one persisting in its own character while accommodating more or less successfully to the other stabilities impinging upon it. That accommodation is peculiar to us humans because we alone in nature are able to alter the manner of our relatedness to the things about us in order to satisfy some law of our own making. These laws are meant to revise the unconsidered relations among reciprocally related systems in order to achieve a value that has come to be endorsed by some of the stabilities, i.e., by people who want to alter or regularize the manner of their relatedness. How, for example, shall we minimize conflict while acknowledging each system's autonomy and the opposing interests of stabilities affecting one another? How shall we weigh the universal desire for participation within a larger network of stabilities against the claims of dominant individuals and oligarchies?

Each of these questions reminds us of the discrepancy between the current state of our reciprocal relations and some imagined, i.e., represented, ideal. We respond to these disparities by formulating the laws that will regulate and revise some currently established mode of relatedness. But now we have in addition the idea of categorial form to remind us of our circumstances, the constraints upon us and our objective. Each of these laws is, we realize, nothing more than a stipulation giving voice to our procedures for regulating the mutually affecting relations of stable systems. This is an instance of the commonplace that stabilities act to sustain themselves by altering or securing their relations to the other stabilities of their environment. Each lays claim to some place just by virtue of occupying it, though no stability is altogether independent of every other one in regard to its existence and character. Each is typically nested within some systems while overlapping others. Each sometimes deters other stabilities while pursuing its own interests. Laws regularize or alter these relations, e.g., by making each one's behaviors uniform and predictable to the others. But always, there were and are myriad ways of altering any current mode of reciprocity, so that we weigh the general requirements for autonomy and reciprocity against the more specific benefits achieved by altering the manner of our engagement with one another. Usually, we prize uniformity and predictability, though we needn't always do that. Some of our rules and laws might have the aim of scrambling our social relations, making them unpredictable for some imagined advantage. There are, apparently, many ways to tune the relations among reciprocally related systems.

Consider, for example, John Stuart Mill's proposal that there are three concentric circles of liberty: first, the circle of thought and conscience; second, the one of personal choice and behavior; third, the circle of joining voluntarily with other people for specific objectives.[7] The justification for affirming these claims is uncertain, for there is Mill says, no way of demonstrating claims about ultimate ends.[8] There are no empirical or logical tests for their validity, because these claims are not true or false. What other status should we ascribe to them?

We do best by describing Mill's proposal as a recommendation. It is formulated as we think about our experience as stabilities. What are the conditions for our well-being? How shall we regulate ourselves in order to achieve it? We discover, in the course of this reflection, that autonomy and our reciprocal relations to others are equally significant for our lives as self-regulating systems. We also remark that people often suffer under political regimes that ignore one or the other of these considerations. Here, in Mill's proposal, we have a policy for defending the interests that have come to seem paramount. Stable systems, at least the human ones, shall have a "right" to that privacy they already possess, when internality is characteristic of every self-equilibrating stability. They are to have additional rights for behaving in ways determined by their internal states (e.g., hunger and curiosity), and finally rights for accommodating themselves to other systems (e.g., the right of making contracts). Every human being already does these two things as well, so that Mill's three circles of liberty are only the demand that each of us should have the "right" for doing what we would inevitably do if we were not forcibly prevented from it.

How shall we live as autonomous but reciprocally related agents? Mill's three circles of liberty speak to this point. They acknowledge categorial form as it applies to us, while prescribing that certain of its effects be meliorated. The actual balance of power among stable systems, speaking only of humans, is vastly unequal. Add that previous moral rules have further distorted our relations, and we see the virtues in a recommendation for altering the balance between autonomy and our engagements with one another. Many of those other political, legal, and moral systems have ignored the twin claims of autonomy and reciprocal relatedness, as slavery and despotism ignore them. Mill has a sharper eye for these basic facts about us. He would create a domain of legal and moral rights in the way that landscape gardeners exhibit some of the natural contours of the land. In both cases, we judge the intervention by its results. Does it acknowledge the character of things, shaping them in ways that express their proclivities while securing one or another version of what is arguably their well-being?

I don't mean to suggest that Mill's three circles of liberty are an adequate characterization of both our autonomy and our reciprocal relatedness. Mill has proposed that we save ourselves from despotism by ignoring too much of our essential embeddedness in a network of nested, overlapping, and reciprocally related stabilities. He would restrict every individual's autonomy at the point where he or she harms some other one; but then he too much ignores the supports and security provided by the system of mutually engaging relations among us. Mill is too much the social atomist. His theory neglects those constraints laid down by the categorial form prevailing within nature.

Does my argument, nevertheless prove too much, namely, that *is* entails *ought,* where an accurate theory of categorial form supplies some or all of the prescriptions for moral life? Do we achieve moral virtue merely by being ourselves, as every shark is a good one? This is half of the story, but only that much of it. For we cannot have an effective morality that ignores what we are and our situation while being it. Nature is, however, protean and determinable, rather than narrowly determining. It tolerates a diversity of accommodations, hence a diversity of rules for redirecting behavior. Where physical size is decisive for some relations among people, thereby reducing the autonomy of those who are weaker, we may alter these relations so that autonomy, rather than strength and size, is the decisive value. Here is a case where alternative kinds of relatedness are considered before one is chosen. We then contrive the rules and procedures for having a social order reshaped in this way.

There is also this corollary: An ethics of character and virtue is incomplete apart from the context of rules and laws that mediate and direct the accommodations and coordinations of stable systems. We know by way of these norms what honesty, for example, is and why it is virtuous if costly. The rules alone are moral abstractions; though conversely, every particular sort of moral character and virtue is displaced and unintelligible apart from the context of those rules and relationships prescribing that we have this sort of character. There are, accordingly, three foundations for our character and virtue: (1) the natural agency of mutually engaged stable systems; (2)

the rules introduced as we choose among contending sets of rules on the way to creating a certain kind of society within the determinable natural base; (3) those behaviors encouraged and performed by agents who have learned to regulate their behaviors in the ways directed by the rules. Morality, this implies, is one part nature and the other part convention, where thought reflecting upon nature and alternative ordering relations chooses the norms that regulate behavior.

8E. Anomalies of Thought and Experience

There is, finally, this other point to consider as we apply this sample hypothesis about categorial form to ourselves and our experience: Anomalies are generated when we try to explicate all of human nature and experience within the context of some theory about categorial form. These anomalies result because of a conflict between our theory of categorial form, and the tacit, usually *ad hoc* assumptions made as we interpret some aspect of experience.

There is, for example, the opposition of our alleged direct self-perception, as in Descartes' "I am, I exist," to the implied absence of any power for self-intuition in self-regulating stable systems. This raises a question: How should we explain our intimate self-knowledge? We say that everyone's idea of him- or herself is a construction having these elements: (1) a body that perceives its own states; (2) memories of a past that coheres with one's present circumstances; (2) more or less stable expectations and plans; (4) the name by which one knows oneself and is known to other people; (5) their stable expectations and demands as one sometimes regards him- or herself as the cynosure of their attention; (6) the frequent use of personal pronouns as they focus and consolidate these other factors. These six considerations are the core of our self-recognition. They explain the conviction that we are self-perceiving, but also they dissolve the anomaly resulting when Cartesianism is set against the hypothesis that we humans are self-regulating stable systems.

Equally troubling among the anomalies of experience is the fact that the time of space-time precludes some of the claims that may seem to be justified by our experience of time. Two claims about it seem well-founded within experience: the belief that passing time is directly experienced; and the belief that time is separable from space. The direct perception of time seems apparent in our perception of things moving or otherwise changing, as we hear the successive notes of a flute and see the finger moving across a page. Hearing the flute is also evidence for the separability of space and time, as we may hear nothing of directionality or some other clue that the sounds are generated in space as well as time.

49

We might demand that every plausible notion of categorial form be consistent with, even explain, these "facts" about our experience of self and time. Why prefer some abstraction about categorial form to the compelling features of experience? The answer is that these descriptions of temporal experience, like the ones of self, may be defeasible: We may be able to explain the experience of time as a construction of something else.

Consider the alleged separability of time from space. Isn't "space-time" merely a fashionable abbreviation with a good scientific ring? Isn't that cachet too expensive, because misleading, when aural experience shows their separability? The answer I suggest is that hyphenated "space-time" is more than stylish. With motion as our point of reference, space and time are two of its necessary conditions. There is no motion without both of them, so that they are distinguishable but not separable where motion is assumed. Aural experience, interpreted as confirming the separability of space and time, is therefore anomalous with the claim that space and time are joint conditions for motion.

One response will be that the inseparability of these two as regards motion is irrelevant to the various other occasions where we experience duration or succession in time, but no motion, hence nothing of space. Suppose, for example, that Kant is right in describing time as the form of inner sense,[9] so that everything occurring within experience has a place in the temporal order, though some contents of experience are not also spatial. Why ignore these examples while insisting that time is not both distinguishable and separable from space?

There are two reasons. First is the universal applicability claimed for a hypothesis about categorial form: If nature is a protean flux where stable systems are constantly formed, sustained, and dissolved, and if we humans are exclusively natural creatures, then all of experience originates in motion. The space and time conditioning that motion will be distinguishable but inseparable. Our interpretation of experience as revealing a time separable from space must be mistaken if this hypothesis about categorial form is true. The second reason for giving precedence to our theory of categorial form is the suspicion that descriptions of temporal experience are misdescriptions. Locating these misdescriptions would enable us to eliminate the anomalies, for there is no conflict between categorial form and our experience of time if it is only our misdescriptions that generate the apparent exceptions to a hypothesis about categorial form.

How should we describe the experience of time? Imagine again some experience that is temporal but not spatial, e.g., a melody or the changing pitch of a continuous sound. Notice that the fact of having these experiences is not in question; only their interpretation is problematic. What are the properties ascribed to time on the basis of these experiences? Four are conspicuous. *First* is the succession of notes, or pitches: Terms related within the succession occur *before* or *after* one another. *Second* is a feature experienced as the passing away of each previous term. For temporal succession is not cumulative, with each sound continuing as the others are added; rather, the sounds are heard with diminishing force, until they are heard no longer. With some current sound marked as *now*, the ones before are *past* while the others anticipated are *future*. This passing away is the basis for saying that time is irreversible, as that which has passed away is inferred to be irretrievable. *Third*, each of the sounds endures, however briefly. *Fourth*, sounds may be contemporaneous: they may be heard "at the same time." These four attributes are corporately the experience of time. The first three are characteristic of every temporal experience; only the fourth is, contingently, a feature of some but not all these experiences.

What shall we say of this complex experience? Is temporality itself the object or content of experience, or is something else being described, misleadingly, as temporality? I prefer this second alternative: Temporal properties are represented within experience by considerations not themselves the core of temporality.

Consider the three notes of a familiar tune just now being heard. The second note displaces the first one while the first note is remembered and the third one is anticipated. Three of the four properties credited to time, plus one other not mentioned above, are ascribed to this brief experience. There is succession in the relation of the first two notes. Passing away is experienced when the first note is succeeded by our memory of it. Duration is provided for when the temporal spread of either note has two constituents: the note heard; and the augmentation of that sound by our memory of it. There is also a basis within the experience for the directionality of time, though this is more accurately the directionality of the developing tune. It is often important to some evolving experiential content, though not perhaps to time itself, that this directedness is confirmed, as when the anticipated third note is heard.

The anomaly that concerned us is now eliminated, for there is no conflict between the inseparability of space and time alleged by our hypothesis about categorial form, and our experience of time as separable from space. That conflict is only apparent, when the experience of a separable time turns out to be something quite different from this characterization of it: namely, that complex of percepts, memories, and anticipations construed as the experience of time. The experience-of-time is, I mean to say, a construction that is not in any way a direct perception of time itself.

We do of course infer from this experience-of-time to time's own properties, though the experience is equivocal because of allowing for a diversity of interpretations, including some that are contrary, e.g., that time is continuous or corpuscular. The experience-of-time is, therefore, an inconclusive basis for our hypotheses about time.

There is, finally, this last consideration: Perception, memory and anticipation may be the activities of a physical system, especially the brain. The motions producing them will presuppose, as our hypothesis about categorial form declares, that space and time are distinguishable but not separable.

8F. Summary

This is a place for taking our bearings. The spiral of reflection had carried us from thinking about practice and its conditions to nature's categorial form. Now, we have descended from these claims about nature's pervasive least features and its blueprint to the more ample consideration of us human beings and our place within nature. Using the idea of self-regulating and reciprocally related stable systems as a sample theory of categorial form, we have understood that some at least of the features distinguishing human life are explicable in the terms of this hypothesis. This descent from categorial form to human nature has been speculative in the way that applying a generality to some new particular is speculative: We have wanted to confirm that our universal hypothesis is applicable and adequate to this class of particulars. I shall suppose, though nothing about thought's spiral hangs on this claim, that this hypothesis is or might be confirmed. We are located within nature as its creatures, with nothing to exempt us from its constraints, and nothing about us that is not explicable in its terms.

9. Nature's Conditions

There are two additional tasks for metaphysics, one of them speculative in all the ways that positivists deplore. Somewhat less controversial is the question of being: How shall we characterize everything previously studied in regard to its being? Is there one sort of being only, or does being have distinctive modes? Thinkers who find these questions thin to the point of emptiness might nevertheless accept them as harmless. There is likely to be no equivalent charity for the prior task of asking about nature's self-sufficiency. Is nature, in its parts and altogether, self-sufficient, or does it have extranatural conditions?

There is, for example, the finding that words and sentences are meaningful. A sentence is meaningful if it is syntactically correct, meaning well-formed, and if the arrangement of its descriptive words is semantically correct, as 'It's raining numbers' is one but not the other. Both conditions need be satisfied if a sentence is to be meaningful. Yet these are necessary, not sufficient, conditions for meaning. This is so because words and sentences are the signs for extralinguistic matters of fact. There are two other conditions to satisfy if words are to have that force. First is the requirement that the words be construed as signs. Imagine a sentence in English, then one in a language we do not read, where both sentences satisfy the syntactic and semantic combination rules of their respective languages. Is the apparent meaningfulness of the English sentence merely the result of satisfying these rules? This is one of the relevant considerations, but not the only one: The English sentence is meaningful because of being construed as the complex sign for a possible state of affairs. The possibility signified is the other condition for meaning: viz., a word or sentence is meaningful if it is construed as the sign of some possible property or state of affairs. Material truth is definable now as the relation between a sentence and that actuality which instantiates the possibility signified by the sentence.

The idea that something within nature, i.e., meaning, has an extranatural condition, i.e., the possibilities signified, has its complement in the idea that all of nature is conditioned by something extranatural. Remember the first lines of Wittgenstein's *Tractatus:* "The world is all that is the case"[10] and "The facts in logical space are the world."[11] The facts in logical space are the possible states of affairs represented by meaningful sentences, logical space being just the aggregate of these possibles. The world that "is determined by the facts, and by their being *all* the facts"[12] is the world of instantiated possibilities, the world of actual states of affairs. Wittgenstein has supposed that every possibility in logical space is independent of every other one, but in this, he is likely to be mistaken. For possibilities seem to be organized in various ways, as a possible world is one that satisfies a certain least degree of complexity in the relations of its constituent possibles. These least organizing features are apparently common to all possible worlds, so that any actual world, ours included, is conditioned by these internal constraints.[13]

Let us follow this hypothesis one step further, for there beyond the limits of nature, we see the conditions for actuality merging with the conditions for meaning and the unrealized but sometimes realizable objects of desire. That happens when the possibilities signified by our sentences, words and thoughts are the possibles from which our world is instantiated; when true sentences represent a subset of all the possibilities signified; and when ideals are possibilities uninstantiated, i.e., possibilities that we may signify, then work to achieve. This is one of the several convergences we should expect if being is arranged economically, with a relatively small number of factors reinforcing one another in ways that integrate the whole.

There is, however, the greatest reluctance to make these inferences from nature or some of its features to extranatural conditions. Sometimes this caution is justified by the assumption that nature is and must be self-sufficient, so that it has and needs no conditions. More often, the antipathy to these inferences expresses the suspicion that we have no way of testing them. This suspicion is most important, for metaphysical hypotheses, like the ones of practice and science, should be responsible because testable. What tests are classically available to us, and how do they apply in these circumstances? Consider these alternatives.

One test requires that we look for the observable difference that would result if the possibility signified by our hypothesis did obtain. Observability implies that the thing instantiated is accessible to us by way of the sensible differences it makes in us. The reverse is not implied: that the sum of sensible differences, or an infinitely denumerable class of them, is identical with the thing observed. Apples do not reduce to the sensory differences they make, as more generally reality is not identical with the things that are or might be set before our inspecting minds.

An apple's perceived color is the effect of light reflected from its surface. This example illustrates just one of the several kinds of relation holding between empirical effects and the things observed. For many of the properties ascribed to things observed do not correlate, as proximate cause and effect, with those sensory data which are evidence for our hypotheses about them. So, electromagnetic fields and migrations are observed, though observation in these cases requires that we infer to the existence and character of these things from the sensory differences that are made by some other things observed, e.g., magnets and birds flying. Observing a migration is a complicated act, one that requires some current observation of birds in flight coupled to memories or reports of previous observations, all of this joined to the inference construing the behavior as a migration. Still, we do reasonably say that migrations are observed. We have only to agree that the inference from sensory effects to their causes is always complex, mediated, and fallible.

The alternative test requires that we prove the truth of a hypothesis by demonstrating that its negation is, or implies a contradiction. There are several objections to tests of this sort, but one of them especially can be acknowledged, then discounted. We suppose that the logic appropriate to demonstration is the one including the law of excluded middle, i.e., either *p* or *not-p*, though there are alternative logics available for making inferences

54

about the world. The use of a logic including excluded middle is provisional so long as we have no proof that this logic is the only one applicable to relations within nature, and to nature's relations to its alleged conditions. Some interpretations of quantum theory deny the universality of this rule's application, though the question is unresolved.[14] We have in the meantime no compelling reason for believing that any other logic does apply to the relations to which demonstration might be pertinent.

There are, of course, some other objections to using demonstration for testing our claims about the world. Many of us suppose that the necessities confirmed in this way are only tautologies: They are stipulative definitions, e.g., 'Bachelors are unmarried males', or they result from organizing the logical constants within a sentence so that it is true for every consistent substitution of truth values for its variables. This idea of necessary truth is too narrow, if, for example, the laws of motion derive from the geometry of space-time. For then we cannot assume the negation of one or more of the relevant geometrical features of space-time without implying the negation of these laws. Demonstrations regarding relations within a geometrized space-time do, accordingly, represent constraints upon every change occurring there. As the rules of a game limit or determine every next move within it, so is a geometrized space-time, with the laws deriving from it, the matrix of constitutive or merely regulative factors limiting whatever changes occur within it.

Suppose, for example, that we demonstrate some necessary characteristic of the trajectories occurring in a particular kind of space, e.g., they are great circles, not the straight lines of Euclidean geometry. This is a parochial truth, i.e., a truth local to spaces of this sort. It is, nevertheless, necessary to these spaces that straight lines be great circles, as it is necessary to chess that bishops move on the diagonal. Having this parochially necessary truth is not, however, a sufficient reason for saying that anything has been demonstrated of our world. Confirming its applicability here requires the additional, empirical premise that space in our world is curved. Now having that premise, we say that the demonstrated claim about curved space does apply in our world, e.g., straight lines here are great circles. We do not allege that some necessary constraint operates within nature, or in nature's relations to its conditions, until we have both a demonstration, and some relevant empirical claim confirmed by observation.

These necessary constraints make an empirical difference, as Mercury's perihelion causes the subtle but particular sensible difference appropriate to a curved space. Understanding this difference requires a process having several steps. It begins as we infer from the empirical effect to its possible conditions. These are, most often, conditions to which this effect seems to relate contingently, as choice may seem to be more or less arbitrary as regards the things chosen. There may, however, be some hypothesis specifying conditions from which this effect would derive necessarily, in the way that the great circular trajectories of light are necessary in a curved space. There might be several hypotheses of this sort, each one identifying some different ground having this effect as a necessary consequence of itself (as we might begin explaining a move in an unfamiliar game by hypothesizing to those alternative sets of rules that would sanction it).

We could not know in advance that the effect at issue relates contingently or necessarily to its conditions, though we might hope to progress, as Leibniz said we should, by moving from a contingent truth to the constraining and sometimes sufficient generating conditions for this effect. Our objective, one that is rarely achieved, is the formulation of those factual judgments which Kant might have called analytic *a posteriori*: Starting from the observation of apparent contingencies, we hope to identify the identity-determining conditions for all of their features, or for one or more of their generic features. How shall we do that when there might be no suspected necessary ground, or when there are several competing hypotheses, each of them specifying a different ground? The one prospect might express the shallowness of our current thinking. The other one would require that we find some empirical effect, independent of the effect which has provoked us. We could use this other effect for choosing among the competing hypotheses, if it would not occur unless one of these sets of conditions were to obtain. The hypothesis explaining both it and the original effect would be the one more likely to be true.

The obstacles to formulating, then confirming our claims about any one set of generating, constraining conditions are formidable. Still, we needn't avoid or deride these hypotheses, and the proposed demonstrations for them when, for example, a geometrized space-time is our evidence for saying that truths about the parochial necessities prevailing within nature can be formulated and tested.

We have still to consider the domains in which the tests of these two sorts apply. Both tests, the empirical one and demonstration, are applicable to hypotheses about nature's categorial form: that much is explicit in the examples proposed above. Is this also true of nature's conditions: Are both tests also pertinent to them?

The answer is plainer when we have noticed that there are conditions of two sorts: causal and noncausal. We normally suppose that empirical differences are the effects of causes, where hypotheses are true if they signify the causes of perceived effects. Every cause falls within nature, where nature is described for these purposes as the matrix of things causally accessible to one another. (Relativity theory limits this accessibility, though not in a way that subverts the formulation: Two things not accessible to one another may be accessible, in the remote past or future, to some thing that links them.) The empirical test might seem to have application only within this network, for nothing outside it could be the cause of sensible differences within it. Even the God of cosmological arguments would have to be described in either of two ways: as an agent acting as a cause within a nature extended to include it, or as an extranatural condition that is not a cause. A God acting as a cause would make a visible difference, by virtue of creating the visible universe. The God acting outside of nature would make the same difference, but not as a cause.

There are various examples of extranatural conditions that would make an empirical difference, as the possibilities conditioning actualities make an empirical difference. Our problem is that hypotheses about these extranatural conditions are usually precarious to the extreme. We may not succeed very well in specifying the conditions; or the evidence construed as favorable to hypotheses about them may be easily interpreted in another way, as someone who explains a noise by ascribing it to the voice of God is likely to be told that what he hears are people talking in the next room. We do better, therefore, if we are scrupulous in construing the empirical hypotheses allegedly having an extranatural ground. Where the very plausibility of a hypothesis is an issue, we prefer a more decisive test for its truth: A well-formed, apparently substantive hypothesis should not be ignored, we say, because its negation is a contradiction. A nontrivial hypothesis that fails this test might still be true, as no claim about God is, so far, successfully demonstrated. Still, we cannot be surprised when people wanting a decisive test doubt the plausibility of those hypotheses about nature's conditions which are not demonstrated.

Are there any plausible examples of hypotheses about nature's conditions that are necessary truths? Yes, there are: Many truths of number theory satisfy this requirement, if we suppose that any world embodying a plurality of things would have to satisfy them. A less familiar but equally important example concerns the modalities. Whatever is not a contradiction is a possibility, so that something is either a contradiction or a possibility. Its being a possible is, therefore, necessary, if that something is not a contradiction. Something that is necessarily a possibility is eternally possible. This argument is mute regarding the "something" or "somethings" which are possible. What might they be? It is, I suggest, properties, both simple and complex, which exist as possibles. There is, this implies, a domain of possibilities, construed as properties and their complexes, existing eternally. Add now the demonstration that actuality presupposes possibility, as nothing that cannot be, i.e., nothing that is not possible, is actual. Any actual world presupposes a possible world. But is anything actual? Here we intrude this empirical premise: Our world is actual by virtue of being a distribution of properties in space-time. This actual world, i.e., nature, is conditioned, by the possible world instantiated here.

This may be disappointing as an example of hypotheses that carry beyond nature to its conditions. We might admit this realist interpretation of logical possibilities without seeming to have additional information about the world. I believe that information of a significant kind is forthcoming if there is an ascertainable hierarchical structure to possible worlds, a structure that is prefigured in them and identifiable in our world.[15] The inference to a domain of possibilities does, on these assumptions, provide a condition for nature, and information about it.

Our concern, however, is not this example but only the point it makes: that nature may have conditions, and that hypotheses identifying them are testable in a way that combines demonstration and observation. We shall not, of course, be able to use this test in every case. Some of our most ambitious hypotheses about nature's conditions never are demonstrable, as we speculate about the existence and character of God. Speculation exceeds testability: We cannot tell if these hypotheses are true or not. What shall we say of them?

We might insist that every untestable hypothesis be rejected. For here, at this nearly final turn of thought's spiral, we have reached the place where metaphysical hypotheses are not distinguishable from religious myths. Emotional or communal values may supersede the interest in truth. We risk losing the rigor and discipline that have carried through out speculations from practice and science to the testable orders of metaphysical thinking.

We might want to eliminate every untestable hypothesis in order to minimize the chance that these considerations might dominate our thinking. I suggest a different policy. Imagination is and ought to be liberated for speculating at the borders and foundations of reality. We do no harm by hypothesizing beyond the limits of testability if we have carefully marked the hypotheses which are not testable. These are sometimes the most powerful myths and metaphors shaping our views of the world, as Plato's claims about the Forms direct our thinking of it. Why now allow that some hypotheses about nature's conditions may be the figurative expressions of truths that we may sometime translate and test? Any demand more restrictive than this one reinstates the peevish concern for intuitionist certainty, though the restless way of our thinking makes it likely that we shall always speculate untestably about nature's conditions, however settled we are about its categorial form.

10. Being

One more task remains. This one is less speculative than retrospective: We need a space for reflecting upon the generic features of nature and its conditions. This will be the time for considering being *qua* being, the being of nature and the being of its conditions, being in its modes, and being in the relation of these modes. We shall want to characterize and summarize all that has gone before. We might say, for example, that being has actuality and possibility as its expressions, one as the mode of determinacy in quality and quantity, the other as the mode of qualitative and quantitative determinability.[16] This too is a hypothesis, indeed, a hybrid deriving one part from our observations of determinate nature, the other from our speculations about possibilities defined by their determinability. This hypothesis, like every other one that is meaningful, may be true or false, though here, at this farthest reach of careful reflection, our characterizations of being are conjectures stretched thin. We shall likely say too little or too much. Wanting to be responsible, we find ourselves almost having to be reckless. Yet these claims too may be testable in one or the other of the ways considered above, as the existence of actualities is observed, while that of the possibles is demonstrated. "Reckless" does not have to mean portentous or dogmatic.

11. Conclusion

It may seem, from my way of describing it, that thought's trajectory through science and metaphysics is easily discerned, and extended. Nothing so banal is intended. Never mind that most people, most of the time, are too preoccupied with saving their lives to rise much beyond these concerns. Nor do I suggest that categorial form is plainly intimated to most scientists. Metaphysicians are all the more distracted, by two things especially. One is the intuitionist bias that affects so much of philosophic thinking. We too often suppose that some feature of reality might stand before our minds as an inspectable given. We allow that there may be a diversity of contents satisfying this description (as words, thoughts, feelings, and the mind itself are said to be inspectable), but we hardly concede that reality might surpass inspectability. Second is our preoccupation with the history of metaphysical thinking. Why launch ourselves on this most ambitious of inquiries, if we can loiter instead in the theories of our antecedents? Notice, however, that their thinking is usually tainted by their intuitionism, so that we find them forever turning about the conditions for certainty in regard to things whose only reality depends upon the fact that they are or can be set before our inspecting minds. How should we use the history of philosophy for the purposes of the reflection I have proposed when this intuitionist bias is endemic to the practice of philosophy? What is left of that history when we have rejected intuitionist method, with its demand that we have certainty as regards the subject matters inspected, and its ontological claim that nothing is real if it is not inspectable?

Two aspects of our history survive to inform the more speculative but experimental inquiry proposed above. One consideration is the eye-popping diversity of hypotheses about us and the world, some curious and trivial, others evocative and deep when stripped of their intuitionist bias. The other useful consideration is the dialectic animating and propeling the instinct for metaphysical thinking. This is, at one level, the dialectic of the many theories, each one promising to do better than its adversaries. More fundamentally, this is the dialectic of regulative principles. The one and the many, is and ought, actuality and possibility, particular and universal, any difference and its sufficient condition: these are some examples of the ideas and principles that have come to define the arena in which we think metaphysically. Each of these pairs establishes one of the tensions addressed as we formulate and appraise our hypotheses about the world. It is not so important, therefore, that the first statements of these principles are usually formulated within an intuitionist theory; there are naturalized versions which survive when that bias is removed. Like the keys that stretch the surface of a drum, these principles supply the oppositions on which our hypotheses resonate.

The history of philosophy is, therefore, crucial to the spiral of reflection, though its worth is less in the recounting of particular doctrines, and more in the dialectical tensions that drive the many theories. It is not surprising if the equable progression implied by my description of thought's spiral is regularly disrupted by the discovery that some currently favored theory has ignored one or another of the oppositions that establish the conceptual field within which inquiry progresses. For theorizing looks these two ways: to the phenomena which hypotheses are meant to explain, i.e., to nature and its conditions; and to these dialectical oppositions. Anyone who does the one while ignoring the other has missed the metaphysical boat.

Notice too that inquiry is incomplete, until we have asked about the status of these dialectical pairs: Are they effectively regulative because of representing pervasive relations within the world, or because we use them to establish the field of significant discourse? Kant supposed that regulative principles need not be true of anything beyond themselves while controlling inquiry. He denied, in particular, that these principles could ever be shown to have their foundation within the world.[17] But is that right, when regulative principles seem to have two faces: they direct our inquiries into a world apparently instantiating these very principles. Kantian intuitionists, i.e., prescriptivists, would say that this is a case of thought seeing its own shadow, as form is projected onto sensory data. Consider the one and the many, a difference vital to everyone trying to live within, or govern, a big city. Is this difference merely a rubric for thinking about diversity and totality, or does it represent real features in things themselves? There are some principles that practice or science has shown to be irrelevant to inquiry because of being false to the world: "like knows like" being one of them. Some other principles are useful devices for keeping track of things, or merely for organizing our thoughts about them, e.g., "canonical" form. But equally, there are principles, like the one and the many, that endure as organizing or directing principles of thought because the preponderance of logical or empirical evidence speaks for their validity as representations of real differences and relations within the world. The history of philosophy chronicles our discoveries of, and justifications for, these principles. That may be its primary utility when the intuitionist bias is rejected. The generation of these principles, as claims about the world and as directives for inquiry, is, however, mysterious. Chapter 4 describes their source, and the objective basis for their applicability.

2

The Intuitionist Alternative

The reflection that starts as we turn upon our circumstances and problems moves beyond us, first as it locates us within nature, then as we characterize all of being. There is, however, this other view.

1. The Intuitionist Notion of Reality and Inquiry

Intuitionism requires that everything real be presentable (or more radically, that it be presented) for inspection. No thing exists if it is not, or cannot be set before mind as its determining content. Sensations, ideas, words, sentences, theories, and mind itself are alleged to be inspectable, hence real. Other things, e.g., material objects or eternal possibilities, have no claim to reality because they are not inspectable. This idealist result is a consequence of the intuitionist demand that we eliminate every chance of error by closing the gap between thought and its objects. Error is precluded where nothing is concealed, and all the things set before our minds are seen as they are, with no gap or medium distorting our view of them.

Intuitionists would have us devote ourselves to providing within mind for whatever differentiations and relations are required for a self-sufficient world. Nothing essential to the world is to be left outside of mind, where knowledge claims cannot reach. It is incidental to this generic point that we identify the world with sensory data or the articulations of a comprehensive scientific theory. All of the world is, in either case, to stand before our minds, nothing hidden, all of it thinkable.

One might argue, like Plato, that finite minds exceed themselves on the way to confronting reality, i.e., the Forms.[1] More often, the argument assumes that mental activity and its content are contained within the horizons of finite self-consciousness. Every thing then claimed as real earns that title because of being one of mind's inspectable qualifications. Even mind itself would have no claim to reality were it not self-inspectable. Descartes' *cogito* is, on this later view, the fundament for all of being, and the crucible within which being discovers itself.[2] This hermetic idealism is usually individual and solipsistic, but we make it cultural by extrapolation. For thought's horizons are fixed by mind's own structure, or by the language or theory used for thinking about the world. Reflection is, on either telling, a kind of light that mind directs first onto its own determining content, then onto itself. The spiral described in Chapter 1 is reduced to being a small, closed circle.

Descartes' *Meditations* and Kant's First Critique are the emphatic challenge to views like mine. Metaphysics is first, not last, Descartes supposed, because the truth of "I am, I exist" is prior in knowledge and being to every claim except the one affirming God's existence. His *cogito* is the unqualified foundation for every truth when Descartes' successors have dispensed with God. My concern is Descartes' legacy, not the full scope of his views. There are these four points to consider.

First is the claim that knowledge of one's own existence is assured, even necessary, in the moment of self-discovery, though our every other belief might be false.[3]

Second is the claim that mind, now secured in the knowledge of its own existence and character, reviews every other proposal about matters of fact in order to decide which ones are true. We are to look for the clarity and distinctness that are sufficient marks of truth, withholding assent from any idea that is not clear and distinct.[4] Notice what this implies: that an idea or belief might satisfy this condition for truth without our having any empirical evidence of the things signified by our clear and distinct ideas. Every truth is to be a demonstrated truth. We confirm, for example, that two plus two are four by showing that the negation of this complex idea is a contradiction, not by counting the beads on a string. This *a priori* appraising of ideas, not the search for confirming empirical evidence, establishes that the ideas are true. A mind having this posture is not yet the arbiter of truth, a posture to which later Cartesians will elevate it. Ideas are clear and distinct in themselves without regard to any judgment of ours: Their negations are, or are not, contradictions. Still, we have a first glimmering of mind's power as it selects among the candidates for truth, certifying some, rejecting the others.

This authority is all the more apparent when, *third,* we consider the many ideas whose negations are not contradictions. These are the contingencies. In them, clarity and distinctness do not have the logical force that Descartes claims for truths whose negations are contradictions. He supposed that these, usually material ideas would eventually be resolvable into ideas of mathematical properties and relations, as our idea of wax is, ideally, geometrical.[5] This ideal is never realized: Negating or altering our idea of the sun produces another idea, not a contradiction. This is an example of the many ideas for which clarity and distinctness come to be reformulated as a discretionary criterion, meaning one that mind interprets in a way congenial to itself. We decide what properties shall qualify these contingent ideas for being "clear and distinct."

Fourth is the elision of existence and truth. This is the result when mind's power for deciding what ideas shall count as true has the consequence of giving mind responsibility for determining what does or can exist. Suppose that an existing state of affairs corresponds to every true sentence, where "existing" signifies whatever matters of fact are signified by true sentences or ideas, whether positive or negative, e.g., 'There are no unicorns' as well as 'There are crickets'. The power for deciding the conditions for truth is at the same time the power for deciding what sentences shall count as true, hence for deciding what things shall exist.

These four claims have this effect. Being Cartesians of a literal sort, we use clarity and distinctness as the test for truth. But then, where no contradiction results from negating a multitude of ideas or sentences, we are left with a domain of truth claims for which there is no infallible test. We decide that particular sentences are true or not, after we have interpreted clarity and distinctness in some other, not strictly logical way. We might even repudiate clarity and distinctness as our criteria, saying that they are too impressionistic. We might, for example, prefer saying that sentences are true if they cohere, more or less tightly, within a story or narrative of some kind, as the sentences of a novel or scientific theory cohere. We add that the sentences cohering within an "interpretation" must also satisfy the requirement that we be able to use the interpretation for organizing our sensory data in a systematic and reliable way. This interpretation creates the experience of a "world," and, because of its criterion for truth, both a set of truths about that world and, derivatively, the set of existences current within it.

There might be any number of interpretations that are coherent and effective in this way, though each of them might differ from others in regard to the differences, relations and entities ascribed to the world. Mind has authority for formulating, then accepting any one of these interpretations, then the freedom for taking up one interpretation after another: Mind is empowered for creating a succession of coherent experiences, truths, existing states of affairs and worlds. Where some of these interpretations are mutually exclusive, mind creates a succession of contrary worlds, meaning worlds that could not obtain "in the same place at the same time."

The modern sources for this prescriptivist creation story are Descartes and Kant. Plato is their more remote ancestor. His Forms may have been suggested by the ideas in our minds, rather as Husserl's eidetic reduction moves from sensory data to the essences they exhibit.[6] Plato too makes clarity and distinctness a criterion for truth, as one cannot be mistaken about seeing the sun. Still, Plato's remarks about Forms and truth do not encourage the view that either one is psychologistic or discretionary. His Forms have an existence and character that are independent of our finite minds. Each of us looks beyond himself, when knowing them, to a cosmic, rational order, one that we have not made. It is, however, Plato who suggests that the whole evidence for truth might be the state of mind induced by the ideas themselves, as we who are blinded by the sun can hardly doubt our idea of its force. Descartes is more cautious. He localizes the content, activity, and authority of mind, ascribing ideas to our finite minds, then to God. Ignoring God and his guarantee has the effect of giving mind the unchallengeable authority for deciding what thoughts or sentences shall be counted as true. Where existence correlates exactly with material truth, we are left to concede that autonomy in setting the conditions for meaning and truth confirms mind's power as world-maker.

This idealist, prescriptivist result cripples the spiral of reflection. Its boundaries are now reduced to the ones of inspectable self-consciousness, or to those transcendental activities to which we infer as we argue from a characterization of experience to its still intrapsychic conditions. We get introspection or transcendental psychology, but nothing that would extend the domain of our thinking so that it might reach beyond us into a world that is independent of the ways we think, perceive, and talk about it. There are, instead, the various prescriptivist foundations for experience including the "logical geography" of ordinary language, Husserl's eidetic reflection, Carnap's semantical frameworks, Gadamer's interpretations, and the fields of interanimating sentences described by Quine. Mind is first in being and authority (through all these variations) as it lays down the differences and relations with which to think an intelligible world, then the criteria for deciding what shall count as true claims about that "world" schematized by our thinking.

How ironic that Descartes should be celebrated for deflating metaphysics, when he espouses a different metaphysics, one that turns skeptical about the external world while focusing exclusively upon mind and its products. Descartes recalls us to that psychocentric ontology which has sometimes poisoned metaphysics from classical times onward. For there is no claim more speculative and precarious than the one affirming that mind is a self-sufficient world-maker, where every other thing "exists" only because mind has rendered it thinkable. This is the view to repudiate if we agree that thought and action locate us within a world we have not made. Talk about thought's spiral is then a useful orienting metaphor. It suggests that sequence of reflections which pass from thought-directed action, with its plans and regularizing norms, to hypotheses about our place within nature, then to hypotheses about nature's more general features and conditions.

2. "Empiricism" as a Kind of Intuitionism

There are, of course, many philosophers who object to the claim that mind makes experience, hence the world, either by creating a thinkable experience, or by establishing the criteria for meaning and truth. Most of us agree that mind is not the measure of all that is, or is not. Isn't Hume our example, as we test our claims about a world we have not made against the empirical evidence? I suggest that this defense expresses only the appearance, not the real drift, of our inclinations. There are two things to notice as we realize that Descartes' idealism, and even his a priorism, are fundamental to Hume's empiricism.

One consideration is the affinity between Descartes and Hume. Both of them are intuitionists; they agree that something qualifies as real only if it can be set before our inspecting minds. God is the one exception to this rule for Descartes. There is no exception for Hume; nothing exists, he argues, if there is no impression of it.[7] The things that do exist are not separate from us; existence is, for Hume, only the force and vivacity of our impressions. Consequently, the fact that Hume waits for impressions to show us what is present in the world should not incline us to say that Hume locates reality in states of affairs having an existence independent of our minds. He shrinks reality to the horizons of inspecting mind.

Hume might seem to refute this interpretation by his insistence that there is no encompassing, inspecting mind having impressions and ideas arrayed before it. This objection reminds us of Hume's assertion that mind never discovers an impression of itself; there are, he says, only the impressions and ideas of other things.[8] Mind has disappeared, though we cannot escape having to specify those conditions for experience which Hume ignores, for surely there are no impressions and ideas, no simple inferences, and no habits without the mind empowered for inspecting and organizing its contents. All of Humean experience is the qualification or suffusion occurring within that mind.

A second consideration requires that we look beyond Hume to the thinking of subsequent empiricists. Many of them distrust the clarity that Hume ascribed to percepts, a clarity sufficient to make every percept immediately recognizable. There are two other possibilities: Impressions are obscure in themselves, requiring ideas or words to differentiate and clarify them; or experience overwhelms us because of its richness and diversity until we simplify and differentiate it by using a relatively small set of concepts or words. Husserl speaks for the first of these claims as he says that impressions would be obscure but for the ideas which signify and exhibit the relevant differences.[9] Carnap disagrees, saying that mind is baffled by the diversity of sensations until it introduces the concepts which differentiate the myriad percepts.[10] Both sides agree that the intelligibility of perceptual data is founded partly or absolutely in mind, as we make or discover within ourselves the concepts or words used for thinking the data. But then it follows that every difference credited to the world, however specific and empirical, is founded in thought or language, not in the data themselves. Impressions are opaque, meaning too obscure or profuse for thought, until mind introduces the concepts which make them discriminable.

This is the progression as empiricist intuitionism is reclaimed for Cartesian a priorism. It is contingent that the flash I see is red; though red is an *a priori* difference, one that I project onto the sensation occurring within me. Every more abstract notion, e.g., dog and cat, gene and proton, property, number, and law, are all the more plainly notions which mind has introduced for differentiating and organizing experience. We are acquainted with these concepts, because we have formulated or discovered them within ourselves. They might be extracted from experience, then refined and used for differentiating subsequent data, or they might be innate. Either way, we are to suppose that an articulated experience, meaning experience of the sort we humans have, requires that mind should have whatever concepts or words are required for differentiating and ordering its sensory data.

This is, I agree, a misdescription of Hume. Mind, as he described it, is passive to its impressions, managing nothing more than habits to anticipate recurring impressions, ideas to copy them, and simple inferences. Still, Hume has reduced existence to the force and vivacity of the data inspected, so that he no more than Kant allows that thought's objects might be located outside the arena of conscious awareness. Descartes, by comparison, has tried to provide for extra-mental realities. He does not suppose that

68

thought provides access to them, for thinking is only the analysis or synthesis of the ideas set before our minds. Still, he does affirm some postulates entailing the existence of extra-mental things when certain contingencies are satisfied. Descartes argues that there must be as much reality in the cause as there is in its effect; and that our finite minds do not have the power for creating all of their sensory data and ideas.[11] This point is claimed as decisive evidence for the reality of God, when our idea of an infinite being is said to have that being as its cause. This God is to secure the truth of our clear and distinct ideas, though later, when Descartes' successors reject the speculative assumptions that seemed to justify his claims about God and material things, all reality reduces to the matters set before our inspecting minds.

3. The Socialization and Autonomy of Intuiting Mind

This summary characterization of thinkers past may seem to have an antiquarian interest only. Why bother with discredited views when contemporary thinkers agree that meanings and experience are public? Meanings, we remember from Dewey[12] and Wittgenstein,[13] are conditioned by public criteria. There are rules to which all of us defer as we show by our conduct what we mean, believe, and intend. We are mistaken, therefore, if we carry on saying that mind creates the world as we think or talk about it. For no mind is intelligible, even to itself, until it learns the rules enabling us to think and communicate about a common world. Mind is forced out of itself, into the public world, just because of having to be intelligible to others and itself. Thought and meaning, even personal identity, have a social basis.

This argument, with Hegel inspiring it, is only superficially opposed to the mentalism apparent in Descartes, Hume, and Kant. Reality, Hegel says, is Substance-for-Subject, not merely Substance.[14] This Subject is the *cogito* writ large: It is the Absolute or God. With all of reality lodged within God's mind, or derivatively within the social "mind," it is not surprising that forms of thought, e.g., the ideas, presupposed by the world's intelligibility should also originate there.

The socially founded rules responsible for whatever is meaningful and thinkable within a culture might begin as ideas in the mind of God; but that is their more remote cause. The proximate causes are finite, human minds. The rules start as conventions formulated by particular thinkers, before being learned and refined by the other members of a culture. These shared rules prescribe whatever differentiations, relations, and values this community ascribes to its corporate reality. World-making passes from be-

69

ing an individual to a communal activity, though the result is not different from the one that Kant described; i.e., the only thinkable reality is the one we schematize.[15] All the rest is unknowable because unthinkable.

The reality that Kant described as the product of individual minds is now socialized. Still, the two objections considered above are pertinent and unanswered: We are asked to believe that reality depends for its character and existence on our ways of thinking or talking about it; and that thought is only the organizing of sensory data, the production of significant discourse, or the rule-governed directing of behavior. We never admit that thought might formulate and test hypotheses representing a world it has not made. Mind's product is socialized, though we have not altered the Cartesian view that nothing is better known to mind than mind and its works. Nothing else, we have conceded, can be thought or known. Minds are world-makers. First laying down the conditions for intelligibility, mind uses these differences and relations for creating a thinkable experience, and thereby a thinkable world.

Why should we suppose that minds have this autonomy and power? Two reasons are assumed. First is the dread that a world independent of our awareness might forever elude our knowing it. We do, however, seem to know many things so that, second, we turn this skeptical fear into the unabashedly idealist claim that mind itself prescribes the conditions for a thinkable experience and world. This is, still more fundamentally, the intuitionist assertion that nothing shall be alleged of the world unless that thing can be set before our inspecting minds.

Mind satisfies this intuitionist requirement only as the differences and relations used in "making" a "world," then that schematized "world," are the content of its self-reflection. Where "I am, I exist" is the elemental expression of our knowledge, mind knows itself by catching its reflection in some other content known, as I know something of myself in thinking or perceiving any other thing. We add that mind's contents are, for this intuitionist, psychocentric view, its determining qualifications. Everything else, i.e., everything whose existence and character are independent of mind, is dismissed as unthinkable. There is, by the time of Kant, only the idea of negative noumena to mark the place that was once occupied by the world known, a world owing nothing to mind for its existence and character. Even this vestige disappears when Carnap distinguishes the questions internal and external to a conceptual framework. The external questions, those concerning a world independent of mind and language, are, he says, meaningless.[16]

Some important things have been confused. When the applicability of our ideas or sentences was contested, because we could not guarantee the existence of their referents, three claims were introduced. *First* was Descartes' proposal that the ambit of truth shrinks to whatever ideas are seen to be irrefutably true. The bearers of truth are to be inspectable; their truth is to be discerned as they are inspected, without additional, confirming evidence of the matters signified. This means, in practice, that we prove the truth of arithmetic ideas by showing that their negations are contradictions. We do not supplement this proof by counting the apples in a basket. *Second* was the shift from ideas to rules. Ideas "about" something that is not directly inspectable reach dangerously, unverifiably, into the void. It seemed better that ideas be redescribed as rules. This redescription has two advantages: it eliminates the uninspectable, extra-mental referent for ideas, while freeing mind to invent and apply its own rules. This confirms mind's autonomy. Individually or corporately, mind or minds are acknowledged as world-makers. For there is no extra-mental consideration to which mind defers as we appraise our rules, their applications and products, i.e., the worlds created. Mind has formulated the rules appropriate to some activity, and the norms for appraising them. The *third* point is here, where truth is reduced to being one of these norms. Mind confirms that the rule-governed relations of thoughts or sentences are true or not, as it confirms that some other activities are legal or not. Where truth prefigures existence, mind's authority regarding it is sufficient to determine what is true or false, existent or not.

There are rules for making truth claims and other rules for playing and winning at chess. The similarity between these examples is superficial, as it is a well-founded theory, not a well-played game, that is true. We can decide what to search for within the world; but then we are not also free to decide, by creating the rules for meaning and truth, all that is present there. We do stipulate what *red* shall signify, but not that anything is red. We have obscured this difference by emphasizing the activities best expressing our autonomy, as novelists create fantasy worlds and legislators write the laws creating a social order. These examples are distractions from the task of formulating and testing hypotheses about those things whose existence and character are independent of thought and language. It is most important, therefore, that we recover the distinction between the two sorts of activity, the one performed as we construct certain things, the other performed as possible matters of fact are represented by our hypotheses. We create novels, constitutions, signs and their interpretations. We also represent them, together with the many things minds have not created, by thinking and talking about them. We usually know the difference between doing the one thing or the other. Predicting panic may cause it, but this result is not so typical as the one of talking about the weather while making no difference to it.

Let us acknowledge that mind thinks constructively and hypothetically, doing one or the other as circumstances justify and require. Why not start our metaphysical reflections by locating ourselves within nature, then by explaining that our situation there requires constructions and hypotheses too? The "spiral of reflection" is a way of characterizing thought's activity as we do both these things, creating a livable space for ourselves, while making and testing speculations about nature, our place there, and its conditions. Thinking has these two effects. They are complementary, but different.

World-making and mind's perfect autonomy are a delusion, one resulting when the truth of hypotheses is misdescribed in the terms appropriate to mind's responsibility for its constructions. We cure ourselves because of that innate *telos* which forces us beyond the urgencies of practical life to a concern for what and where we are.

3

Hypothesis

1. Interpretation

One assumption about metaphysics is often shared by those who renounce it. Metaphysical theories are not true, they say, because of being neither true nor false. Opponents of one sort excoriate the theories as meaningless. Others say that truth and falsity are irrelevant to metaphysics, as they are to literature. Like novelists and playwrights, we metaphysicians are said to formulate the stories used for thinking about possible worlds, e.g., the imaginary ones of fiction and this actual world. Metaphysics, this implies, differs from literature only because its stories have a wider scope. Where novelists devote themselves to incidents and personalities, metaphysicians tell stories that emphasize the categorial features of a world. Either way, these activities are motivated by a single objective: We formulate interpretations in order to use them for creating thinkable worlds. All of the intelligibility credited to any possible world, i.e., all its differentiations and relations, originate within these interpretations. No one should suppose that interpretations are true or false; for these are not the representations of preexisting states of affairs. They are, instead, the very condition for the existence of possible worlds. Why? Because these worlds exist only as they are prefigured within, and created by, the interpretations used for thinking them.

My concern is this emphasis upon interpretation, not the alleged meaninglessness of metaphysical claims. I worry about the mix of skepticism, relativism, and idealism tangled within it. How does it happen that a conceptual system creates a world? That is the result when mind schematizes sensory data, thereby creating experience and our life-worlds. Claims about the truth of these experience-creating interpretations are misconceived in the way that we err in believing that a cook's recipes are true. Isn't it enough that a recipe is a directive for baking a cake, where having and eating it are proof enough that this is an effective recipe? No theory need be true or false, if every theory, whether practical, scientific, or metaphysical is appraised in this other, "pragmatic" way.

This emphasis upon interpretation is the expression of Kantian themes in the conceptual relativism of late twentieth-century philosophy. *World* has changed its referent. Before it signified nature, including us humans as we are located within it. Now, *world* refers only to the experience created when sensory data are differentiated and organized by the system used for thinking them. That system might be a paradigm directing scientific inquiry, the interpretation expressing a social interest, or a problem-solving plan. Each of them may be regarded, in the manner of Kant's empirical schemas, as a rule for creating a differentiated and organized experience.

Metaphysics, Kant said, is an impossible discipline because of striving to know a world that everywhere exceeds the boundaries of sensible experience. We could abandon metaphysics, or transform it. Kant and his successors have transformed it. No longer the discipline promising to formulate and test some very general claims about the world, metaphysics has become, for many thinkers, the activity of world-making. How do we make a world? We do it, as indicated above, by using a conceptual system to schematize sensory data. That system is a complex of thinkable forms, so that projecting its differences and relations onto the data makes them thinkable too. Mind, now having this experience arrayed before it, inspects a "world" that mind has itself created.

Who are these world-spinning metaphysicians? They include scientists and poets, but also each one of us. For every intelligent behavior requires an interpretation, so that each of these activities creates a thinkable world. There is only this one significant difference: Literature invents the possible worlds of fiction, while science and practice apply their conceptualizations to sensory data, thereby creating the actual worlds of experience. This Kantian style of world-making has one other effect: It exiles us philosophers to a kind of exalted limbo. We are unique for not being world-makers. Instead, Kant makes us responsible for describing the "transcendental" activities that create worlds. In our time, when transcendental psychology is scorned, we reflect upon or formulate the thinkable forms, i.e., the conceptual systems, used for making experience. Philosophy can abjure metaphys-

74

ics, this implies, only as every other thinker is a world-maker, and in that respect a metaphysician.

This idealist project tortures belief. Why suppose that every thinker is a god, empowered by the consistency and coherence of his interpretation for creating a world? Why not concede that sensory experience is the effect of our interactions with a world whose existence and character are independent of the ways we think and talk about it? That world is represented by the natural signs of perception, while being representable by the conventional signs of language. It is known as we formulate and test hypotheses about it. Why reject this naturalistic account for the emphasis upon world-making?

The Kantian answer is that knowledge of the world is precarious if our access to it is forever mediated by signs. Judgments construing the signs will often be mistaken, so that skepticism is the likely result. Kantians want to eliminate error-breeding signs as they separate the knower from the known. Knowledge is assured, they suppose, only as we knowers address a world that is set before us in the moment of our schematizing it. Our problem, as Kantians, is the one of arguing that sensory experience might be grounded altogether in mind's productive activity. Is there some less problematic example of a thing created and sustained by our minds?

Consider the rules prescribed so that experience may be differentiated and organized. There are, for example, traffic and business laws. They establish the circumstances where behaviors are intelligible to potential agents, hence predictable and safe. This network of civil laws is the conceptual basis for an experienced "world," in this case, the one of public order. Here is a "world" first created, then sustained by thought.

Examples like this one help justify our saying that all of sensory experience might be the expression of mind's autonomy. With imagination (after Fichte) or an unthinkable I-know-not-what (after Kant) to generate the raw data, everything determinate within experience is to originate in the interpretation used for making the data thinkable. This is a world to which mind would have a privileged, even infallible access, though only because that world's whole character would be the one that mind has imposed. We would have only to examine civil laws, the rules of ordinary language, or the syntax and semantics of our theories and plans to know whatever is intelligible in the experience they have schematized. Here is the realization of Artistotle's claim that we humans are closest to being gods when we make the laws for organizing ourselves. Kant's world-making ego is all the more grandiose: It makes everything, culture and nature too. Everything we do or can know is to receive its differentiations and organization from the conceptual system used for thinking it.

Philosophers who defend this Kantian thesis in our time sometimes describe themselves as "pragmatists." They couple a perfunctory critique of realism in knowledge and being to the claim that interpretation is, or ought to be, the paradigm for all our knowing. We may have supposed that pragmatism is a theory about thought and action. They are allied, we might have said, for the purpose of solving real problems in ways that enable us to secure ourselves within nature. This version of pragmatism is different. It has just one problem to solve, and a single instrument for solving it. Our problem is the one of making the world intelligible, hence thinkable. Our instrument is a conceptual system. Which system should that be? Whatever theory is recommended by our values. Wanting a simple theory, we are materialists. Preferring mystery and the promise of a being more sublime than ourselves, we are theists. Either theory provides a coherent experience, though neither one is true or false. Value, not truth, dictates our choice of theories.

This style of instrumentalism is oblivious to fish-hooks, smelters, and subways, but also to that intelligence which revises its plans when the behaviors they direct are confounded by circumstances that were nowhere anticipated. This is a prescriptivist, not a fallibilist pragmatism. It cares only that the world be rendered thinkable. We satisfy this demand merely by using any theory that is internally consistent for projecting differentiations and relations onto sensory data. The world has no power to frustrate us if its every nuance originates within the interpretation we use for thinking it. And anyway, we can obliterate the things offending us by using a different interpretation. The only limit on substitute interpretations is the requirement that they satisfy the values which impel us.

Only two considerations are prior even to our values. One is our freedom to choose and revise them. Nothing is to constrain us as we select among the infinity of internally consistent interpretations; any one of them may satisfy us, for a moment, a lifetime, or anything in between. The other consideration is mind as it creates an experience consistent with its values. Being democratic pluralists, we acknowledge a diversity of minds, each one having a right to the integrity of its experience. We are, accordingly, a self-established kingdom of ends. Our principal obligation as members of this community requires respect for other minds, and their "worlds."

Pragmatists of this sort combine the virtues of tolerance with an exaggerated regard for human power. All the world, they believe, can be turned to human designs. Nothing will confound us, because we are free to create, in thought and language, whatever world currently satisfies our values. William James's "Will to Believe" resonates in thinkers who suppose that the truth of a claim is only the defensible consequences of believing it. First writing the novel or play that suits us, we are to climb into the world it

76

creates, living our lives within the congenial furnishings that we have contrived. Where tolerance is a value, we are to be mutually respectful when our differing interpretations and worlds are mutually incomprehensible.

The pragmatists I am describing tell an epistemological creation story. Knowing is making, where using an interpretation to create a thinkable experience makes a world. Still more dangerously, this pragmatism encourages a tacit contempt for those people who cannot think themselves out of one world, and into a better one merely by changing their interpretations. Richard Rorty's "conversation of the West"[1] has that possibility within it. The dialogue he recommends is too much the social patter of those leisured people who need not be right or wrong, because their social positions are well-defended against the demand for relevance, or the threat of error. Art and literature may sometimes share this privileged status. Practice and science never do. They are effective or not, true or false, in circumstances where need may be urgent, and error is palpable.

Let us admit that claims about mind's freedom as world-maker, and the autonomy of its mind-dependent "worlds" are an embarrassment. Everyone who stubs his toe in the dark is rightly suspicious of them. Here is evidence that we cannot do or believe anything we like if we are honest about failure, frustration, error, and death. Let us acknowledge that we are constrained by a world we have not altogether made, a world whose intrinsic forms are a limit upon every change, those we make and those we merely suffer. We are reminded of Peirce, and his description of the idealist drunk: He careens out of a bar into a lamppost. It is Peirce, the realist, not the romantic side of Dewey and James, who is or ought to be our example.

Peirce supposed that the world has a decided character of its own. Thinking is not making; and we do not create the world merely by affirming an interpretation while enjoying its coherence and implications. We want to know if a theory is true of a world it has not made. Which is better: the philosophic theory celebrating hermetic, self-justifying interpretations, or the one acknowledging error and the procedures for testing our claims about matters of fact? I prefer this second alternative, because this is the more accurate description of our circumstances and aims, both in practice and in science. This is also the preferred alternative for metaphysics, if we agree that metaphysicians are neither world-makers not transcendental psychologists.

Our problem is the one of formulating testable metaphysical theses. How shall we do that? The intuitionist answer goes either of two ways. Prescriptivists suppose that mind lays down the rules for meaning and truth. Other intuitionists, like Plato, Descartes (as against the prescriptivist Cartesians who succeed him) and Husserl, are more passive to the given.

They suppose that mind is a crucible where every datum reduces to its essence before mind's purifying gaze. But then intuitionists of both kinds hide, disguise, or ignore all the paraphernalia and assumptions which make the process go. They are slow to tell us about the presuppositions of their method, including minds' self-sufficiency and its structure, power, and freedom as a self-creating self-consciousness. When these assumptions are acknowledged, the intuitionist activities claimed for mind seem a pretense. We stop caring about prescribing, inspecting mind, and look for a different method.

The alternative is close at hand. Philosophy is sometimes irony, analysis, or the stipulation of rules directing some kinds of thought or activity. This other role is, nevertheless, more fundamental. Philosophy is theory. We lay down a conceptual network so that we may tell a coherent story about the world. This story is more than fiction, for we intend that our theories be meaningful, cogent, and true of the matters they signify. Where speculation drives thought beyond practice and science to metaphysics, we hypothesize about nature's categorial form and conditions, and about our place within nature.

This chapter is a survey of the issues significant for making and testing hypotheses, metaphysical ones especially. Here to start are some remarks about their form, meaning, and use.

2. Hypothesis

There is a speculative attitude pervading most of our thinking, and many of our linguistic expressions. There are, for example, the many times when we begin by saying "Suppose," "Pretend," or "Imagine." Every factual claim, down to and including perceptual judgements, is a hypothesis, as when we call *red* something that may not be red. Speculation extends from these most particular and easily verified claims throughout all that part of our thinking that applies to matters of fact, up to and including all the material truths of science and philosophy. The only kinds of thinking exempt from this generalization fall within one or another of these three rubrics: (1) declarations of value, e.g., "I call this good"; (2) constructive thinking, as when buildings are designed or constitutions written; (3) the act of using a rule, e.g., when playing games and making inferences. Even this third rubric is sometimes speculative, as we suppose when applying a rule that it does have application to these particular circumstances. The distinction between our hypothetical and nonhypothetical reasoning is, therefore, plain. On the one side, we speculate about some aspect of the world when its existence and character are independent of our thoughts about it. On the other side, thinking is controlling and creative as we stipulate or construct some rule, standard, argument, or design.

Also pertinent is the difference between hypothesis as the speculative attitude of mind addressing the world, and the grammatical notion of hypothetical sentences. 'Rain if the wind turns' is grammatically hypothetical, though it does not become a hypothesis until uttered by someone proposing that the possibility signified is or will be actual. This tentative, speculative attitude, not the grammatical form of a sentence, makes our use of it hypothetical. We allow, therefore, that categorical sentences too may be used hypothetically. "The sky is blue" is used in that speculative way when its speaker addresses a matter of fact about which his claim is true contingently, if at all. Even "Tea is served" is hypothetical, when announced by the steward on a soon-to-be-sinking ship. Every thought or sentence addressed to possibilities that may be, but are not necessarily, actual (as none are) is a hypothesis.

Hypotheses are problematic in several ways. How do they come to be meaningful? What are the conditions for their truth? Here are the answers proposed in Chapter 1, followed by their explication, and some objections to my claims.

2A. Meaning and Truth

The meanings of our thoughts, words, and sentences are possible states of affairs. Meanings, this affirms, are the extraconceptual, extralinguistic objects signified by signs. Behaviorists and ontologists who despair of subsistent entities will find this view abhorrent. Their objections are considered below. Just now, we consider the spare outlines of this view. We say that a cat's being on a mat is a possibility, but not only because there is a cat and mat such that one could sit on the other. That is material possibility, not the possibility required for this notion of meaning. It requires logical, eternal possibles, as the cat's being on the mat is possible because of embodying no contradiction. Actual states of affairs are a subset of these logical possibilities, namely, the ones instantiated. True thoughts and sentences have these instantiated possibles as their referents. They are vastly outnumbered by the array of meaningful but false thoughts and sentences, as 'Asterix lives' is meaningful because of signifying a possibility, but false.

This notion of meaning has two parts: words and thoughts are meaningful because they are construed as the signs of objects. The construing of signs is *intentional meaning*; objects are the *senses*, i.e., the meanings, of thoughts, words and sentences.

79

2Ai. Intentional meaning

Intentional meaning is anathema to behaviorists because of seeming to require that there be a succession of conscious acts as we regard and interpret successive thoughts and words. Nothing of that sort is implied by the notion recommended here, for the introspectionist version of intentional activity is troubled indeed. Cartesians who defend that version are left to answer a bewildering array of challenges: Is each of the words in a sentence construed separately? Is there an additional act required for integrating the several construings within a sentence so as to create a unified if complex interpretation for it? How do we treat words that are not the signs of objects, e.g., 'sake', before integrating them into the unitary sense intended when the sentence is construed as a complex sign? Answering these questions as Cartesians requires that mind be credited with contemporaneous or sequential acts having a diversity of spans. One act might comprehend a complex thought or sentence with the span appropriate to a truth-bearing grammatical unit, i.e., a sentence, while a sequence of acts construes its separate thoughts or words. The larger scale of this grammatical perception might also be sensitive to the difference between subjects and predicates, and also to the difference between such words as *sake* and *snake*.

This idea of mind, so much like the one of spotlights in a circus tent, some having beams wide enough to illuminate all of the floor, others lighting only a single ring or performer, is not complicated enough. We shall need other acts of awareness with a scale large enough to comprehend the relations of sentences, then acts of a larger span to integrate paragraphs, and so on. What is more, these larger-scale comprehendings will not have the advantage of grammatical form, i.e., the forms of sentences, to serve as grids for organizing the separate sentences, paragraphs, speeches, pages, or whatever. The devices used for integrating everything beyond the words of individual sentences will be very much in doubt. Organizing rules or ideas might serve this purpose; but they are not easily formulable apart from the ordered sentences and paragraphs that express them. Remember now the intuitionist demand that mind be able to confirm, by inspection, every claim about its own activity. This Cartesian program is discredited, in its own terms, when we do not discover these multiply layered and focused acts within ourselves.

Here, where the introspectionist apparatus exceeds mind's capacity for keeping track of itself, we jettison this idea of construal for a different one. We say that construal is association, where construing a word or thought locates it within a network of words, thoughts, behaviors, and observations.

2Aii. Construing thoughts and words as signs

There are two associative networks relevant to the meaning of thoughts and words. First is the association of words or thoughts to one another, in speech or on a page. Second is this network of thoughts and words together with the behaviors and observations relevant to construing any particular thought or word as the sign for an object.

Associations of the first kind justify the identification of meaning with the rule-governed use of words with words. We are often persuaded that this is all of meaning, for the good reason that we can understand hours of speech or hundreds of pages without ever breaking through the tide of words to construe any one of them. We inhibit associations of the second kind in order that we not be distracted while listening or looking for every next word. We are satisfied when any particular sequence achieves coherence as a detailed and organized thought or message.

The rules controlling these skeins of thoughts or words are often hard to discern. Where the negative rules, e.g., contradiction, are easily stated, we are confounded by the multiple layers of rules used to produce a coherent message. How, for example, do we distinguish information organized systematically from a more fragmentary message? Deductive form is one way of distinguishing them; though we easily decide while reading something not having that formal rigor, that it is more or less coherent. The rules applied in making this judgment are only a surmise, though we readily make the distinction in particular cases, thereby convincing ourselves another time that all of the conditions for meaning are founded in the rules for associating thoughts and words.

We do sometimes visualize the things signified by our thoughts and words, but these accompanying associations rarely exhibit details sufficient to represent the complexity of the things signified by a sequence of thoughts or words. Even a physicist's images of neutrinos do not count for much in construing his thoughts or words about them. More often, there are inhibitions within the physiology of these first associative networks to prevent us from moving through the sequence of construing associations. There are some words defined ostensively, as *red* means red; but these definitions are the only concession to the view that linguistic and conceptual meaning cannot be altogether autonomous. We do associate the complexes of words and thoughts to the world beyond them; but it is enough that we do this at the margins where phenomenal words are ostensively defined. All the rest of meaning stands apart from the world, as music may be oblivious to it.

We might hope to support this impression of autonomy by pressing the analogy between assembled thoughts and words, and those other complexes constructed under the direction of rules. That strategy does not help us. Music, games, recipes, and boarding schools supply many examples of rule-governed behaviors, but little or nothing of meaning. What distinguishes the meaning-bestowing rules of thought or language from these other rules? The answer is that rules of music, for example, generate complexes having no empirical applications. This is not to say that the music cannot be played, only that the bars or measures within it do not signify anything beyond themselves. Compare thought and language as they show their applicability to matters of fact by describing, explaining, and predicting them. The analogy fails: Linguistic and conceptual meaning are not autonomous, and not merely because some few ostensively defined words break the surface of language by signifying something beyond themselves. Most words do that.

This aspect of meaning is plainer if we consider an example. Suppose that someone finds the grammar book for a dead language, and that all of us learn to speak the language grammatically. Our sentences are well formed syntactically, and well formed semantically; i.e., there are no solecisms. All of us have learned the same rules, so that each of us recognizes the good form in another's words. Yet none of us has any idea of what the words signify. Their meaning escapes us. The situation is eased only a little if there are color patches and shapes in the book coupled to the words signifying them. That leaves all the rest of the words undefined. This might be an especially thorough book with a dictionary defining every other word by way of the few words defined ostensively. Still, this dead language is different from every language known to us, for none of them supplies definitions by way of words ostensively defined for all the other words. There is no definition of that sort for 'cousin' let alone for 'third cousin twice removed'. Yet these words are meaningful, and not merely because of being associable with other words. The skein of thoughts or words is not nearly autonomous, connecting to the world only by way of the few thoughts or words defined ostensively. There are, to the contrary, the thousands of words and thoughts that are meaningful because of being used as signs signifying possible properties or states of affairs distinct from themselves.

Construal is the order of association used for connecting these signs to their objects. Associating the word to be construed with other words and thoughts, and finally with behaviors and observations, we connect the word to its referent. I assume that the first referents are actuals, not possibles, as we learn to say *dog* when seeing dogs. Our first signs are rooted in these actual encounters. But then three other mental acts become significant: We *abstract* from our observations before *varying* and *combining* the information thereby acquired. Seeing shades of blue, we abstract from these particulars, representing their generic property before formulating a more or less accurate rule for determining the increments among discriminable shades of blue. Observing several of its shades, and using them to confirm our rule, we vary the rule's application so as to produce Hume's missing shade of blue, or a sign for it. We also combine the thoughts or words for things observed, or the ones for abstractions and variations, thereby producing signs for things which have never been observed. We create an array of thoughts and words signifying possibilities exceeding the things observed. Our experience of nature's apparent geometry is, for example, the basis for extrapolations to possible geometries nowhere instantiated.

This genealogy is all-important for explaining that the use of signs is no foundationless bridge into the void of properties somehow possible but uninstantiated. Our first encounters with possibilities, i.e., with possibles instantiated, are superseded when abstraction, variation, and combination enable us to signify possibilities that are nowhere realized. Construal then carries on without regard for the fact that the possibilities signified by our words are instantiated, as *red* signifies a possibility whether or not anything is red.

2Aiii. Theoretical terms

How do we confirm, in particular cases, that a thought or word alleged to be meaningful does have a referent though it represents something that is in principle unobservable, i.e., a possibility? This question has its sharpest edge in our doubts about the meaningfulness of theoretical terms. The possibles signified by terms such as *red* are perceived as instantiated. The instantiated possibilities signified by theoretical terms are, by contrast, not observable in themselves but only indirectly and partially by way of their sensory effects. Reference is all the more obscure when the possibles signified by theoretical terms are not instantiated. Every term of this sort is theoretical and speculative, because its reference is not firmly established. How should we satisfy ourselves that these terms do signify possibles rather than being nonsense syllables?

One solution to the problem of theoretical terms—what do they mean, and how is their reference fixed?—proposes that the terms be defined implicitly before their empirical sense is established. Implicit definition requires that the terms appear in sentences related to one another by rules of inference. These rules establish an uninterpreted calculus of sentences. Individual non-logical terms within the sentences are defined in the respect that the sentences and rules together determine the range of their permissable combinations within the system, i.e., sentences whose terms are arranged in these ways are deducible from it. These formal definitions are supplemented by correspondence rules. They relate a term defined implicitly to sensory data. Where *atom* receives its implicit definition by way of an abstract calculus, it receives its empirical meaning by way of the rules correlating the term (and sentences containing it) to whatever sensory events are adduced as evidence for our claims about atoms.

The two conspicuous failings of this account are its appeal to the logical relations of sentences in formal systems, and its assumption that factual reference devolves only upon the correlation of terms in an abstract system to sensory data. This first assumption is no help whatever as regards all the theoretical terms appearing in sentences not codified within deductive systems. That is the status of most theoretical terms in most sciences, and all the terms of metaphysics. None of them is more than partially defined in this formal way. The second assumption is also flawed. With a nod to phenomenalist intuitionism, it identifies reality and the referents of all nonlogical terms with sensory data.

We need some other way of explicating theoretical terms. One crude idea refers us to the terms lodged within true sentences, irrespective of the fact that they do or do not appear within theories. These sentences are assumed to be true because of predicting sensory affects that do occur within us. The theoretical terms are presumed meaningful because these predictions are confirmed. Their signification is dubious, however, until we determine what role any particular term has played in making a prediction. Like a mere noise or random mark, it might have no effect upon the prediction. Removing the term, then getting a different prediction, proves that it did have some responsibility for the prior one, though we may have no more accurate way of telling what role that is. This solution is also deficient in another way: It repeats the error of supposing that theoretical terms are meaningful only to the extent of signifying sensory data. That cannot be true when these data are altogether different from the specific meanings ascribed to theoretical terms within true sentences and theories, as the complexity of the theoretical language used for representing light compares to the simple shock of walking out the door into a sunlit street. Notice too that false but meaningful sentences may not have even the satisfaction of confirming data, though we can specify the observables that would be available if they were true. It is these false sentences, most conspicuously, which remind us that the complexity of our references often surpasses anything that is or might be observed.

How shall we establish that a theoretical term does have a referent when implicit definition is unachievable for want of a fully deductive system, when false but meaningful sentences may have no actual data to which to appeal in defining their terms, and when sensory data underdetermine the referents of even those theoretical terms appearing in well-confirmed sentences and theories? There seems to be no procedure other than the one supplied by the genealogies used for confirming that rule-governed words signify something beyond themselves, as rule-governed chess pieces do not.

Consider, for example, the notion of *possibility*. Its genealogy begins in the observation of things, and then proceeds to their characterization as actuals. We remark that these actuals have not always existed, and that they do not forever exist. We coin words to characterize the existence of these things. *Necessity* is introduced to signify the modal property of those things existing always because they could not fail to exist: Their non-existence would be a contradiction. *Contingency* signifies the state of those things existing although they are not necessary, and may sooner or later cease to be. *Possibility* is introduced as we couple the notion of contingency to the inference that something which was not but has come to be was, before its actuality, that which could be though it was not, hence a possibility. We also distinguish material from eternal possibles, i.e., those possible events for which one or more causes are in place, from possibilities called *logical* because of embodying no contradiction.

This analysis exemplifies the more general point that we can tell what difference a theoretical term signifies, and how we have come to use this sign. Genealogies are, in this spirit, justifications for the intentional meanings of our theoretical terms. They tell how the terms are construed, and how we come to ascribe particular characters to their senses, i.e., to the possibles they signify. *Ether, boson, phlogiston* and *gene, property, law,* and *disposition* are all terms of this sort. Each one has a specifiable intentional meaning. Each one is construed as a sign having some particular, more or less complex difference as its object.

Genealogies may be more or less successful. There is, for example, no generally agreed philosophic or even theological sense for the word, *God*. This is not merely the result of its being equivocal, for negative theology may be correct: We may be unable to specify a sense for *God* as other than the limit to an infinite series of extrapolations from properties known to us, as God is infinitely better than good and wiser than wise. Some other terms fail altogether to achieve meaning, when we don't know what sense to construe them as having. Kant's *negative noumenon* is close to being one of them, because of signifying that-to-which-no-predicate-is-ascribable. We are properly dubious of the place-holding *that* in the hyphenated phrase above, because anything having no properties should be a nonbeing.

Other theoretical terms, including many important to metaphysics, do have a specifiable intentional meaning. Positivists demur, saying that metaphysical terms and even the inapplicable scientific ones, e.g., *super-luminary velocity*, are meaningless because of being undefinable by way of terms definable ostensively. This compulsion for securing meaning by iden-tifying sense with sensory data expresses the misplaced fear that we shall lose touch with the senses of our words if we cannot observe them. It hap-pens, nevertheless, that theoretical terms of all sorts are made to have a sense when the mind's powers for abstraction, variation, and combination enable us to construe words as the signs of possibilities which may be no-where instantiated, hence unobservable.

2Aiv. Possibilities as the objects, i.e., the senses, of our signs

I have suggested that the senses of our thoughts and words are prop-erties existing as possibles. The ether, for example, is a possible, whether or not it is instantiated. Why is this notion ridiculed? For a reason implicit in the dominant ontologies of this century. We are physicalists or phenome-nalists, with no place in either of them for the possibilities just mentioned. Even their characterization as "logical" misleads us, given one or the other of these ontological persuasions, for logic is understood as a set of rules, not as the principles of order expressed in every domain of being, including language, music, and physics. Logical possibilities are, this implies, the shadows cast by rules; they are not entities of any sort.

No one who refuses to consider a world richer than the one of objects in space-time, or the sensory data set before our inspecting minds will acknowledge the reality of eternal possibles, or their role as objects of our signs. What is the motive for this aversion, apart from the unyielding com-mitment to one or the other of these two ontologies? The short answer is our discomfort with *subsistents*. Two of their alleged qualities are especially galling. First is their irreducibility to one of these two favored ontologies, as though we can endure the reality of physical objects or phenomena, but nothing else. The second, more serious objection is that subsistents are "known" as objects of the intentional acts performed when concepts or words are used. Round-squares, for example, are to be acknowledged when the notion *round-square* is used for thinking about round-squares. This sec-ond objection is one I share: It contests the idea that mind is a kind of theatre where ideas are used projectively, like beams of light, to posit their referents on the stage or screen where these things are perceived, by way of rational intuition.

This idea of mind as a theatre is the tacit paradigm at the heart of in-tuitionist method. If the entities postulated as referents of our thoughts and words are only these intentional objects, then surely thought and lan-guage do fall into the solipsist abyss, where nothing but a generous God secures the reference of any thought or word beyond the stage of our private theatres. There is, however, nothing of these mental lights, beams, stages, and intentional objects in the suggestion that the referents of our thoughts and words are possibilities.

That is so because eternal possibles are not any sort of mental creature. They exist whether or not anyone thinks about them, just because of embodying no contradiction. They are, as Wittgenstein described them, the facts in logical space. They limit all that is or can be. Everything actual is one of them, or more exactly, a possibility instantiated. Thought and language secure their grip on the world by signifying these possibles. Starting with the signification of possibilities instantiated and observed, we quickly extend the range of meaningful thoughts and words by signifying possibilities that may be nowhere instantiated, hence nowhere observed. Meaning, this implies, is prior to truth, as possibilities signified are prior to the ones instantiated.

2Av. Material truth

Suppose that some possibilities are instantiated, so that the question turns from meaning to truth. Where the unit of meaning is the word, the unit of truth is the sentence. Contingent sentences are true or false only as they are affirmed or denied, but it is these sentences, not the acts of assertion or denial, which are true or false. Why? Because the possibility signified by a well-formed sentence is instantiated or not. The sentence is true if that possibility is instantiated, false if it is not.

Well-formed sentences, not words or phrases, are the least units of truth. That is so, because sentences, not words, represent the elementary facts of being; i.e., that something is or is not; that something has a certain character; that things or properties stand in some relation to one another. Facts of these three sorts may be particular or universal, as we show by using sentences that are appropriately quantified. They may be represented in a variety of grammatical modes, as the question "Are all men mortal?" represents a possible state of affairs. Yet all the while, truth and falsity devolve only on the considerations mentioned above, i.e., the sense intended is a possibility; it is instantiated or not. Where most readings of Tarski's semantic definition of truth allege that his notion is ontologically neutral, I am supposing that truth and falsity are substantive: something is actual or not, because a possibility is or is not instantiated. 'Snow is white' is meaningful on this telling, because of signifying a possibility, and true if that possible is realized.

All of inquiry, I suppose, is devoted to formulating meaningful sentences, then to testing for their truth. There are many occasions for doubting that any particular hypothesis is meaningful or not, and true or not. The conditions for meaning and truth are, nevertheless, simple enough.

2Avi. A political implication

My emphasis upon the association of thoughts, words, behaviors and observations has a political corollary.

Association is private, and idiosyncratic. Each of us may differ from the others and some "normal" standard as regards the intentional meanings of his thoughts and words. Regularizing social rules prescribe the "right" thing to say in particular circumstances. Respect for these rules is obligatory as we normalize usage so that each of us uses *red* to mean the same thing. Establishing and confirming the univocity of our meanings is, nevertheless, a test for meaning, not meaning itself. Nor should we expect that regularizing rules will eliminate all of the discrepancies in our separate construings of any particular word or sentence.

Compare this implication to the antipathy for private intentional meanings, and the preference for rules enforcing linguistic, hence conceptual, uniformity. Notice the fear that individual thinkers might be innovators in regard to meaning. Why emphasize this aversion? Because the appeal to rule-governed usage implies that thinkers and speakers who break the rules, perhaps by inventing rules of their own, are unintelligible to their fellows, therefore unpredictable and dangerous. Poetry, especially as it challenges us to understand poets' meanings, should be much less threatening to established sensibilities if this view of meaning were correct, for then the poet would be unintelligible even to himself if he did not use words in the ways sanctioned by the publicly established rules. Equally, radicals who dream of a justice unintelligible to other people should be more easily diagnosed as sociopaths.

It is too bad that the behaviorist and ontological motives for discounting intentional meaning and sense generate theories inadequate to the meanings they are meant to explicate. It would be shameful if these morally neutral motives were used to justify a pernicious uniformity of meaning, thought, and action.

2B. Behaviorist Objections

My claims about meaning, truth, and possibility violate the assumption that we might describe the method and instruments of metaphysical inquiry without making any radically speculative metaphysical assertions. That promise of neutrality was encouraged when I proposed that metaphysical theory be continuous with practice and science. They are sometimes conducted without our making egregious metaphysical claims in their behalf. Perhaps metaphysics too might be launched without our having to justify some disruptive claims in its defense. That hope was naive. That meaning and truth do require extraconceptual and extralinguistic referents, and that these referents cannot always be actualities are facts that might have perplexed us from the first moments of ordinary practice when well-conceived plans proved to be misrepresentations of the world. Meaning, representation, truth and error are considerations as urgent at the beginning of inquiry as they are at the end of it. That we do finally address these issues when describing the conditions for metaphysical inquiry, and the last spirals of refection, is not so much a surprise as it is a relief. Practice and science are assumed, with only metaphysical inquiry still to consider. This is our last chance. Where the extraconceptual and extralinguistic referents for our thoughts and words, i.e., their meanings, have been neglected until now, it is more than timely that we finally acknowledge both these referents among possibilities, and the behaviorist strategy for eliminating every referent not publicly observable.

Consider for a moment the behaviorists' claims about meaning. Stimulus-meaning, e.g., bringing a slab when someone in authority says "Slab!" is barely adequate for describing our use of a small number of terms. We object, even with respect to them, that appropriate behavior is not the basis for meaning, but only the evidence that the actor understands, in a way independent of his actions, what the words signify. The idea of stimulus-meaning is still less cogent with those many words whose meanings are known though no behavior is appropriate when hearing them, as *gross national product* evokes no response in most of us though we know its referent. Nor is it satisfactory that people regarding the same stimulus are provoked to utter contrary claims about it, e.g., "A bat." "No, a bird." These sentences are not knee-jerk reactions to a stimulus. They are uttered by speakers who disagree about the possibility instantiated by this fluttery thing. Seeing it has provoked their response, though neither the stimulus, the responses, nor their combination supply the meanings of the words used.

Behaviorism is equally evasive when it refers us to notions of meaning which ground it within the rules for coordinating thoughts and words to one another in socially regularized ways. These rules do supply the necessary conditions for social coherence and communication; but they limit the referents for our meanings to the practices or things commonly observable. They defer too much to a consensual notion of the reality present within, and apparent to a group's members. This socialized behavior assures that the words of one tribe are meaningless in the experience of other tribes, unless their socially constituted "realities" overlap in some discernible way.

We confound these behaviorists by using words to signify realities of which we have no socialized experience. Novelists and scientists do that repeatedly as they signify possibilities exceeding group experience. The rest of us may come to use their words, as scientific and literary expressions enrich ordinary language on the way to becoming jargon. More important here, these words are meaningful, because of signifying possibilities, before they are socially approved.

Behaviorism is the undisguised strategy for explaining linguistic meaning without appealing to intrapsychic activity, or to extraphysical or extraphenomenal referents. This fails if words are meaningful because of being construed as the signs of possibles, and if most possibles are uninstantiated. Nevertheless, we may withdraw somewhat from the ontological characterization of these referents. Rather than describe senses as properties existing eternally as possibilities, rather than say that possibility is a mode of being complementary to actuality, we retreat into the familiarity of the word, saying only that thoughts, words, and sentences are meaningful because of signifying logical, as distinct from material, possibilities. Surely, metaphysics will have to tell, sometime, what these possibles are, how they relate to actualities, and how we gain access to them so that we may construe our thoughts and words as their signs. We may, however, suspend curiosity and judgment about these questions, merely affirming two things: first, that thoughts and words are meaningful because of being construed as signs of objects, where these objects, their senses, are possibilities; second, that thoughts or sentences are true when the possibilities signified are actual.

3. Why We Need to Think Hypothetically

What are the circumstances where formulating meaningful and true hypotheses is important, even vital?

A creature having innate ideas appropriate to every situation would have no use for hypotheses because of having an array of responses triggered by stimuli in its normal environment. Every creature incapable of learning is equipped in this way. All of them live in circumstances to which they are adapted, meaning that they respond to stimuli with appropriate behaviors. "Innate ideas" is too generous a description of the reactions provoked by stimuli; but we can imagine a person for whose capacities this phrase would be apt. He or she would be like us, except for having innate ideas for every difference encountered. This thinker, like the one that Descartes describes, would only need some percept to occasion the mind's awareness of an appropriate idea, though we should allow that any single percept might provoke a variety of ideas, as one might think both fruit and tart when seeing a lemon. This creature would never err. Having endowed it with speech, we could only explain its errors by citing a mechanical breakdown between perception of the stimulus and the idea provoked, or between an idea aroused and the speech center. Where fallibility is the symptom of a gap between thought and its objects, these utterances would not be hypotheses. We do better to describe them as the responses of a system that behaves as though evolution had suitably wired it for one particular niche within the world.

Our human situation is not like that. Our cognitive responses are not only reactive. We have considerable autonomy in creating, then construing the words or other tokens used as signs. Signs mediate between stimulus and response to the point where altering the signs inhibits some behaviors while impelling others. Equally, it often happens that we do nothing overt, being satisfied by our cogent representations of the things about us.

Here, as in Chapter 1, we need to distinguish among the several kinds of representation. Interpretations are first. They express the differentiations and relations used projectively for making experience intelligible. Sometimes less explicitly, they express the values motivating any particular reading of things. This amalgam of values and factual claims is probably our universal first response to the need for making sense of our circumstances. Though we risk misrepresenting the world because of the values distorting our claims about it. We correct this bias as we distinguish interpretations from plans. Plans too are motivated by interest, though a successful plan requires that we identify our values well enough to discount them for the purpose of achieving the desired result. There are some plans that work just because we are reckless in pursuing them. But even they presuppose what is usually more apparent, namely, that two kinds of representation are critical to the success of a plan. One is a good representation of the instrumental relations tolerated in nature, as we might propose lighting fires with matches but not marshmallows. The other is a map of the terrain in which a plan is to be enacted. Maps and plans engage us within the world, always in behalf of some value, but equally with regard for the actual shape of things. The third kind of representation is more disinterested. These are the hypotheses formulated as we amplify and extend the information acquired by acting upon, hence testing, our maps and plans. They represent the character of the world about us. Maps and plans have enabled us to secure a place for ourselves within the world. Now, the urgency for accommodating to the world or controlling it gives way to the desire for understanding both it and ourselves.

4. The Metaphysical Uses of Hypothesis

Suppose that attention is restricted, for the purposes of metaphysical reflection, to knowledge rather than action. How should we use our hypotheses?

4A. *Two Kinds of Metaphysical Hypotheses*

Whitehead is rightly celebrated for insisting that metaphysics be speculative, and for affirming that hypotheses are its principal instrument:

> Philosophy will not regain its proper status until the gradual elaboration of categoreal schemes, definitely stated at each stage of progress, is recognized as its proper objective. There may be rival schemes, inconsistent among themselves, each with its own merits and its own failures. It will then be the purpose of research to conciliate the differences. Metaphysical categories are not dogmatic statements of the obvious; they are tentative formulations of the ultimate generalities.[2]

One endorses these sentiments while objecting that speculation has a rigor of its own, a rigor from which Whitehead turns. Let Plato be our example of good speculation. Acknowledging both change and the fixity of thought's objects, he explains that which is prior in experience, i.e., perceptual flux, by reference to that which is prior in being, namely the Forms. This is an instance where speculation is daring: It specifies the generating condition or ground for the phenomenon at issue, as Forms are the source for whatever is differentiable within our perceivings. Starting from something observed or alleged, thought has speculated about a generating condition that may be unobserved. That we may confirm the hypothesis by searching for and observing this condition, with the eye or the mind's eye, is important to verifying hypotheses but incidental to their speculative character. The point decisive for speculation is different: Plato's hypothesis *explains* the intelligibility of our perceivings by identifying, however fallibly, those conditions necessary or sufficient for making percepts thinkable.

Whitehead's speculative style is weaker. His hypotheses are generalized descriptions, not explanations. As Whitehead describes his method:

> The conclusion of this discussion is . . . the assertion that empirically the development of self-justifying thoughts has been achieved by the complex process of generalizing from particular topics, of imaginatively schematizing the generalizations, and finally by renewed comparison of the imagined scheme with the direct experience to which it should apply.[3]

This says that hypotheses are to be speculative in the way that every inductive generalization is speculative: Will the next swan resemble the last one? Whitehead's speculations are never speculative in the manner of Plato's explanations; he does not try to identify the generating conditions for those phenomena regarded as paradigmatic for all of being.

But surely Whitehead knew the difference between explanation and description, so that his preference for description was reasonably motivated. What could that motive have been? We see it in this other passage from *Process and Reality.*

> Descartes modified traditional philosophy in two opposite ways. He increased the metaphysical emphasis of the substance-quality forms of thought. The actual things "required nothing but themselves in order to exist," and were to be thought of in terms of their qualities, some of them essential attributes, and others accidental modes. He also laid down the principle, that those substances which are the subject enjoying conscious experiences, provide the primary data for philosophy, namely themselves as in the enjoyment of such experience. This is the famous subjectivist bias which entered into modern philosophy through Descartes. In this doctrine, Descartes undoubtedly made the greatest philosophical discovery since the age of Plato and Aristotle.[4]

This passage comes several pages after the paragraph where Whitehead lists Descartes' assumptions:

> The subjectivist principle follows from these premises (I) The acceptance of the 'substance-quality' concept as expressing the ultimate ontological principle. (II) The acceptance of Aristotle's definition of a primary substance, as always a subject and never a predicate. (III) The assumption that the experient subject is a primary substance.[5]

This third assumption is the decisive one for Whitehead's own ontological views: He "fully accepts Descartes' discovery that subjective experiencing is the primary metaphysical situation which is presented to metaphysics for analysis."[6] Whitehead reformulates Descartes' subjectivist principle, eliminating many of the features that identify it as an exclusively human perspective. It is nevertheless this Cartesian notion that is paradigmatic when Whitehead writes that

> 'actual entities'–also termed 'actual occasions'–are the final real things of which the world is made up. There is no going behind actual entities to find anything more real. . . . The final facts are, all alike, actual entities; and these actual entities are drops of experience, complex and interdependent.[7]

Whitehead could not be plainer: subjectivity, however purified, is the elementary stuff of which all the world is made.

These passages emphasize description and ignore explanation. Why? Because "subjective experiencing" is the primary datum for metaphysics. This is a datum available to us as we turn self-consciously upon it. Analysis describes this datum without explaining it, because explanation would require that we specify constituents or grounds more fundamental than the datum itself. That we cannot do, for subjective experiencing is like the Sun of Plato's *Republic*; it is the creative source for everything existing, and the source of that light which makes all its creatures visible. Subjectivity has no elements or grounds more fundamental than itself, when God and eternal objects are discounted. There is nothing ulterior to which we might refer in explaining it, not even those two things just now set aside. Subjectivity is ground and cause of itself. Turning upon ourselves, we are to discern those essential and organizing differences constitutive of any possible reality. Every issue regarding substance and change is to be resolved with only the resources available as we examine the elements, structures, attitudes, and aims of these momentary experiences. They are described, not explained.

4B. Some Obstacles to Hypothetical Thinking in Metaphysics

Whitehead and Plato speak for the two attitudes, or procedures, constitutive of metaphysical theorizing. Speculation, says Whitehead, is descriptive generalization. But then Plato, Aristotle, Thomas, and Kant exploit the inferences Peirce calls "abductive." Those are hypotheses moving from the characterization of something thought or observed to its conditions, as we infer from smoke to fire, or from the unity of experience to the unifying act of transcendental apperception. The conditions may be causes, constituents or constraining laws. They may be necessary conditions, as apperception is said to be necessary for the unity of experience, or merely sufficient, as fire makes smoke when there is wood or paper to burn. Conditions that are necessary may also differ in this other way among themselves. Some are necessary for the particular expression of a property, as the zero curvature of a surface is necessary for a triangle's having interior angles equal to 180 degrees. This is parochial necessity, necessity of the sort applying when every change in nature is constrained by the physical laws applying here, though not by those laws applying within other possible worlds. Other conditions are necessary universally, as space and time are universally necessary for motion, whatever its specific character. There is, finally, this other difference among the conditions to which we infer abduc-

94

tively: Some are separable from the things conditioned, as grapes are separable from vines; others are inseparable from the thing conditioned, as being a right triangle is inseparable from the fact that the sum of the squares of the sides is equal to the square of the hypotenuse. There are, plainly, a great variety of these abductive inferences, so that using them extends our speculative thinking in ways never contemplated by philosophers who identify speculation with descriptive generalization.

We concede that hypotheses of both sorts are problematic. Generalizations remind us of the need for a hypothesis (probably an abduction) justifying induction. Explanations recall the need for justifying the principle of sufficient reason, i.e., that any state of affairs has conditions to which we may infer when explaining either its existence or character. What right do we have for generalizing or explaining when neither principle is justifiable in some universal and *a priori* way? The altogether defensible answer is that induction and sufficient reason are used as leading principles, i.e., as directives for inquiry. This means, in practice, that we generalize or infer abductively from claims that are well-confirmed in themselves, before testing for the further evidence that would confirm our generalizations or abductions. Accordingly, we justify these leading principles in this *ad hoc* way, i.e., by using them in particular cases; we do not wait for *a priori* justifications that no one supplies.

We allow for the possibility that these principles may not apply in every case. It may be contingent that the principles do have instances, or there may be some intrinsic though currently unknown limit to their application. We acknowledge the possibility of this contingency or this limit; while proceeding as though induction and sufficient reason do apply necessarily and universally. This attitude is apparent as we consider phenomena that baffle us, because of seeming to have no reason in themselves or another for their existence or character. The principle of sufficient reason seems inapplicable to them, though we persist in using the principle when thinking about them, as we have explained the mystery of action at a distance by identifying the intermediary conditions for gravitational forces. Where the phenomena important to quantum theory challenge this principle again, we hope that their conditions too will be discovered. We may eventually concede that there are no conditions for certain quantum effects, thereby implying that sufficient reason does have exceptions. But even that concession would hardly make the principle less useful as a regulative principle for inquiry. For there are those myriad things which do seem to be conditioned. Where successive obstacles to the universality of the principle have fallen to it in the past, and where doubts about the finality of quantum theory in its current formulations make us wary of declaring the principle inapplicable there, we may reasonably suspect that sufficient reason is universal, and even necessarily applicable to every difference. Suspecting this is less than proving it. Not having that proof, we go on using the principle as before: We conduct our inquiries, whether practical, scientific, or metaphysical, on the assumption that anything specified does have conditions in itself or in another, or we generalize from the matters observed or inferred to all of a class. We agree that applications of these principles may be limited by factors intrinsic to nature; but then we challenge every apparent limitation, supposing that it may be the artifact of superficial hypotheses or clumsy experiments.

We have, accordingly, these two procedures for metaphysical inquiry. We may describe matters of fact, and then generalize from our descriptions; or we may characterize some thing, and then argue from that description to conditions for, including the constituents of, the thing described. Each of the two steps in both procedures is hypothetical; i.e., we describe then generalize or describe then infer, so that risk and error are prominent whether we generalize about some aspect of the world, or explain it. There is, of course, the offsetting fact that we look for, and often find the sensory data confirming our generalization and abductions.

5. Hypotheses Used as Descriptions and Explanations

Metaphysics as much as practice and science wants to answer both the *what* and the *why* questions, supplying descriptions for the one and explanations for the other. Its hypotheses, in either case, are speculations about matters whose existence and character are independent of the ways we think and talk about them. We might suppose, however, that some metaphysical descriptions and explanations are not hypothetical. We need to consider them before moving on to those descriptions and explanations that are incontrovertibly hypothetical.

5A. *The Intuitionist Reduction of Explanation to Description*

One sort of empiricism affirms that descriptions might be infallible, and that abductions to unobserved or unobservable conditions are abjured. This is an intuitionist claim. It supposes that the only appropriate objects of philosophic reflection are the ones set before an inspecting mind, as sensory data, words, ideas, theories, or mind itself are alleged to be inspectable. Hume is a familiar example.[8] All of the realities he acknowledges, i.e., impressions and ideas, are subject to description only. We do make simple inferences, Hume allows, but only among ideas that have been conjoined in the past, and are conceivable again. Explanation to something unobservable is not so much irresponsible as impossible, when reason has no power for inventing ideas of things unperceived or unimaginable. Words used to signify them are meaningless, because there is nothing for them to signify.

Hume supplements these claims about meaning and inference with one equally destructive for speculation: Explanation presupposes the principle of sufficient reason, though explanation is merely a deception because everything distinguishable is separable. Nothing, this entails, has the conditions it may seem to have. This is the argument applied when Hume infers that there is no reason in nature or metaphysics for supposing that any event need have an antecedent.[9] Causes are assumed to be antecedent conditions; and causality is notoriously the principal victim of this attack. Where no thing requires an antecedent to condition its existence or character, it follows that nothing needs or has a cause.

This conclusion overstates the force of Hume's argument. He assumes that mind is the one significant arena for being, so that separability among our ideas—we may conceive one without conceiving any other—confirms the essential separability of all things, hence the refutation of sufficient reason and its more determinate expression in the causal principle. But surely, Hume has only confirmed the separability of our representations, not of the things represented. Hume thinks otherwise because he has identified existence with the force of our impressions, but that is, again, merely the intuitionist doctrine that *esse es percipi,* i.e., that nothing exists if it is not set before our inspecting minds. The only things "before" our minds are representations so that Hume could only have demonstrated their separability. Hardly anyone supposes that representations *qua* representations are subject to the same relations binding the things represented, so that an argument proving the separability of thoughts, words, or percepts says nothing about the separability of the things represented. Sufficient reason is, therefore, as good a leading principle for inquiry as ever it seemed to be. We have all the history of its successful application to justify our continued use of it.

Hume demurs. Writing as an intuitionist, he supposes that the fundamental task for knowledge is the one of discerning, then describing the matters set before our inspecting minds. Even generalization is suspect, for there is no assurance that things shall appear in the future as they have in the past. We do acquire habits encouraging these generalizations, but this is one of the unconsidered aspects of our thinking. More careful regard for our circumstances should make us cautious, even to the point of saying, for example, that the distinction between impressions and ideas may not apply forever within experience. That would leave us no authority as knowers but the one of describing the things before our minds. Descriptive nominalism should be the attitude and practice that directs all our claims to knowledge. Hume never goes quite this far, as he never suggests that the difference between impressions and ideas might not obtain some time in the future, but this is the disabling spirit of his views about inquiry and our prospects for knowledge.

Hume has pursued intuitionist method and its psychocentric notion of reality to something near its limit. Doing this exposes the method in its simplest form: Matters are set before our inspecting minds; knowledge is achieved merely by discerning them, though we may also describe what we see. This emphasis on description is also apparent in all the versions of phenomenology where there are, as Husserl remarks, an infinity of phenomena that might be described after the first reduction, then an infinity of ideas on which to reflect as we discern the essences exhibited more or less obscurely by the phenomena first discovered before the mind's eye.[10] The preference for description dominates each of the four styles of explanation commonplace in philosophic practice.

First is analysis. Starting from some complex of obscure phenomena, we describe both its elements and the rules for assembling them. This is the procedure recommended in Descartes' *Rules*,[11] and by Locke as he applies his historical plain method.[12] Both of them propose that we reconstruct some idea or complex sensory datum within the imagination, never departing from matters directly perceived and describable.

Second are those explanations that make a particular intelligible by setting it under a pertinent universal, or within a framework of universals. Ordinary language analysts explain the individual uses of words by citing the rules that constrain them, where the rules are said to be perceived by way of their particular applications. A different example concerns the "existence" of such disputed things as numbers. Do they exist? One response would have us explain their existence by locating number terms within the semantic frameworks where there are rules for saying, 'There are numbers' and 'Five is a number'. These frameworks, like the reconstructions Descartes and Locke describe, are presumed to stand before our inspecting minds, so that explanation is again description.

A *third* style of explanation acceptable to intuitionists requires that we deduce or otherwise derive one sentence or term from another. There are, for example, the lower-order hypotheses or test sentences of a formalized scientific theory. We are to explain these sentences by describing their derivation from the theory's higher-order sentences. With all of these sentences laid out before us, we locate this particular sentence within the formalization, always satisfying the demand that we are merely to describe the relations of things set before our minds. Similarly, we explain a number by showing that it is the product or sum of some other ones. Here as before, explanation does not exceed the domain of things accessible to inspection and description.

Explanations of the *fourth* kind describe correlations, as we explain smoke by citing its regular occurrence with fire. Hume identified cause and effect with these correlates, after insisting that every part of the causal relationship be inspectable. Where nothing but these correlates is discernible, nothing else is ascribable to their relation. Explanations of this last sort are, therefore, like the other three; no reality is acknowledged but the ones discernible and describable by an inspecting mind.

5B. *Reaffirming the Difference Between Explanation and Description*

Is it plausible that explanations might be nothing more than descriptions? This is dubious when explanations regularly surpass the range of currently inspectable and describable phenomena. That happens in everyday practice when the explanation for a mechanical or procedural failure is an inference to some thing that may be unperceived and unknown, and for those reasons indescribable. There are, for example, headaches, palpitations, and the behaviors of farm animals before an earthquake. Imagine a time when nothing much was known of physiology or the earth's structure. Explanations for these phenomena would have required the citation of factors undescribable in every way except this one: We might have identified them functionally as conditions for the phenomena observed, as geologists might have speculated about the features sufficient to have caused the shifting, trembling ground. Scientists of our time do regularly speculate about the unobserved conditions for various phenomena, so that their hypotheses do have this functional character, with inferences going from characterizations of things observed to specifications of what may plausibly be their conditions. Sometimes, these conditions are eventually perceived and described. Other times, we continue inferring their presence because of their effects, though we never do get the chance to describe them more directly because of perceiving them. The inference to gravitation in the absence of more direct evidence for gravitons is an example.

These hypotheses to inferred conditions require three steps: (1) We remark the existence or character of something, asking about its constituents or conditions; (2) We formulate a hypothesis specifying those factors which may be responsible for this effect, as its constituents or causes; (3) Our hypothesis signifies a possible state of affairs, so that we test the hypothesis in order to confirm by way of the sensory difference it makes that this possibility is instantiated. We do sometimes find that the possibility cited by the inference is instantiated and observable. Then, explanation can give way to description. We see, for example, the fire causing the smoke from which we have inferred the fire. Other times, the instantiated possibility is known only by way of its effects without being otherwise observable, gravity being an example.

These considerations help to show that *why* questions are different from *what* questions. *What* questions may be satisfied by descriptions of things observed; *why* questions encourage us to extend our understanding of the world by specifying the conditions for the things observed. It is, accordingly, explanation not description that reaches beyond the range of our current information to identify constituents or conditions previously unobserved and probably unsuspected. Descriptive generalization does extend the promise of understanding to particulars previously unexamined, but it is abductive explanation that propels understanding in directions where observation has not yet gone and may never go. It is abduction, not usually descriptive generalization, that makes us speculators.

5C. Metaphysical Explanations

The force of abduction is well known to practice and science, as we speculate that rain dances might cure a drought, or infer to viruses, genes, and magnetic fields. Where are the examples of metaphysical speculation, for granting that we regularly press against the limits of current knowledge, using abductive explanations to catapult us beyond those limits, what things does metaphysics explain? Is there any single thing that metaphysicians have ever explained abductively? We may think of Plato's Forms as an explanation for sameness through change; but too many of us discount that idea as a pseudo-explanation founded in a metaphor, i.e., the allegory of the cave. We are apt to catch our breaths, not being sure that metaphysics does work abductively. Could it be that we have come this far only to admit that metaphysics never explains anything, except perhaps in the four intuitionist ways described above?

We might hope to salvage metaphysical inquiry by emphasizing the prospects for "descriptive metaphysics," even if this phrase is mostly a euphemism for the intuitionist demand that we restrict ourselves to describing the matters set before our inspecting minds, as ideas, words, theories, or the mind itself might be described. Explanations of the four descriptive varieties listed above would satisfy this demand, though abductive explanations surely would not. Most of contemporary and modern philosophy encourages this descriptivist, intuitionist point of view. Though what should we say

100

of its assumption, that mind is the ample theatre where the matters appearing before it are exhaustively visible to the one auditor who appreciates and describes them. He, she, or it may have a comprehensive view of the theatre's architecture, and of every contingency playing within it, while knowing nothing, and taking care never to speculate about the conditions for this spectacle. The rest of us may want to avoid taking our seats in a theatre that is not so much the heart of being as it is the back of the cave.

Could it be true, nevertheless, that metaphysicians attracted by the idea of abductive explanation are misled by an analogy? Everyday practice and science use the abductive method, but it does not follow that metaphysics can use it too. We suppose, for example, that the things to which scientists infer are observable in themselves, even if technology or current theory have not yet succeeded in making them perceptually available to us. Metaphysical entities are presumably unobservable in themselves, so that no amount of theoretical or technological progress would render them observable. This is, I suggest, an altogether mistaken assumption about the matters to which metaphysicians infer when making abductive explanations. There is no reason whatever for supposing that the entities and relations vital to these metaphysical explanations do not make observable differences. Indeed, one might reasonably say that no entity important to practice, science, or metaphysics can be known in any way but for the observable difference it makes. We need only allow that the empirical evidence for some condition not be like that condition. If some percepts are the icons of their causes, as the image of a circle is like a circle, most perceptual evidence is different in some or many ways from its conditions. No one mistakes flashes in a cloud chamber for the properties of the particles causing them. Similarly, we need not suppose that the entities identified by metaphysical abductions are like the perceptual evidence they condition.

What explanations might these be? What are the subject matters to which metaphysics might contribute its abductions? Chapter 1 argues that all of inquiry starts in practice, as we begin reflecting upon the character of the world and our place within it. Metaphysics was said to have these four tasks: specification of nature's categorial form and conditions; the determination of our place as humans, within nature; and the characterization of being. Only this fourth task is principally descriptive, as our claims about being are a summary description of nature, its conditions, and ourselves. The other tasks are accomplished as we supply abductive explanations. Suppose, for example, that our focus is categorial form. Observing and describing the mix of stability and change in nature, we want an explanation for it. What is the character of the things sustaining part of their identity while being transformed? Are they atoms, Aristotelian primary substances, or the stable systems described in Chapter 1? We infer to things of one sort or the other. We also infer beyond these things to conditions distinct from them, as laws are distinct from the things whose behaviors are lawful. Then too, abductive explanation is all the more conspicuous as we locate ourselves within nature, explaining that human beings no more than stones are exempt from physical laws, that consciousness may be neural activity, and that even human values, especially the ones of securing and satisfying ourselves, may not be different in kind from the values of every system having to sustain its internal equilibrium while accommodating itself to the ecological order within which it nests. We are reminded that metaphysics was first conceived, as it continues to be, the quest for explanations. What are the conditions for sameness and change, for unity and plurality, for fact and value, for meaning and truth? Description marks out the domain of matters provoking these questions. Abductive explanation supplies the answers.

Sometimes the things specified by our explanations are later described, as the character of a hit-and-run driver may be inferred, then confirmed by observation. This later confirmation and description is incidental to the different roles played by description and explanation as we extend the range of our knowledge. For it is mistaken to suppose that the things identified by abductive explanations should eventually and invariably be presentable for observation and description. That expectation only reaffirms the intuitionist demand that nothing be credited to reality if it is not inspectable, though many things, including some of our own constituents and causes, may be known only by way of inference. We are always delighted when some new instrument makes the deep structure of matter visible, though we may have to acknowledge that the lattice of molecules or atoms in a crystal is not paradigmatic for all of being. Some physical things, and not only such conditions for nature as the domain of eternal possibles, may not be observable in any "direct" way, but only remotely by way of their effects. The hypotheses citing these things will be no less explanatory for that.

There is also this other responsibility. We want speculations that are responsible, and explanations that are true. How shall we test our hypotheses?

6. The Testing of Metaphysical Hypotheses

Philosophy is sometimes oblivious to the requirement that its hypotheses be applicable to matters of fact, and testable. That happens in part because we are distracted and confused where applicability resembles a two-barreled gun, each barrel splayed to an opposing side. One side aims at other theories, as we suppose that a theory is applicable when it speaks to, and solves their problems. The other barrel aims at possible states of affairs; the theory is applicable if these possibles are actual, i.e., if it represents things as they are. This second focus is ignored when philosophers speak mostly to one another, and usually for the purpose of defending themselves against dialectical attack. Our fascination with the rhetoric of assault and defense, together with our vanity in defending a favored position, makes truth and testability a marginal issue. We forget that no theory is worth the time spent affirming it if the theory could not be applicable to matters of fact. We may sometimes try to obscure this point by saying that theory is merely interpretation, where any theory defensible against its competitors while making experience thinkable is reasonably espoused. But then we also agree that the plausible story placing someone at the scene of a crime is not sufficient reason for hanging him. Truth is more demanding than interpretation. Metaphysical inquiry is deficient if its hypotheses are clever but untested.

6A. *Testable Hypotheses*

Hypotheses that might be true or false are grammatically well-formed specifications of possible states of affairs. They would be true if the possibilities signified were actual. A testable hypothesis is, therefore, one whose truth would make a factual difference, specifically the difference signified by the hypothesis. This is a general formula only. It may be no help to us as we consider any particular hypothesis, asking what it represents. For what are the meaningful thoughts and sentences? How shall we determine that some candidate thought or sentence does signify a possible state of affairs? How shall we distinguish those sentences from the rhymes of nonsense syllables or from Delphic slogans? What, for example, should we do, or stop doing, and what is the matter of fact signified when we are told to "Let being be." Metaphysical proposals in general, even this one, may signify some possible differences, but how are we to ascertain that they do?

The short, unhelpful answer is that knowing the meaning of a hypothesis is equivalent to knowing what possible state of affairs it signifies, hence what factual difference would obtain if the hypothesis were true. This is unhelpful in the way that formulas for getting rich are mostly useless to the poor; there is no telling how to apply their good advice in any particular situation. And equally, what is the state of affairs signified when the injunction quoted above is honored so that "Being is let to be"? We can supply a sense for this phrase within the dialectic of philosophic discussion, where it is used to recommend that interpretation and theory should stand aside, so that being might exhibit itself to the mind registering its unmediated presence. Still, this way of explicating the proposal locates its meaning in an act or procedure that we might perform, not in a claim about mind-independent matters of fact. We might hope to avoid having to tell in every case what matter of fact is signified by a metaphysical hypothesis, always telling instead what procedure mind is to follow in some context. But this will not clarify very many of the things we want to say of the world. Compare this slogan to hypotheses about matters of fact independent of our thinking: The one counsels that we rip the scales from our eyes, the other represents possible states of affairs. How should we proceed when testing hypotheses of the latter sort?

6B. The Four-step Procedure for Testing Hypotheses

There appears to be no rule for establishing in an *a priori* way that grammatically well-formed sentences do or do not signify possible states of affairs. Identifying the meaningful, hence testable, hypotheses is a problem. Where Lewis Carroll's rhymes are well beyond plausibility as candidates for testability, we have to admit that fluent speakers of a language are rightly puzzled by assertions like the one of my example. Needing a procedure for confirming the meaningfulness and testability of any particular hypothesis, we invoke the one that follows. It has four steps: exposition, the search for empirical evidence, dialectical defense, and integration into the body of hypotheses already found to be meaningful and confirmed.

6Bi. Exposition

Exposition is amplification. It moves up, down, and sideways in a style that may be formal or informal. We start with these various directions, telling what they imply before considering the difference between expositions that are formal or informal.

6Bia. Particularity, generality and collateral information

The typical hypothesis is general, hence determinable. We say, for example, that something is a crow. This limits the range of applicable properties without telling what specific expression they have in this bird. What is its subspecies? How big is it? How uniform is its color? The typical bird-watcher ignores these details as the bird flies out of view. He has seen many crows, is not much interested in this one, and is happy to classify the bird before dismissing it. Then again, this might be someone having a special interest in crows. It may be important to him that subspecies and even particular birds be distinguished. 'Crow' is too general for him. It requires exposition making it more specific. This is exposition in the downward direction. It supplies information of the sort enabling us to distinguish lower-order kinds and individuals, as no one ordering a suit of clothes is satisfied by the assurance that the material is colored. What color, we want to know? It is amplification that tells us.

We might also care to know that crows and ravens are the particular expressions of generic properties having a certain regulative force throughout the range of their many variations; or that suits of clothing like the ones currently fashionable are expressions of a style that is constraining across the range of its many versions. There are, for example, buttons on the sleeves of jackets, as one also sees buttons on the sleeves of military uniforms, and the formal suits of diplomats. Someone knowing the history of fashion locates the hypothesis, 'This is a man's suit' within the typology of styles, as a hypothesis about one of the force laws might lead to an explication showing that all force laws are more determinate expressions of the laws of motion. This is exposition in the direction of generality. It locates the hypothesis at issue within the higher-order determinable to which it relates as a lower-order, more determinate expression.

Exposition moves sideways as we locate our hypothesis within the network of collateral information. There is, for example, a degree of mutuality in the influence of men's and women's clothing. There may be evidence in this man's suit of a decorative flourish first introduced into women's apparel. This is lateral exposition as it locates our hypothesis within the larger setting of information that may help to specify the possible state of affairs it signifies. Lateral exposition is, by implication, indefinitely extendable, as there are successive domains of information that may be pertinent to the claim of any hypothesis.

Ordinary usage is somewhat equivocal in regard to the word *theory*. I suggest that a hypothesis deserves being called a theory when exposition has located it within the network of higher-order determinables, lower-order determinations, and collateral information. For then the hypothesis, whether descriptive or explanatory, has been generalized and extended in its relation to other pertinent information. It is, moreover, projectable onto some domain of significant particulars. The hypothesis is now a theory.

There is also this implication for the intentional meaning and sense of the words within hypotheses. We may construe these words so that the possibilities signified are narrowly drawn, as the referent for 'point' is specific. Probably most words and many sentences are narrowly, i.e., "literally," interpreted. But dictionaries are misleading in their implication that meanings might always be rendered with this near perfect specificity. There is always a penumbra of indeterminacy about every word and sentence. The context of its use and our intention when construing it may require that we draw more or less from this penumbra. But then we do or can move in one of these three directions, downward to greater specificity, upward to greater generality, or sideways to collateral information.

6Bib. Metaphysical hypotheses that are vague, fragmentary or metaphorical

Exposition helps to resolve our doubts about hypotheses that are, at first sight, puzzling. What do they mean? Amplification, in the three directions described, provides the only hope of an answer. For if specificity, generality, and collateral information fail to supply a reading of the hypothesis, there is not more that we can do to make it intelligible. It is, for example, collateral information about the obscuring effect of interpretation that makes it possible to interpret the aphorism considered above. Amplification is, more generally, our substitute for the natural light: a hypothesis still obscure after rigorous exposition is probably irreparably obscure.

Metaphysical hypotheses are especially vulnerable to the charge of obscurity. Metaphysicians are so preoccupied by having to criticize other positions that they are careless in making sure that their own views are applicable to matters of fact, or we prefer rhetoric to testable hypotheses. Either way, we risk formulating hypotheses defective in any of these three ways: They are general to the point of vagueness or vacuity, with no way of telling what more specific application they might have, hence no way of knowing if particular states of affairs would be their instances; they are fragmentary, so that we cannot specify either their application or their higher-order or collateral contexts; they are metaphorical, so that we cannot tell what literal sense they make, or the factual differences that would obtain if they were true.

There are prominent examples of all three defects. Materialism is a generality without established applicability to mind until we can tell how a material system might perform as minds do. Materialism is a vital leading principle for directing the inquiries that may ultimately satisfy this demand. But it is, in the meantime, a generality without confirmed application to mind. Hypotheses emphasizing time while acknowledging change are fragmentary, because they ignore space, though space is as fundamental as time to those changes that are motions. Hypotheses are only metaphorical when there are no resources within them, and none available to exposition for translating their evocative notions into something that is literal, applicable, and testable. Plato's description of the Good as being like the Sun is affecting in this way, though we have no other evidence or plausible interpretation for the claim that all of reality derives from the Good.[13] There is also Whitehead's claim that his "actual occasions" are "drops of experience" hav-

106

ing "feelings" and "subjective aims."[14] These allusive phrases do not carry the burden of theory so long as there is no way of telling how those anthropomorphisms might be applicable to all of nature.

Our aims, wherever hypotheses are vague, fragmentary, or metaphorical, is the one of amplifying them so that we can tell what factual differences would obtain if the hypotheses were true. There are of course thinkers who ignore this demand for amplification, all the while denying that their hypotheses are vague, fragmentary, or merely allusive. Isn't it enough that we tell a dramatic story about reality and our place within it? Why insist that our claims be literally applicable and testable? Perhaps literality is the enemy of depth, so that a testable philosophic theory is sure to be pedestrian. Isn't Plato's eminence just the measure of our contempt for the ordinary demands of meaning and truth? Plato is the Homer of our philosophic tradition; his myths are the flash of insight at the core of otherwise atrophied disputes. Squelch his myths, and philosophy is reduced to theory-mongering and analysis. We might as well be scientists or bookkeepers. We will surely be scholastics.

We do want a middle-way between the mythic and the banal. But what is the point of saying that the Good is like the Sun if we cannot tell what factual difference would obtain if this were true? Does it entail that Hitler should have been invisible because of being evil? If evil is a privation, then a nearly absolute evil should be nearly nonexistent, and nearly invisible. Hitler was neither. Is this a test the hypothesis fails? It is hard to know. Consider, too, any brick. Are there drops of experience comprising it? Should we ask about the subjects of these experiences; or is that irrelevant? Supposing that we know the meaning of this hypothesis—bricks, like us, have feelings—how shall we test for its truth? What is to count as evidence for or against this claim about a factual difference?

We ask these questions while agreeing that large-scale hypotheses may sometimes be vague, fragmentary, and metaphorical, at least in our early statements of them. There is no harm in this, if amplification enables us to bring these hypotheses to bear upon possible states of affairs. Great metaphors are the heart and soul of our intellectual culture, even while being the engine of its practical success. Plato's allegory of the cave, and especially his figure of the divided line deserve that description within modern scientific culture. It is Plato who taught us to assume the difference between ephemeral particulars and stable universals having mathematical expression. It does not matter to this point that Plato is not the originator of all these ideas, or that the implications of his allegory and figure are not always adequate to the matters at issue. The direction he supplied may be enough to explain our sense that reality has a certain design, a design that we can know. Other great cultures lack this metaphor, and their science may have been crippled for want of it.

Is this admission a bald inconsistency, coming as it does after my saying that metaphors are deficient because of resisting exposition? Can we require literality and testability for metaphysical hypotheses while agreeing that the most gorgeous of metaphysical ideas, and by practical measure the most successful, is a metaphor? There is no inconsistency if we amend Whitehead's remark that the history of philosophy is a series of footnotes to Plato. Why not say instead that our history is often a succession of expositions calculated to make Plato literal and testable? Surely, the evidence for some core of truth in his ideas is apparent when we use his speculations as a regulative idea. It would be odd that we should have learned so much about the world if the distinction directing our theories and experiments—the one of forms, universals, or laws versus particulars—were not applicable to the world itself. The best formulation of this difference is a dispute unresolved, though all of our debates about nature and knowledge turn upon the assumption that this is a fundamental difference. Perhaps our circumstances are clarified a little by acknowledging that metaphysical theories move in cycles, and that some of them may dominate our thinking as long as Plato is remote from us. Exposition and confirmation may take millennia, even while the culture about us successfully applies the cruder notions that metaphysicians struggle to amplify and confirm. Not all of our hypotheses have a career so momentous or perplexing, but some do.

6Bic. Modal structure

Suppose that exposition has moved up, down, and sideways, thereby supplying the detail which justifies redescribing a hypothesis as a theory. More than that, exposition will have supplied the modal structure of the possibility signified by the hypothesis. Motion, for example, is contingently fast or slow; but always it presupposes space and time, whatever its specific character. So are the many possible arrangements of furnishings in a room constrained by its shape, as the array of words in a sentence are meaningless if the sentence is not well formed. Even our bodies are necessary in the respect that variations in the styles of our clothes are constrained by the shapes of torsos, arms, and legs. What does *necessity* signify in all these cases? Just that character which conditions and limits some other property or set of properties.

The necessities revealed by exposition may sometimes be universal, as space and time are universally the conditions for motion. More often, these necessities are parochial, as there is nothing universal in the fact that we have two arms rather than the six of an Indian goddess. Necessities of both sorts are the invariant in respect to which contingencies are variable. It is not significant to this difference that parochial necessities are themselves variable, as the laws of nature invariant in our world have no application in worlds characterized by other laws. The relation of invariants and their variable expressions is, therefore, usually contextual, and in that respect contingent. Still, the invariant, whether universal or parochial, is necessary to its variables as that which fixes their generic character while leaving open their differing realizations of that character.

Exposition will have discovered this difference between an invariant and its variable expressions on the way to articulating the meaning of a hypothesis, hence the structure of the possibility it signifies. We infer that exposition, itself, is experimental and probing as it determines the degree of constraint exercised by an invariant in regard to the domain of its variable expressions. The question will always have been: How much can some particular invariant be altered while preserving this same domain of variations; or conversely, how much can all of them be altered within the limits prescribed? Occasionally, we discover an absolute limit. Those are cases where the identity of the variables does not survive a change of the invariant. Nothing of that sort happens, for example, when the furnishings constrained by the size of a room are moved into some other space, or even as the words suited to one kind of syntax are reorganized in the way required by some other one. Still, it does sometimes happen that the relation of an invariant to its variations is absolute rather than contextual, as when motion presupposes space and time for its every expression. Notice too that there is a division in the class of absolutely necessary invariant conditions. In some cases, it is the particular expression of a generic property that has a particular necessary condition, as it is a plane of zero curvature that is a condition for a triangle's having internal angles of 180 degrees. Other times, the absolutely necessary condition applies throughout a range of variations, as extension is a necessary condition for every shade of color.

These instances of absolutely necessary conditions are also important in this other respect: We may use demonstration to testify that denying either the conditionality of some of them, e.g., the conditioning of motion by space and time, or the bi-conditionality of others, e.g., the relation of hypotenuse and sides in a right triangle, produces a contradiction. What does contradiction indicate in these cases? That a necessary condition so determines the identity of the factor conditioned that denying the necessary conditionality of that factor violates the identity of the variant conditioned: the variant could not be as it is if the invariant were not as it is.

The fact that exposition does sometimes produce these demonstrations is not at all the same as affirming that these are *a priori* proofs about matters of fact, for it does not follow from the fact that space and time are necessarily presupposed by motion that there is any motion in our world. Affirming that motion does occur here is an additional, contingent claim based upon our observations. There is, nevertheless, the anticipation justified by exposition that some hypotheses do represent *de re* necessities in the possibilities they signify. Equally, we may suppose that these *de re* necessities would be imminent in our world if the relevant possibilities were instantiated here, as motion in our world does presuppose space and time.

6Bid. Sensory evidence

We need evidence before saying that relations of any sort, necessary or contingent, are instantiated in our world. Exposition should carry on until we have specified whatever consequences implied by a hypothesis would serve as evidence of its instantiation. What is to count as evidence? Only those sensory effects that would result if this state of affairs did obtain.

Observability is the measure of instantiation, and of truth, although we must avoid the easy confusion of sensory affects in us with the possibilities instantiated, i.e., the actual things observed. Sensory data are the evidence *of* these things, and the evidence *for* our hypotheses about them. For if there are no *a priori* illuminations regarding the world, and if necessary truths cannot be known to have application in the world without empirical evidence that the factor represented by the conditioned term within them, e.g., motion, is instantiated, then observation is the only source for the evidence we have of instantiated possibilities. Exposition, as a kind of disciplined association, is pressed to tell us, for any particular hypothesis, what the pertinent sensory data would be.

There are also these two cautionary remarks. *First,* we typically prefer data thought to be iconic with their causes, so that we might know a cause merely by regarding the data. We sometimes resist having to acknowledge that most sensory data are not like their causes in any significant way, even though we often infer from the data to the character of their causes, as we infer to the properties of electrical phenomena from pointer readings, and to those of atomic particles from the marks on photographic plates. *Second* is the fact that sensory data are a test of truth, not always the content of meaning. It probably happens that meanings are generated from reflection upon our observations, as *red* is used within the true sentence, "This is red," to signify the perceived redness of something. Truth and observation are, therefore, the original conditions for fixing the meaning of this observation word. Later, abstraction, variation, and combination extend the range of meanings well beyond the perceptual data. Possibilities, not those data, come to be the senses of our words. Philosophy, under the influence of empiricist intuitionists, is addicted to forcing meanings back to these remote origins. This project necessarily fails, because sensory data are impoverished when compared to the diversity of possibilities signified. Observation is, nevertheless, decisive for truth when nothing else supplies the evidence for saying that the possibilities represented by our hypotheses are instantiated.

6bie. Observability as a test for metaphysical hypotheses

Our special concern is the exposition of metaphysical hypotheses. There are, curiously, two attitudes regarding the importance of observation for them.

One one side are the intuitionists. They suppose that no claim about reality has any currency if it is not confirmed by some matter set before our inspecting minds, e.g., as evidence for the existence of Plato's Forms is the fact that *nous* perceives them. The other side supposes that observations are incidental to the truth of metaphysical claims, though the reasons for saying this diverge. One reason is that competing claims may have the same sensory data as evidence for their truth, as phenomenalism and physicalism appeal to the same data. Someone insisting that a true claim must have observable consequences finds himself having to concede that sensory data are not evidence enough for choosing between these two theories. That leaves economy, coherence, fruitfulness, and plausibility as the criteria to be used for deciding between them. The other reason for ignoring observation is a certain contempt for the idea that we should, or could, test metaphysical theories by showing that they imply or predict certain observations. We discount the effect of sensory data—they could only confirm a claim, never demonstrate it—or we are distracted from the demand for proving a theory applicable to the world by our fascination with the dialectic of contending positions. Truth, we suppose, could only emerge from the contest of theories, as each one is used to ditch its competitors while defending itself. This view is compelling for everyone captive to the beauties of his own theory, and determined to live his thinking life within it. We come to adore our theory's idiosyncracies. Defending it, while declaring the flaws in other theories, is, for us, the sufficient condition for our own theory's truth.

These several attitudes are not equally respectable. The first one, that of identifying reality with the things inspectable, is the sure route to the psychocentrism affirming that the only reality is mind and its affections. The third alternative, commitment to dialectic without regard for the observables, loses itself in dispute after forgetting that the truth of a theory depends upon something more than our determination to defend it. Only the second alternative is a severe obstacle to testing hypotheses, for it is sometimes true that contrary hypotheses do have the same observable consequences. We are obliged to introduce some other consideration when choosing between or among them.

This is fortunately a rare outcome, one that we can defer while considering a prior issue: we need first establish that metaphysical hypotheses, like the ones of practice and science, do represent possibilities that would make, were they instantiated, observable differences. Exposition is to tell what sensory effects there would be if our metaphysical hypotheses were true. I am assuming that we address the world by way of our hypotheses, and that the world has to show something of itself if we are to gauge the truth of our claims about it. There are, we assume, no *a priori* tests for their truth.

Is there, perhaps, a special domain of evidentiary phenomena to which metaphysicians can resort when testing their hypotheses? The question is suspicious, for this is likely to be the barely disguised appeal to that illumination intuitionists claim when they suppose that disciplined reflection is our access to Forms or ideas of a sort are invisible to more vulgar perceptions. One wants to say that there is no evidence for these privileged data, but that is question-begging when some people claim to have them. One says instead that their reports of those data are misdescriptions of something more commonplace, e.g., as the alleged intuition of ideas may be only a facility with words. That leaves us with nothing but the array of sensory data with which to test our hypotheses, whether practical, scientific or metaphysical.

There is also this other resource: We have some latitude in characterizing the perceptual data and the things thereby observed, where our aim is the one of describing the data in ways appropriate to the generality and claims of the hypotheses being tested. What veterinarians and their owners call dogs and cats, we describe as physical objects or as congeries of sense data. What others call migrations may be regularities for us. Physical objects, sense data, and regularities are actual, so that observing these various things justifies our saying that actuals are observable. It is, not a special domain of sensory data, but only the power for characterizing things in salient language that distinguishes metaphysical from other uses of this data.

This freedom for characterizing sensory data and the things observed by way of them is, we know, subject to abuse, though nothing in this is peculiar to metaphysics. Every child lost in the woods may overdescribe or misdescribe the sound of wind in the trees. These characterizations of sensory data and the things causing them are tacit hypotheses in their own right, as describing a bird flying south as a migrating bird is a multilayered hypothesis, even before we christen this behavior a regularity. A properly self-critical exposition will signpost these more or less tacit interpretive hypotheses so that the ultimate confirmation or falsification of the hypothesis being amplified will be seen to have depended upon these ways of characterizing the observables. It often happens that nothing illicit was introduced or assumed when the observables cited within the exposition were characterized in some particular way. Other times, we return to an apparently confirmed hypothesis, remarking that its apparent confirmation was the result of a question-begging characterization at the time of its exposition. That would happen, for example, if our characterization of awareness as beamlike, hence as justifying the distinction between a subjective act and its content, were upset by the discovery that conscious activity is never more than the sequence of associated multilayered, overlapping acts, with neither beams of mental light focused upon them, nor a division between subjective acts and objective contents.

Exposition, this implies, risks the introduction of hypothesis-distorting errors at the point of characterizing sensory data and their presumed causes. This is an ineliminable risk as long as we refuse to be intuitionists. They would avert the difficulty by supposing that the only justifiable hypotheses are the ones reporting whatever matters stand before our minds. We are to report these things exactly as they appear to us, every other characterization being an instance of false and reckless misdescription. Satisfying this intuitionist demand would produce the sparest possible phenomenology, where every description risks being an under-or overdescription, as *red* signifies a property that is much too determinable for anything perceived. We might be reduced to nodding in recognition of the phenomena perceived.

No thinking of any sort, practical, scientific, or metaphysical, accepts this restriction. Not wanting to be intuitionists, rejecting their view that mind is the crucible in which every other thing is set before our refining gaze, we characterize sensory data and the things to which they give us access on the way to finding our way in the world. We take care that our specifications of the data and the things thereby observed are flagged so that these descriptions may be reconsidered. Just as urgently, we do not encourage these later reexaminations by misdescribing the sensory data or their presumed conditions, e.g., by describing the wind in the trees as the voice of a god so that, yes, this god as much as the trees is observable. There is no tightly drawn rule for preventing these excesses, but we can be scrupulous when introducing only those characterizations that seem neutral regarding whatever issues are disputed. 'Physical object' is relatively neutral in that way if we have rejected intuitionist phenomenalism; *regularity* and *actu-*

ality are safer still. But no characterization of sensory data or their grounds is completely innocent, so that we expect to be challenged some time or other as we work through an exposition on the way to specifying the perceptual evidence for a metaphysical hypothesis.

Amplification in the direction of sensory data and their observable grounds is also problematic in another, quite different way. I have been assuming that we should be able to specify first the factual difference that would obtain if a metaphysical, or other, hypothesis were true, and then the observable effects of that factual difference. This claim makes three suppositions, each one needing elaboration.

First, why should we assume that every factual difference makes an observable difference? There is no proof that this must be true; but only the consideration that something which gives no sensible evidence of itself will never be discovered. We don't mind that the evidence is remote, requiring a subtle chain of inferences, perhaps of the sort required for estimating the character of black holes. We only demand that there be some evidence. Metaphysics could only claim exemption from this requirement if there were some other sort of evidence available to it. Intuitionists of one sort claim the light of reason, but intuitionism is or ought to be renounced in all its forms. That leaves metaphysicians with no resources but the ones available to practice and science. Where evidence for our hypotheses is the issue, that resource is only sensory data.

Second is the reminder that metaphysics is concerned as much with nature's conditions, if there are any, as it is with nature itself. We must anticipate having to tell what perceptual evidence there might be of nature's conditions. These data will typically be gross differences, as a world that is internally contradictory cannot be observed in any way, because it cannot exist. Conversely, the fact that a possible world is instantiated implies the perceptual evidence of, first, the actual world, then more remotely of the possibility instantiated.

Third is the difficulty of choosing between different, even contrary hypotheses implying the same sensory evidence. Phenomenalism and physicalism do that: Every sensory difference implied by or consistent with one is implied by or consistent with the other. This entails that expositions specifying the sensory differences that would obtain if hypotheses were true are not sufficient, when joined to confirming experiments, for establishing the truth of these hypotheses. This is the reason for acknowledging dialectical defense as one of the essential steps in testing hypotheses: Each confirmed hypothesis must be defended against its equally well confirmed contrary.

6Bif. Formal and informal expositions

Exposition proceeds in either a formal, or an informal way. Formality makes it disciplined, so that we are better able to check some extended exposition to confirm that nothing inappropriate has been introduced. We may suppose that nothing less than an axiomitized system is formal enough, but that is too much like saying that perfect pitch is the only pitch, or that color-blind people can't see at all. Other, nonaxiomitized expositions may also be formal to some extent. In them as in the strictly formalized ones, there are rules for directing the exposition, and these same rules to serve as criteria when we appraise the warrant for some previous amplification. We have a spectrum of expositions, with axiomitizied theories at one extreme and free association at the other. Our problem is the one of identifying the rules used for directing those expositions which lack the explicit formality of axiomitized systems.

Specifying these rules is hard, because the rules are usually applied without having been expressly formulated. How can we justify saying that exposition has produced the appropriate associations for some hypothesis when the determining rules are unspecified? The answer seems to be that exposition is directed by two things: first, by the hypothesis itself, especially by its constituent words or phrases and the grammatical form integrating them; second, by some general rules of association. One quite general rule directs us to look for sameness or difference in regard to quality, quantity, or relation. Another, equally general, rule encourages us to suppose that terms have relations, and relations terms so that, having one, we look for the other. These rules are heuristic or leading principles. Applying them to the hypothesis at issue supplies exposition with both the content and general procedures required for amplifying it. I assume that the rules directing association are themselves more or less transparent hypotheses about the world, as we claim that it has quality, quantity, relations, and the terms related. This is another instance of the fact that exposition is not metaphysically innocent: Amplifying a hypothesis requires that we operate upon it in ways implying some claims about the world. Here, as in the case of terms used to characterize sensory data or their grounds, we acknowledge these assumptions.

A full list of the general rules directing exposition has never, to my knowledge, been formulated, though one presumes that associationist psychologists have identified some of them, and that engineers simulating human intelligence would also need to identify them. Perhaps one motive for wanting to formalize scientific theories is the unuttered suspicion that nothing less than a mathematical formalism supplies reliable rules. This would imply that every exposition short of this formal ideal is unreliable, or the instance of an undisciplined free association. Expositions are almost always more cogent than either of these alternatives would allow.

6Big. *Exposition as an end-in-itself*

Exposition is not an end in itself, though philosophers sometimes behave as though it were. We pride ourselves on being analytic, caring only for the exposition of ideas or sentences, not about their truth. Truth itself may become a topic for exposition, although making it so is different from wanting to confirm that particular hypotheses are true. Perhaps this devotion to exposition is a defense against the inclination to speculate, and the fear that our hypotheses will be untestable. Rather than dare to say anything important that might be false, we settle for amplifying the meanings of our words and regimenting our sentences. More parlous still, we take in laundry, meaning other people's words and sentences, promising to return them in good canonical form.

This caution is sometimes useful, as when we determine that a hypothesis is irreparably incoherent, fragmentary, or metaphorical. Yet we pay for these successes by forgetting our aim, i.e., amplifying hypotheses on the way to testing them. We come to resemble those painters who are always checking their paints and brushes but never painting, or the parachutist who folds and unfolds his chute but never jumps. This habit is all the stronger in philosophers, for we have intuitionism to remind us that words or ideas clearly articulated and set before our inspecting minds are a good in themselves, one satisfying the standards which Descartes prescribed for us in his *Rules*. Descartes supposed that truth is satisfied when ideas stand clearly and distinctly before our minds. Contemporary analysts repudiate the psychologistic overtones of this formulation, while agreeing that clarity in exposition, meaning exposition satisfying logical rules, is a good and sufficient aim.

We might hope to justify this activity by founding it within that psychocentric ontology where a mind discerning and describing the things arrayed before it accomplishes all that could ever be demanded of knowledge. But how shall we explain this fascination when the intuitionist program is rejected? For then we have nothing to justify the paralyzing concern for analyses serving no interest apart from themselves. We recover our bearings only as we remember that speculation is exigent when we have to accommodate ourselves to the world while having no innate ideas of it. Exposition is the first step in testing hypotheses about our circumstances. It is not the aim, and fulfillment of our philosophic thinking.

6Bii. Searching for evidence

Let us assume that the hypothesis being tested does represent a possible state of affairs. Exposition has shown that much. Even the rare demonstrations of hypotheses do not establish, however, that the possibles they represent are actual, for these are so far truths about possibilities, not about actual states of affairs. We are concerned that our hypotheses be true of the actual matters of fact obtaining in our world. Our problem is the one of searching for evidence that the possibilities signified by our hypotheses are instantiated.

One of our descriptions alleges that someone is a Muslim. Exposition instructs us that such a man is likely to read the Koran and observe Friday as the Sabbath. Do we observe this man behaving in either way? Or the description is metaphysical: it affirms that everything actual occupies some position in space-time. Here too, there are observables pertinent to the hypothesis, and a further implication for testing the universality of this claim: i.e., is any thing actual but *not* located in space-time? Explanations, like descriptions, require this same next step. We say, for example, that minds are only the activities of material systems. We then locate the relevant systems within our own brains, or we construct machines that think as we do.

There are two kinds of art in this search: knowing what to look for, and knowing how to search efficiently for it. Exposition has, presumably, settled the first question, so that our present concern is the one of finding the evidence that will falsify or confirm a hypothesis. This is the place where inquiry is *experiment*. That word is too often reserved for tests using machinery to achieve some predicted effect, though testing the water with one's toes is no less experimental. Why not say that testing the world for some anticipated observable always merits this description?

Tests for metaphysical hypotheses cover the range of technological subtlety. Some of these hypotheses require the best efforts of experimental physicists, because those are hypotheses formulated, then tested by physicists. Probably most of our information about space, time, matter, and motion will derive from these scientific hypotheses and tests. There are, however, the many claims about categorial form for which the evidence is obtained more easily. There is, for example, evidence for saying that some things are past. It includes their perceived effects, e.g., children. So is there evidence in the regularities we perceive for the claim that similar causes usually have similar effects. No special equipment is required for confirming these predicted observations, though searching for them is no less experimental than the procedures that do require it. Some data are harder to achieve and discern, but this is a fact peculiar to the evidence for particular hypotheses. It is incidental to the character of experiment. That probing of the things about us is common to every experiment.

It follows from these considerations that the evidence testing metaphysical hypotheses is no different in kind, or even sometimes in particulars, from the evidence significant for practical and scientific ones. Metaphysical inquiry has no access to the world except the access available to everyone else. Metaphysicians may describe the predicted evidence differently because of the different emphasis of their hypotheses, but these metaphysical concerns, e.g., for generality or modality, are the only basis for distinguishing metaphysical inquiry from inquiries serving practical or scientific interests. This similarity is not surprising when science and metaphysics are overlapping orders of reflection coming after the maps and plans of ordinary practice. Indeed, much of the evidence relevant to our metaphysical hypotheses will have been available at the moment of our first encounters with the world. Science and metaphysics have only refined our early maps, sometimes finding more subtle ways of educing and controlling the experimental effects. The salient evidence may not be new or arcane, though the hypotheses predicting it may have required several turns of reflection.

There is, for example, the question of knowledge. Do we have knowledge of material, contingent things? We do not, if knowledge implies infallibility, though we do have, or seem to have, many true beliefs. These beliefs extend from knowledge about the conditions and locations of our bodies through beliefs about other things and their behaviors to more abstract beliefs about some general features of the world. A skeptic might contest these knowledge claims, but that is incidental to this other point: What should count as evidence for the hypothesis that we do have true beliefs? Only the obvious and hardly disputable fact that people, ourselves included, are observed doing things they apparently know how to do. The evidence counting for or against this hypothesis is close at hand and no mystery to anyone. This is one of the many occasions when a philosophic hypothesis is tested by the available evidence. We are not obliged to invent evidence, or to discover a special domain of privileged philosophic evidence. The data serving as evidence of the things existing apart from us are, of course, located within a special place. But their site, in our heads, is not a special metaphysical place. There is nothing about the data or their locale to justify an important difference between evidence for metaphysical hypotheses and evidence for hypotheses of every other sort.

6Biii. Dialectical consideration of empirically confirmed, but competing hypotheses

Suppose that the predicted observables are discovered: There is evidence for the truth of our hypothesis. It is still premature to say that this successfully tested hypothesis is true and that all its contraries must be false. For we pass now to the dialectic that evaluates competing hypotheses, all of them confirmed by the observables. Where falsified hypotheses have been rejected or revised and tested again, we consider the competition among or between the hypotheses confirmed. If only a single hypothesis survives, we ignore dialectic passing on to integrate this confirmed hypothesis into the network of those other ones already accepted. Suppose, however, that there are two or more confirmed hypotheses. This is the more familiar situation.

Dialectical competition among the hypotheses confirmed by sensory data presents itself in either of several ways. Sometimes the competing hypotheses have nothing in common but the aim of describing and explaining everything. Other times, the competitors are differing answers to some more specific question. Appraising these alternatives may enable us to choose among them, or it may teach us to improve one of the candidates, even to the point of generating an alternative superior to all the ones previously considered.

6Biiia. *Using dialectic to discover something previously unsuspected*

We start with an example of this last sort, where dialectic teaches us that all of the options before us are deficient as stated. Suppose, for example, that we speculate of reality, as Quine does of rabbits, that it is comprised of things, or of their parts, or of their stages. We do see rabbits; we do see their bodies, noses, feet, and tails; we do see rabbits changed. Which is more fundamental: the entity, its parts, or its phases?

Dialectic resolves this dispute by questioning the adequacy of these several formulations. Granting that all of them are applicable to rabbits, do they also acknowledge all of the considerations appropriate to being a rabbit? Are they adequate as well as applicable? We realize, when asking these questions of the three candidate hypotheses, that something important has been ignored. That something is the difference between aggregates and the wholes resulting when their parts are configured. The sand in a pile and pennies in a jar are aggregates. Rabbits and triangles are configurations; the properties of the whole are different from the sum of the parts. The triangle, for example, is comprised only of its lines and angles, though organizing these parts creates the triangle, thereby making the triangle prior, in this respect, to the properties resulting when the parts are configured. So is the rabbit prior to its parts and stages. The parts are related dynamically to one another within the stable system where relations secure and sustain the identity of the parts. The phases are transformations of this entity as it retains its identity, or its genealogical integrity, through the history of its transformations. It is, therefore, more than a semantic point when we say that rabbits have parts and stages, not the reverse. Being a part or phase presupposes that dynamically stabilized spatial-temporal continuant of which these are the parts or phases.

Quine's rabbit illustrates that dialectical consideration may teach us more of the world than the hypotheses at issue, even as this newly acknowledged consideration enables us to choose among the candidate hypotheses. One is reminded of early pages in the *Republic* where the failure of each successive hypothesis helps us to formulate a hypothesis about the assumption precluding justice in each of them, i.e., they misdescribe human nature. None of them acknowledges the equilibrium required in a just soul and state.[15] It is no matter, therefore, that each of several hypotheses seems well confirmed by the data it predicts. Dialectic discovers that something else – something important – has been missed.

6Biiib. Appraising alternative hypotheses confirmed by the same evidence

Dialectic is, at other times, more perplexing and open-ended. There is, for example, the choice to be made between phenomenalism and physical object realism. Exposition shows that both hypotheses are confirmed by the same sensory data. There is no datum confirming one that is not equally a datum confirming the other. How shall we choose between them?

Dialectic encourages us to challenge each hypothesis in two ways: first, from within, asking if the hypothesis is consistent, coherent, and both applicable and adequate to all the phenomena for which it claims responsibility; second, from without, asking if its claims are plausible in themselves, coherent with other hypotheses already accepted, and both applicable and adequate to all the phenomena for which it should claim responsibility. We may ask questions of both sorts without having to be partisans of either hypothesis. For every acceptable hypothesis should be expected to satisfy these questions. The actual practice of dialectical challenge and defense may, of course, reduce to being the merely partisan exercise of poisoning a competitor's well in the hope of making one's own seem sweeter. But that does not happen if our only concern is the one of identifying the hypothesis more likely to be true. With that as our objective, we look for a standpoint that is neutral between the contested hypotheses. We agree, for example, that sensory data show us a world of differentiated but related properties, where particular sets of properties cohere in stable relations to one another. Which of these two hypothesis is the more likely one in the light of these agreed observations and the questions cited above?

Dialectic is opportunistic. Informed by these internal and external questions, we seize upon a weakness, pressing the charge that a hypothesis is defective in some particular way. When appraising the hypothesis of physical object realism, we question its postulation of entities providing a conceptual backing for our observations without seeming to have any additional justification. Wanting reasons for the phenomenalist alternative, we demand specification of the causes or grounds for the appearances that phenomenalism can only remark but never explain. How do we decide between these hypotheses after asking these questions, and hearing the answers? Is there a number grade for each response? Do we settle for an evaluative *gestalt* when one is "seen" to do better?

The one alternative is too precise, the other too impressionistic. The more accurate characterization seems to be that we prefer a hypothesis that is economical in its use of theoretical terms, systematic and plausible, then applicable and adequate to all the phenomena it does and should claim to describe or explain. A hypothesis satisfying these requirements is hard to fault. Every other one is less than perfectly credible.

These criteria are, of course, problematic in themselves. Economy is recommended because we suspect that anything less is likely to disguise overlapping, or duplication among theoretical terms. There is all the history of theories formulated and revised to support this suspicion. A systematic theory is one whose theoretical terms are mutually supporting, as substance and cause in Aristotle imply one another. Here too we express the learned wisdom of working with theories making the empirically confirmed assumption that variables in nature are sometimes mutually conditioning. Plausibility is more suspect for its situational and subjective bias. Still, we do have at any time a body of confirmed and accepted hypotheses. These hypotheses establish a point of reference for every additional claim about the world. New hypotheses violating assumptions shared by these accepted hypotheses will be implausible. Those established beliefs may prove to be mistaken, but they are the reasonable benchmark for an inquiry that must always start with assumptions of one kind or another. Applicability and adequacy are demands that a theory have instances, and that a metaphysical theory should specify all of a thing's categorial features. These are a repertoire of least considerations that any metaphysical hypothesis should satisfy.

Phenomenalism is implausible because of presupposing that the one reality is mind and its qualifying sensory data. That assumption does not square with the solipsistic claims of other phenomenalists, let alone with the story of one's own birth and death in a world that precedes and survives us. Phenomenalism is not systematic. It tells what mind does, but not what it is, i.e., we describe its passivity to phenomena, but not the structure it need have in order that phenomena be received. There is, furthermore, no explanation for the sensory data. Mind does not invent them, it seems; yet, there is no account of their origin. Mental activity (or passivity) and these phenomena are left hanging in the explanatory void, with the pretense that the data inspected, mind's own acts and affections included, might be self-sufficient. Perhaps the self-sufficiency claimed for the data is only a way of putting the best face on the phenomenalist inability to explain all that needs explaining. Phenomenalism is incomplete and implausibile, two reasons, each one good enough in itself, for rejecting the hypothesis.

The considerations disqualifying this proposal do not secure the acceptability of its competitor. Physical object realism has to be good enough in its own right to justify that further claim, though it does succeed in each of the places where phenomenalism fails. Realism coheres with our practical experience, manipulating things that seem independent of us; it explains the generation of sensory data as the effect of interactions between physical system. This is a better theory; it identifies an economical list of sufficient conditions for the things to be explained.

6Biiic. Is dialectical appraisal invariably subverted by an interpretive bias?

Is this finding a concession to the requirements of interpretation, rather than truth? Haven't we chosen between two hypotheses that are equally well confirmed empirically on grounds having much to do with thought's own standards for inquiry but less to do with the nature of things in themselves? These questions force us to acknowledge a difference of opinion at the foundations of our speculative thinking. This difference is the one underlying the opposition of phenomenalism and physical object realism: Should we restrict ourselves to describing the things appearing before us, or should we also explain these phenomena by inferring abductively to their conditions?

We risk turning in a very small circle, never progressing beyond it if we are not willing to make some elementary determinations. A first choice is the repudiation of intuitionist method and ontology. The idea that knowledge is achieved merely by discerning and describing the matters inspected does not square with the demands or claims of practice and science. Resorting to this otherwise discredited method for the purposes of metaphysical inquiry will seem perverse to everyone not addicted to the hope that we might achieve certainty about some things merely by inspecting them. But then we need an alternative method. Abductive explanation with inferences proceeding from things declared to their conditions does seem to be the principal lever for all our understanding and control, both of ourselves and the things about us. Supplementing these abductions with the descriptions they presuppose (e.g., of smoke before inferring fire) and with descriptive generalizations, supplies a battery of instruments for effective inquiry.

Even this affirmation is subject to reconsideration if the network of previously accepted hypotheses and procedures is revised to the point where claims that were plausible before have come to seem dubious; though it is hard to imagine the circumstances where intuition would seem more appropriate than description and abduction as the method for learning of the world and our place within it.

Is this last sentence, shorn of its last clause, the final concession that our choice of hypotheses is always a nod to the mind's own standards and not the assertion of discovered truths? No, we merely agree that creatures living in the middle of things, but without innate ideas of them, can hope to keep their bearings only if they are prepared to speculate, then to think again, always revising some hypothesis turned dogma when subsequent considerations require justification.

6Biv. Integrating the empirically confirmed survivor of dialectic into the network of already accepted hypotheses

The last of the four steps required for testing a hypothesis is integration. It must be shown that the empirically confirmed hypothesis surviving dialectical challenge can be introduced into the network of hypotheses already accepted, or that the very plausibility of those accepted beliefs has collapsed under the force of this new claim. Revolutionary hypotheses are rare. We are never certain that some new and despised idea will not be the inspiration for the wholesale revision of our current beliefs. But we usually proceed conservatively, on the reasonable assumption that we already know a great deal about the world, and that new hypotheses should not violate, even if they do not support and cohere with, previously confirmed and established beliefs.

Integration is, however, problematic in four ways: (1) Whose beliefs are to count as the body of accepted beliefs? (2) Beliefs change so that beliefs congenial or not to some newly tested hypothesis may themselves be revised, with consequent implications for the acceptability of this currently tested claim; (3) Integration may be more or less systematic and formal; (4) A conspicuously successful integration is no proof against error. Let us consider these four points in detail.

6Biva. Which are the "accepted" beliefs for metaphysics?

Which are the standard beliefs into which some newly confirmed metaphysical hypothesis is to be integrated? Are they beliefs of the individual inquirer, or the beliefs of his or her intellectual community? Are they, perhaps, a selection of the diverse hypotheses proposed over the course of our philosophic history? We usually do best if we protect ourselves against the errors intrinsic to all of these resources by balancing each one against the others, although there is this other, opposed consideration: We may sometimes have to liberate ourselves from a chronic history of error when it affects each one of these three sets of beliefs. In metaphysical tradition, that error is the intuitionism pervading so much of our thought. This is the demand that nothing be acknowledged as real if it is not, or cannot be set before our inspecting minds. Nothing comes from this method and the set of beliefs confirming it except another restatement of its psychocentric ontology, and the renewed demand for certainty in knowledge. Everyone who repudiates these ideas does better to separate himself from this tradition and the community perpetuating it. These dissenters will have to formulate a network of hypotheses independent of the intuitionist dogmas, though there are no rules for doing so. Only the accumulation of hypotheses formulated and tested in conscious rejection of the intuitionist past will supply a more reliable network of metaphysical claims, serving henceforth as a core of reliable, though revisable, hypotheses. Every new metaphysical hypothesis can be tested for its coherence with them.

There are antecedents for this nonintuitionist metaphysics, as in Aristotle and Hobbes. Yet, one must pick and choose even from their books. There is, accordingly, no secure base of agreed hypotheses that might serve as the established network in which to find a place for a newly confirmed hypothesis. One hopes for a future consensus regarding some principal claims about the world, and one supposes that those claims will cohere with the results of scientific inquiry, and some at least of the hypotheses confirmed in everyday life. The more detailed character of that network is hard to discern. Hypotheses about self-stabilizing material systems in space-time, with a backdrop of eternal possibilities, is my proposal for its schematic design.

Integration is, therefore, problematic in three ways that bear upon established beliefs: first, as we require that a newly confirmed hypothesis be tested against a set of established beliefs; second, as we appraise the networks currently available, especially the views so plainly founded on intuitionist assumptions; third, as we create a new and independent network of metaphysical hypotheses into which newly confirmed hypotheses can be integrated.

6Bivb. Shifts within the network of accepted hypotheses

Every set of accepted beliefs is subject to revision, so that there is a certain contingency to the ease or difficulty of integrating a new hypothesis into them: It encounters them at a time when they are more or less congenial to it. The idea that all of life and mind might have physical constituents only would have seemed heretical and unassimilable in the past, though it is plausible enough today. Perhaps there is some unknown constraint preventing us from formulating or testing hypotheses that too much exceed the tolerance of currently accepted hypotheses. Without being able to formulate the latitude for "errant" speculation, one imagines that the margin for "responsible" speculation is narrow, and that it quickly falls into "silliness." Constraints of this sort assure that revision within the network of established hypotheses is incremental, and that revolution, however dramatic it may seem, is usually no more than the recasting of views already held in ways that extrapolate from the increments previously consolidated into the body of accepted belief. Hypotheses exceeding these constraints seem reckless or nonsensical, until, perhaps, later when we describe them as "ahead of their time."

There is an evident difference between these incremental or radical changes within an accepted framework, and the suggestion that we repudiate the established network of intuitionist beliefs because of a deep flaw within it. The one effect occurs when a powerful substantive hypothesis is assimilated. The demise of intuitionism is revolutionary only in the negative sense that we are denied the support of beliefs that had seemed incorrigible.

6Bivc. The more or less systematic organization of accepted hypotheses

The network of accepted hypotheses may be integrated more or less systematically. *Minimal* integration is reminiscent of old cities. Like their many quarters, some new, some old, some of narrow, crooked streets, some with wide boulevards, our hypotheses are collected into diverse sectors. A few may be organized deductively, with higher-order hypotheses serving as axioms, and rules of inference to generate lower-order ones. Most sectors are not organized in this deductive way, and not because of laziness or obscurity in us. It expresses cunning as we acknowledge that we do not have the axioms and rules enabling us to organize all the hypotheses of that sector into neatly deductive form. And anyway, we would lose too much of the detail, or commit ourselves too firmly to axioms whose material truth is suspect. These are sectors where the web of representations is looser, where any one hypothesis is more readily detached from the others, where relationships among the remaining hypotheses are more easily revised. There is, finally, more tolerance in these quarters for new hypotheses. *Maximal* integration is, by comparison, always deductive, with only two ways of integrating a new hypothesis into a maximally integrated set of beliefs: Derive it from one of the hypotheses already situated within the deductive network, or add it as an axiom.

Metaphysical theories are rarely or never deductive for two reasons, one concerning the relation obtaining among the hypotheses of a meta-physical theory, the other concerning their truth. Relations among metaphysical hypotheses are unlikely to satisfy a deductive system because its axioms are mutually independent, no one is implied or entailed by any other. Moreover, these axioms need not be true or false of anything beyond themselves.

Metaphysical hypotheses are different in both respects. Relations among the hypotheses of a metaphysical theory are mutually implicative, in some-what the way that the rules for checkmating a king in chess presuppose the rules for using every other piece. (They are not mutually implicative in the formal sense that *A* and *B* are equivalent if *A* implies *B*, and *B* implies *A*.) A metaphysical theory is, similarly, a grid of mutually supporting concep-tual claims, as Aristotle's hypotheses about substance and cause imply one another. The demand for truth is similarly differentiating. A metaphysical hypothesis purports to be both applicable and adequate to each of the things in its domain. These two considerations are enough to preclude the simple identification of integrated metaphysical hypotheses with an axiomi-tized theory.

Could it nevertheless happen that metaphysical hypotheses might someday relate to the accepted hypotheses of practice and science in some-what the way that the higher-order sentences of a deductively organized theory relate to its lower-order sentences? Wasn't it the contention of Chap-ter 1 that metaphysics is to supply general claims about categorial form and nature's conditions while leaving science and practice to supply the inter-mediate, more detailed claims? Couldn't this structure be organized deduc-tively, if only with the proviso that its axioms be mutually supporting and materially true?

We need be careful that we are not seduced by the exalted status this promises for metaphysics. There would be real substance to a comprehen-sive metaphysical theory, especially as it embodied the most general claims of a well-confirmed physics and biology. These would be hypotheses repre-senting all of nature's categorial form and conditions. This project looks made to order for deductive organization, and sometime in distant millen-nia it might deserve that style of organization. There are, in the meantime, several decisive cautions. Many of the claims regarding categorial form would count as auxiliary hypotheses and commentary, as nothing follows about particular regularities when we have remarked that the laws constraining them are intrinsic to nature rather than being mere sentences representing constant conjunctions. (It is consequential for particular regularities if the laws constraining them are intrinsic to nature because of being founded in space-time's geometrical structure.) A second consideration bears upon the motive and circumstances where deductive form is used. Casting hypotheses into that form is worth the effort only if we need to clarify the relations among our hypotheses, or when the set of hypotheses is complete, i.e., when our theory is applicable and adequate to every matter of fact. The pragmatic interest in clarifying relations among some current set of hypotheses is always justified. We are, however, a long way from having all of the hypotheses required for a science or metaphysics that is applicable and adequate. More, these two interests may sometimes conflict, as a theory that has been deductively organized may come to be used as though it were complete, when it is not. We then have the problem of unlearning the habit of using the theory as though it were more comprehensively applicable than it is. In the meantime, we forego the opportunity for speculating about those areas where the theory is incomplete, so that inquiry withers and dies. There is, this implies, no urgency for reformulating the bare bones of a metaphysics into deductive form, even the merely figurative "deductive" form of hypotheses mutually supporting and materially true.

It is enough that we use a form of integration more akin to the city of disparate but mutually accessible quarters. Doing so allows us to apply these four lessons from the organization of its many neighborhoods. *First,* the new hypothesis can be added to those already in place so that it coheres with, but makes no difference to them. This is odd for metaphysical hypotheses, which are usually mutually coordinated, though it could happen, as one might hypothesize about a disinterested God. *Second,* the new hypothesis may fill a gap in the fabric of established hypotheses, as a bridge might link divided neighborhoods. The hypotheses establishing mind's character as the activity of a physical system links it, thereby, to body's other activities, as we understand better that a broken leg might provoke stress and an ulcer. *Third* are the hypotheses comprehending some others that had been distinct, as people cramped for space may build upon smaller houses in order to create the larger dwelling that combines them. Aristotle's theory of the four causes is an incorporating hypothesis of this sort. *Fourth* are the hypotheses coordinating other hypotheses, thereby making them applicable to some previously undiscovered matter of fact. Leadership that coordinates the neighborhoods enables them to defend the city. Final cause in Aristotle's metaphysics coordinates hypotheses about the diverse behaviors of things, explaining their interactions by citing the result achieved.

There may be some further analogies to urban design, but only this larger point needs affirming. Integration, short of the time when every matter of fact seems to be adequately, i.e. exhaustively, described and explained, is better loose, pliable and revisable, than rigid and tight. We will know when a new hypothesis does not fit. That may not be so obvious as gas stations located in medieval cities, but we do eventually notice that the requirements for linkage, consolidation or coordination have been ignored. We repair the violation, re-creating as best we can a fabric that is disparate but cohesive.

6Bivd. *Empirically confirmed hypotheses successfully integrated into false theories*

It is not surprising that empirically well-confirmed hypotheses integrated into accepted networks of apparently well-confirmed hypotheses should turn out to be mistaken. That failure is likely when sensory data are overdetermined by theory, so that even opposed hypotheses may be confirmable by the same data. Our fallibility is, nevertheless, unsettling when the network of beliefs is accepted all around, when its truth seems almost unassailable, and when the hypothesis that has survived empirical confirmation and dialectical scrutiny is apparently superior to all its competitors. The situation is even more precarious than this consideration implies, for it is not only the hypothesis under scrutiny that may turn out to be mistaken. There may be fundamental (nonintuitionist) errors in the whole network of accepted theory, errors magnified by the new hypothesis.

There is, for example, Aristotle's four-fold theory of cause, and its relations to his other views about the world. That notion of cause is easily integrated into the system of other beliefs, because it helps to create higher-order homogeneity, i.e, theoretical simplicity, within a set of claims that seemed to be categorially diverse. If every cause has matter, form, an end, and a source of motion, there may nevertheless be a diversity of matters, forms, ends, and motions. Thought may differ in all these respects from material things, and both of them may differ from a god. Aristotle is the great systematizer, because of having argued that apparent differences are merely the varying expressions of this small number of categorial notions. Joining his theory of cause to the alleged analogies of being–where everything is presumed to have matter and form though matters and forms differ in the various precincts of being, e.g., nature, thought, and language–we get an ontology that coheres with many, otherwise disparate, claims about particular matters of fact.

Aristotle's hypothesis about causality has seemed to be applicable and adequate to every phenomenon. Yet, there is an unforeseen and costly result when this notion is integrated into the body of other beliefs: The power of the new hypothesis adds credibility to hypotheses that are probably false. Principal among these claims are Aristotle's notion of essential forms and his hypothesis that the world is divided among the many primary substances, each of them comprised of form organizing inert matter. Both claims are good approximations to the appearances, as we do observe common properties and freestanding objects. But only some artifacts are carefully made to satisfy a rigidly prescribed set of properties; while matter is never inert, and individuals are never independent of every other thing for their existence and character. Every thing is to the contrary, a more or less stabilized and dynamic system located within larger-scale systems. Each one may be relatively independent of its neighbors; but closer inspection shows that it overlaps or nests within them, as others are nested within it. This ecological hypothesis, not Aristotle's theory of primary substances, seems to be an accurate representation of our world, though integration of Aristotle's plausible theory of causation has enhanced the credibility of his other inadequate hypotheses. Even his theory of cause is defective, however convincing it may have seemed. Where formal and efficient cause are viable, material cause may be only a disguised version of form. Final cause may be salvageable in some reformulated version, but not as a generalized description of our conscious yearning or intending. We have, therefore, this dismal result: The network of accepted belief, with its newly integrated hypothesis, is flawed to the point of misrepresenting matters of fact.

This outcome is instructive. It shows that the successful integration of an apparently unassailable hypothesis may only disguise our mistakes. But what is the choice? We do not have a single, coherent, and *a priori* illumination of the world. Knowledge is achieved in a piecemeal way, through a succession of amplified, confirmed, defended, and integrated hypotheses. This network of mutually adjusted claims is our only vehicle for representing the world, even as we acknowledge that well-confirmed and integrated hypotheses are a mixed bag of truths, half-truths, and well-disguised errors. Our best estimates of nature's categorial form and conditions might always be nothing better than caricatures. Where every scientific theory turns out to have been mistaken in its previous formulations, there may be nothing better in store for metaphysics.

Nothing in this is solace for skeptics. These "mistaken" scientific theories enable us to send rockets to the moon, or sometime, to breed chess-playing ducks. Theories that are flawed but applicable to this degree ought to renew our confidence that testable metaphysical theories might do no worse than represent matters of fact to some better than crude approximation. If we never do prove the adequacy of our theories, we may very well hope to confirm their detailed applicability.

There is, indeed, something misleading about our notion of error. A miss is not always as good as a mile, as Aristotle's theory is already a decent approximation to nature in the scale to which he studied it. Fallibility provokes the skeptical fear that we may never get it right, though our problem is the very different one of taking care that some important things are not misconceived or misdescribed, as final cause was misconceived. We must also take care that the parameters of our hypotheses are adequate to the full range of pertinent states of affairs, so that we do not mistakenly take some small sample of a domain as paradigmatic for our conceptions, as matter was misconceived. Error may sometimes be the misunderstanding of a thing's character, but other times it is the less severe mistake of claiming universal truth for characterizations suitable only to a subset of the phenomena at issue. Errors of the one sort need to be discovered and replaced; errors of this other sort are a useful basis for revision.

Remember now that we do seem to be placed within nature as its creatures, and that accommodating ourselves to our place within the world, mostly by information-directed behavior, is our principal way of securing ourselves. Errors of a radical sort would quickly kill us all. Where successful accommodation is good evidence that our maps and plans are approximately accurate to their circumstances, where scientific examples carry the same implication, we reasonably suppose that metaphysics too is capable of formulating good, i.e., approximate, representations of nature's categorial form and conditions. Peirce supposed that inquiry would eventually generate applicable and adequate hypotheses about the world, for it has a decided form while we have methods of inquiry appropriate to discovering that form. Peirce was not so familiar as we are with the prospect that the same data may be explained in a variety of different, even mutually exclusive ways. That consideration is no reason for believing that the hypotheses of a mature, naturalistic metaphysics will differ more radically from one another than the difference between rabbits, rabbit parts, and rabbit stages; or that all the hypotheses proposed will survive dialectical scrutiny any better than the latter two of these three. Granting that we might be permanently misled or deluded, there is practice and science to reassure us that good approximations to the truth are regularly achieved, then improved. Metaphysical hypotheses about the same matters of fact should be equally susceptible to the revisions producing good, then better, representations of the world.

7. Objections

These proposals for testing metaphysical hypotheses will seem defective in several ways. Three objections, especially, require a response. One says that inquiry of the sort just described is only a version of scientism, i.e., the view that every sort of inquiry should imitate scientific methods. A second objection rebukes the empiricism I recommend because of the discovery, by Duhem and others, that no hypothesis is ever confirmed or falsified by confronting the sensory data it predicts. That is allegedly so because the tested hypothesis never stands alone, but only as one sentence in a network of hypotheses: Failures of confirmation can be ascribed to any one of the sentences associated to it, though we may never be able to determine exactly which one that is. Third is the objection that knowledge is always perspectival, so that metaphysics must be perspectival too. The comprehensive representation of our place within nature, its categorial form and conditions, should necessarily elude us.

7A. Scientism

First is the allegation that my account of metaphysical inquiry is a kind of scientism. Science provides much of the content for our claims about categorial form; what is more, our inquiry is to produce testable consequences. There is nothing in this to surprise the naive readers of introductory books on scientific method.

This objection is half right, but usefully wrong. Science is one expression of that reflective activity starting in the making and testing of plans. Scientific reflection begins as we elaborate upon the instrumental relations required for executing plans, then upon the maps which anticipate circumstances where plans are enacted. Particularities are generalized. Common features and relations are discovered within apparently disparate subject matters. Categorical explanations become more explicitly probabilistic. Mathematical representations often displace ordinary language. Science is, in all these respects, significantly different from the map- and plan-making of practical life. Still, these differences do not disguise the abiding similarity. For we have no detailed, *a priori* knowledge of the world. We can only speculate about its character, using whatever hypotheses we have for finding our way, here in the middle of things. This tentative, speculative attitude infuses all of our reality-testing behaviors. Scientists too are impelled by it. "Scientism" reduces to the fact that we acknowledge our fallibility when making and testing hypotheses about a world whose existence and character are independent of the ways we think and talk about it. Metaphysicians use the same method, because there is no privileged standpoint available to us as we regard the world, and no special evidence for confirming our claims about it. We too can only speculate about the world, formulating, then testing our hypotheses.

7B. An Outdated Empiricism

A second objection will be that my account of metaphysics is the relic of an outdated empiricism. Hasn't Quine, after Duhem, established in his

"Two Dogmas of Empiricism"[16] that no claim is testable in the way that I have proposed for metaphysical hypotheses? I have assumed the separability of each hypothesis from its context so that it can bear the weight of truth or falsity in its own right, though Quine has argued that every hypothesis is bound inextricably to others within the web of conditioning theory.

Several responses are appropriate. First is a point about meaning and truth conditions. A sentence is meaningful, I have argued, because of signifying a possible state of affairs. That possibility is its sense. The sentence is true if the possibility signified is actual. The truth of the sentence is conditional upon an extralinguistic fact: that the possibility signified is instantiated. The instantiation of one possibility is, of course, a sound basis for inferring that some other possibilities are also instantiated, as umbrellas are likely to be raised in a storm. The truth of particular sentences is, this concedes, important information as we consider the likelihood that other sentences are also true. The mutually confirming relations among sentences are, however, mediated by the relation coupling each sentence to the instantiated possibility it signifies. Sentences P and Q, this says, may relate to one another in truth, but only when the possibilities they signify are instantiated, and furthermore, only if one of the instantiated possibles is cause or condition for the other one.

A second point relevant to Quine's argument is the claim that everything makes a difference to everything else. This notion subverts the more familiar reading of those experimental situations where hypotheses are apparently falsified or confirmed. Sentences connected in the way of Quine's field will not be shown to be true or false in any categorical way; each one will be confirmed by the data confirming some of the sentences and disconfirmed by the data falsifying some others. No sentence will be categorically true or false, but only somewhat likely to be true and concurrently somewhat likely to be false. Truth and falsity will be aggregated probability values, not the relation which obtains or not between a sentence and an instantiated possibility.

Is it true that every sentence is connected to every other one so that the truth and falsity of any one is a function of the truth and falsity of all those others to which it is related? Remember now that Quine's field of interanimating sentences is a device for speaking in the "formal" mode about that set of interpenetrating facts described in the "material" mode. We have, therefore, an additional question: Is it true that states of affairs are connected so that the obtaining of every one makes a difference to every other? There is, I suggest, no evidence for the truth of either claim. The truth of a sentence about the day of the week seems independent entirely of truths about the first five names listed in the local telephone directory. Are the facts themselves connected by Quine's pervasive internal relations? There is no reason whatever for thinking they are.

The inseparability of sentences and facts within these coupled fields is apparently a myth. It is possible, because of being no contradiction, that everything might have been related to everything else, but that is not the world in which we live. Where everything does not relate to everything else, we suppose as before that the network of theory is pulverized, for the purposes of meaning and truth, by the demand that sentences be meaningful because of signifying possibilities, and true if those possibles are instantiated. Where an instantiated possibility is often good evidence for the instantiation of one or many others, there are nevertheless many instantiated possibilities to which this one is irrelevant in every way. Evidence of it tells us nothing of them.

A last defense for Quine's antipathy to empirical testability is the conceptual overdetermination of sensory data. Percepts may be construed in various ways, as the same data are used to confirm diverse, even contrary, assertions. It may happen, for example, that one datum is used for and against the same sentence, as 'It feels good' is true if we regard some current experience as pleasureable, but false if we construe it as painful. Pleasure and pain are unusually contextual, but they are paradigmatic when the equivocal identity ascribed to all sensory data is a potent reason for wanting to make theory exempt from their control. Quine does not tell us to ignore the data, but he does sometimes encourage us to tinker with the sentences of our theories until we have minimized or eliminated apparent disconfirmations. At worst, he says, we may plead hallucination.[17]

We reply that theory's overdetermination of sensory data does not preclude testability. It merely implies that we may be unable to choose between competing theories on the basis of empirical evidence alone, i.e., as two theories confirmed by the same evidence but saying more than the evidence shows will have to be tested in some additional way. Very few competing theories are confirmed, across the board, by the same data. We think of the opposition between physical object realism and phenomenalism as one prominent exception; but each of them is confirmed empirically *before* we use dialectic to establish that these two are not equally plausible or systematic. Are there, to pursue Quine's other suggestion, many occasions when evidence is willfully, but legitimately, ignored? Might there really be a thousand-pound ingot in my apparently empty pocket? Not likely.

None of this mitigates the practical difficulty of ascertaining which of the sentences related within a theory or experimental plan is falsified or confirmed by the sensory data. There is, however, a metaphor suggesting the character and difficulty of testing a sentence bound to some others within a theory or plan: We say that the tested sentence comes to the fore, as the sentences associated to it fall back into a phalanx having this tested sentence at its head. We have tried to organize the test for this sentence so that the matters of fact signified by the other sentences are neutral in regard to the information being sought, as the fact that we have natural light is neutral with respect to the primary colors that might be seen. We cannot always guarantee this neutrality, but we do often accomplish it so that the sensory data produced by an experiment supply a direct hit upon the tested sentence, confirming or falsifying it. This decisive result is not always achieved, and it may sometimes not be achievable, but our objective is plain, and the result of our observations is often decisive: Hypotheses are regularly confounded or confirmed.

7C. Perspective

The last of these objections will be that I acknowledge two limits upon inquiry while ignoring a third. Hypotheses fail to resolve deep anomalies in theory and observation, as there is currently no anomaly-solving interpretation of quantum theory. Other hypotheses may be empirically undecidable, because several hypotheses provide for all of the evidence, though they are not dialectically undecidable; or they may be undecidable because there is no evidence for or against them. Nowhere have I acknowledged that thought and knowledge are perspectival, so that claims about the world are inevitably partial, hence incomplete.

This objection conflates two quite different points. Perspective is a notion having its basis in spatial or causal relations, as every sort of observation is perspectival, and *a fortiori* every hypothesizer has some spatial and causal perspective on the world. It does not follow that the matters expressed by a hypothesis embody a perspective. Consider our theories about perspective: Are they partial because of being instances of the perspectives they cite? This could happen, but there is no necessity for it. Leibniz and Einstein suppose, without apparent inconsistency, that their claims about perspective are comprehensive, not perspectival and partial. That claim is defensible when the content and possibly universal application of a hypothesis are irrelevant to the position of the person formulating it. What we say may transcend the standpoint of our saying it, as a surveyor draws a map representing a terrain that includes his own position.

If we persist in talking about the perspectival character of metaphysical or other thinking, that is because *perspective* has come to be used synonymously with *interpretation*. The incompleteness alleged to any one set of metaphysical hypotheses, however applicable and adequate, is only the fact that this theory may be anomalous with some other one, hence incapable of expressing what that other theory says of the world. But why should modern chemistry have to stretch itself to comprehend all the motives and claims of medieval alchemy? Is our chemistry incomplete because of failing to do that? The answer could be troubled, or affirmative, only if we suppose that metaphysical theories, as against the ones of chemistry, are neither true nor false, but merely useful for projecting intelligibility onto sensory data, hence experience and the world. For then it does matter that some one interpretation does not exhaust all of intelligibility, i.e., that there are other possible, even contrary interpretations. Each will be a partial rendering of intelligibility, and in that respect it will be incomplete.

We have come full circle. We are asked to contend another time with the idea that philosophic theories are neither true nor false, but are required more fundamentally for making the world thinkable. This claim, as suggested before, is only a reaffirmation of the Kantian view that the world has no form of its own, so that we must project differentiation and order onto sensory data if they are to be thinkable. Different interpretations are the various ways of casting these data into thinkable order; the various interpretations may overlap, but no one of them comprehends every other, because every theory, short of demonstrated truths, has its contraries. Why should we say that the world has no form of its own, a form about which to speculate, using testable hypotheses that are true or false of the matters they represent? Because this Kantian view is the expression of prescriptivist intuitionism, hence of the demand that nothing be credited to reality if it cannot be ordered by, then set before, our inspecting minds. The world's intrinsic form would violate this intuitionist demand for immediate access to whatever things are credited to reality. We are to deny, therefore, that the world might have an intrinsic form, arguing instead that its only form is one or another of the forms that we prescribe. What might these forms be? They are the interpretations used for making experience, and thereby the world, thinkable. If there are many of these interpretations, none of them able to comprehend each of the others, then every interpretation is essentially incomplete.

Completeness of this sort is, I agree, unobtainable. But neither is it important or desirable if prescriptivist intuitionism is false, and if the world does have a decided form of its own. For then the problem is only the one of formulating and testing those hypotheses which accurately represent its form. Every other hypothesis is incidental to our concern because of being false. This is the account I recommend. The tolerant, democratic appeal to a diversity of perspectives mistakes the right for having a view with the different and distinctive value accorded to views that are true.

8. Conclusion

Intuitionism supposes that philosophy might be saved from error and the vulgar tests which confirm but never prove the likely truth of what we think and say. Intuitionism promises to do better if we first agree that reality is identical with the matters that are or could be given to, or created by, then set before, our inspecting minds. Accepting this invitation to certainty requires that we acknowledge mind as the only reality, where all the world is only the set of attributes or qualifications inhering within mind. We reduce ourselves, if only in theory and conviction, to monads turned upon themselves. Intuitionism is the metaphysics of the psychocentric ontology dominating so much of philosophic thought, though intuitionism is anathema to everyone engaging a world that will not reduce itself to the tidiness of our theories and expectations.

Metaphysics and all of philosophy resorts to the hypothetical method when intuitionism is renounced. There is no alternative as we formulate our views about a world having an integrity of its own. We too can only speculate fallibly upon a world whose intelligibility is independent of the claims we make about it, a world that will usually show itself in ways falsifying or confirming our claims about it. There is nothing here of pandering scientism, though there is the continuity of method, from practice through science to metaphysics.

Have I nevertheless begged the metaphysical question by making these claims about metaphysical method and its objectives? Don't we presuppose the answers to many important questions if we say that humans live in the midst of nature as its creatures? It may be reasonable, given this assumption, to ask about our role in nature and about nature's categorial form and conditions. But all of this short-circuits an inquiry that should require neutrality regarding these questions, at least to start. Our character and place within the world are, after all, the primary topics for metaphysical inquiry. We should not pretend to solve these questions merely by assuming their answers; neither should we describe metaphysical inquiry in a way that stipulates the answers, then buries them as the presuppositions for a naturalist theory of inquiry and knowledge.

This objection speaks from the heart of philosophic conviction. There is, we are to believe, some neutral standpoint from which to evaluate the many claims about the world, and our place within it. Philosophy is to be different from every other discipline because of affirming its own right to genuine knowledge, while remarking the special, sometimes crippling, biases of every other position.

I don't know what standpoint this might be. Intuitionism forever renews itself by supposing that mind will find this Archimedian perspective within itself. But then mind's "neutrality" reduces to the two ideas that nothing is real unless inspectable, and that mind is the one substance in which every other difference inheres. Renouncing intuitionism, we also renounce the hope of achieving this perspective. Where shall we go for an alternative?

My suggestion is that we cannot have, and do not need, the neutrality that philosophy has praised and promised. We do better to look more closely at the style of inquiry common to practice and science, for they too are legitimate and effective expressions of thought. What is more, they discover, past any shadow of doubt, that we live in the middle of nature as natural creatures. My proposal is the claim that we can assume their position, arguing as they do, learning thereby about nature and ourselves. More, there is no alternative route for metaphysical inquiry. We have no privileged, *a priori* knowledge of the world's categorial form. We can only speculate, as practice and science already speculate, taking care that our hypotheses are responsibly formulated and tested.

4

Sufficient Reason

Something is missing in my characterization of metaphysical inquiry. The formulation of testable hypotheses seems linear and progressive, competent, but bland. There are four kinds of motion discernible within metaphysical controversy and reflection, not only this one. They include the nearly random activity of themes and theories developed in ignorance of one another, like the clatter of music, ads, and news heard as we spin the tuning knob on a radio. There is also the churning of disparate views when some new and apparently significant fact disrupts their hermetic elaboration, causing all of them to turn about this alien thing, each one calculating its resources for neutralizing, incorporating, or surviving it. There are, finally, the tensions stretching us left and right as each theory is made to extend itself in the direction of completeness. All of these motions and vectors may sometimes agitate us at once, but the second one is incidental, like white noise, while the third is sporadic and unpredictable. Only the demand for completeness is a significant addition to the inquiry proposed in Chapters 1, 2, and 3. Describing completeness, telling what it requires, and how it might be justified is the purpose of this chapter.

1. Completeness

Completeness is already familiar to us as an ideal of metaphysical inquiry. The true and comprehensive theory should be applicable and adequate to all of being, hence to every difference within it. Applicability has meant that a hypothesis has instances; adequacy, that a hypothesis or theory signifies every categorial difference within its instances. They are described, for example, as substances having form, matter, and accidents, as well as spatial, temporal, dynamic and teleological relations to other things. Aristotle supposed that a metaphysical theory might be complete in both respects. His example goads the rest of us. There are two other sorts of completeness, both apparent in Aristotle and other thinkers, and both more conspicuous in the past than they are today. We consider these two, before neglecting one to emphasize the other.

The idea to be acknowledged then ignored holds that reality might have an encircling boundary. The idea to be recovered and affirmed is the one endowing our metaphysical thinking with its tensile strength and dialectical symmetry, namely, the principle of sufficient reason. This principle is much despised in some quarters. Hardly anyone dares mention it favorably, and few of us suppose that we might invoke the principle to justify some other claim. This is Hume's legacy. He argued that anaything distinguishable is separable, hence capable of existing without antecedents. Others have agreed with Hume while adding that we have no *a priori* demonstration for the principle. None of this justifies our disregard for sufficient reason, especially when its unacknowledged influence is almost as great as before. Explanation is one pervasive expression of it, as no one hesitates to infer from some phenomenon to its cause or condition, Hume not withstanding. I defer justifying the principle. Just now the question is this one: How can we dispense with the notion of completeness as a boundary when we have the cluster of notions centered upon the principle of sufficient reason?

2. Being as a Bounded Whole

There are, classically, three bounded containers available to metaphysicians who propose a totalizing limit for reality: there is God, space and time, and conscious or self-conscious mind. God is problematic because of being unknown, and because either of the other two may be used to explain God's role as boundary. There is, for example, the suggestion that space and time might be God's sensorium. We have, therefore, only the two practical options: Reality is bounded by conscious mind, or by space and time. One or another of them is alleged to be the limit within which every other thing is contained. Kant joins these boundaries to one another when he applies the idea of God's sensorium to our finite minds by identifying space and time with the forms of intuition.[1] That makes the limits of space and time congruent with the limits of consciousness.

140

This notion of completeness has a powerfully regulative effect within inquiry. Everything contained within these limits is partial in itself, hence incomplete: Every analysis that separates these fragments from their context has the effect of distorting them. Their identity is restored only as we acknowledge the significant relations binding things to one another within their original context. It is no wonder that analysis is thought to denature a thing or kill it, while returning a thing to its context, or merely affirming its place there, restores its vitality. There is, however, this offsetting effect: The part is merged into the whole, losing the identity which made it separable from its place there. We risk committing ourselves to the idea that parts might be mutually entangled to the point of being undifferentiable from one another. The directive for inquiry is, nevertheless, plain: Every property, relation, or phenomenon is to be understood as displaced or distorted until it is located within its whole-making context. Every apparent fragment requires that we find some rubric or relation with which to relocate it within the whole. This is the condition for telling what position it has within space and time, or what significance it has for the other things experienced. We get Hegel or Mussolini, and their holistic notions of society and history.

Revulsion for this totalist ideal, and the practices used to enforce it might be sufficient to make us dubious about using this notion of completeness as a regulative idea for inquiry. There is, however, a different reason, one that is politically and ethically neutral, for replacing this idea. That reason is already explicit in the devices used for integrating fragments into the whole. We don't assume that integration might be achieved merely by introducing the part into consciousness or space and time, as one opens the door for a cat, letting it wander wherever it may care to go. We integrate a part into the whole by applying some rubric. The part is made to fit in a way determined by its own character, but also by some rule. This notion concedes that the alleged boundaries of consciousness or space and time are too remote or uncertain to be a point of reference for integrating the fragments. It also expresses our skepticism about these boundaries. How are we to take their measure in a way enabling us to locate the parts within them? We could, perhaps, fix the addresses of houses within walled cities by drawing a grid of concentric circles; then by orienting the grid with respect to north, east, south, and west; finally by locating each house in relation to the wall and these directions. There is, however, nothing comparable to a city's walls in consciousness or space and time, so that integration of a part never can or does require that we first take our bearings in respect to that boundary. Instead, we locate houses or experiences by reference to one another by using integrative rubrics. Kant is again the decisive historical marker. He implies, in the Transcendental Aesthetic of the First Critique, that space and time might be regarded as bounded wholes co-extensive with bounded consciousness. Later, within the Aesthetic and the Analogies of Experience,[2] it is plainer that space and time are networks of relations, and that individuals are integrated into space or time because of satisfying these relations, not because of being located with respect to a boundary. We have space and time as systems of relations, and also the schemas whose only work is that of relating phenomena, spatially and temporally, to one another. There is nothing left of the intimation that phenomena might be located by way of their distance from a boundary.

This transition from bounded wholes to integrative rubrics is most important because of its two effects. First is the one just mentioned, namely, the displacement of bounded wholes by integrative rubrics. Rather than speak of a bounded space and time, or of consciousness as the great unifier, we explain the coherence of experience by way of the several rubrics required for integrating it. Second is the intimation that there may be other rubrics as fundamental to integration as space and time, or a temporalized consciousness. These two rubrics had seemed fundamental only because space and time, and consciousness were thought to be paradigmatic of bounded wholes. Now, the idea of bounded wholes has lost its force. We discover the possibility that there may be other rubrics fundamental as these two. Cause and effect, whole and part, universal and particular: There are several, at least, of these additional completeness-satisfying rubrics.

3. The Principle of Sufficient Reason, and Its Reformulation

Is there some formal characteristic shared by these rubrics? Is there a principle for generating rubrics, one that is neutral with respect to their content, but sufficient to determine their form? That principle is the one of sufficient reason. It affirms that everything has conditions sufficient for determining both its character and existence, though the principle is indifferent to the fact that the sufficient condition be in the thing, itself, or in another. Conditions sufficient for the truth of the Pythagorean theorem are, for example, present in every right triangle. The conditions for a child's existence and character are its parents, not the child himself.

These examples are simplistic, because the literal reading of *sufficient* requires that we mention not only parents, but all of the infinitely many things that have been required for producing any one child, including all the generations going back to the first life, and beyond that to the origins of the universe. Citing the parents alone specifies only the most conspicuous cause. There is, however, a useful lesson in this example as regards typical uses of the principle. We very often use it to justify the inference from some thought or perceived difference to one or another of its conditions, not only for specifying those conditions jointly sufficient for determining its character or existence. Some of these conditions are contingent, as not every light is sunlight; some may be necessary as space and time are necessary for motion.

We acknowledge this modified statement of the original principle. We say that the existence and character of everything is conditioned, where it is the fact of being conditioned, and not the sufficiency of the conditions, that is stressed. Abductive explanation presupposes this modified formulation, as we infer from the characterization of a thing to one or more of its conditions. Identifying these conditions individually, not as members of the set of conditions jointly sufficient for a phenomenon becomes the objective for most explanatory inquiries. We infer from smoke to fire, not to all the smoke's conditions, e.g., oxygen, flammable material, physical laws, the Big Bang, etc.

Notice that the principle of sufficient reason, even this reformulated version of it, is only a schema. It tells us that everything has conditions without describing any one of them. The principle is, therefore, well suited to being the neutral generator of integrative rubrics. How do we generate any particular rubric? By identifying some aspect of a phenomenon, then by characterizing the condition appropriate to the aspect signified. Surveying the English words for clues regarding some thing characterized and its conditions may seem to be question-begging, when the principle is too easily confirmed, as *effects* goes with *causes*, and *parts* with *wholes*. This semantic serendipity might be trivial, though probably it is not. These pairs may reasonably express the fact that sufficient reason has directed us in coining words to satisfy the tension and symmetry implied by the principle.

How many of these applications does the principle have? There is no finished list of them; we cannot limit the freedom for inventing some new schema short of the time when someone has established that all of the variations possible are only disparate expressions of one or several that are fundamental. We can list the schemas that seem to be fundamental expressions of sufficient reason. They include effect and cause, part and whole, actuality and possibility, consequent and premises, spatial or temporal locale and the system of relations in which this locale is one relative position, particular and universal. The first term in each of these pairs is conditioned by the second one, though the relation of the conditions to the aspect conditioned varies among the schemas in the way prefigured by the difference between the original principle and its reformulated version. In some of them (e.g., effect and cause), the conditions are allegedly sufficient for determining both the existence and character of the aspect conditioned. In the case of some others (e.g., actuality and possibility, particular and universal), the condition cited is not sufficient though it is alleged to be necessary. (There is only a semantic difficulty in saying that we use the principle of sufficient reason for discovering necessary conditions, if it is agreed that necessary conditions are often included within the sets of conditions sufficient for some consequence or effect.)

Can we also tell how these schemas have come to be formulated, so that words appropriate to unexplored aspects of the world and their alleged conditions might be introduced into our language? The very tentative answer recalls the discussion in Chapter 2 of the steps required for introducing the notion of possibility. It was suggested that we characterize things that were not though they have come to be as *actuals,* before introducing *possibility* to signify that which may be but is not. Reflection, in this instance, has carried us beyond the matters observed. Other schemas, e.g., whole and part, are suggested by discriminating observation, as angles and sides are seen to be the parts of triangles. It is also important that we do not wait for any particular observation or reflection to encourage our thinking about these schemas. Sufficient reason is a permanent tension in our thinking. It motivates our discovery of these more determinate expressions of itself.

4. Proving That the Principle of Sufficient Reason is Valid

What status shall we claim for the principle of sufficient reason, whether reformulated or in its original form? Assurance of its truth would enhance our confidence in its various expressions, even when some of them turn out to be invalid.

4A. Sufficient Reason is not Demonstrable

Let us concede that all of practical life, science, and metaphysics very often proceed as though sufficient reason were true. The tension of the various rubrics expressing it is always the energy that carries abductive inference from something thought or observed to the hypothetical identification of its conditions. Perceptual data, or more rarely a demonstration, regularly confirms the existence of the conditions specified by these inferences, e.g., as we infer from parts to wholes, and from street addresses to street plans. The completeness expressed by the symmetry of something conditioned with its conditions is frequently invoked and achieved. The validity of the sanctioning principle is all the while ignored, probably out of fear that nothing can be done to validate it.

There are two reasons for this pessimism. The less important point logically, though it is probably more important to public prejudice, is Hume's assault on some of the rubrics expressing sufficient reason. There are, for example, his condemnations of accidents and their conditioning substances, effects and their causes, act and potency. Each of these schemas is thought to be subverted by the assertion that everything distinguishable is separable. Hume adds that anything conceivable can exist as conceived, so that something conceived as separate can exist separately, i.e., without its alleged conditions.[3] This argument has some bare plausibility when we assume that existence is only the force and vivacity of our impressions, so that something conceived lacks existence only for want of that glow. There is nothing to support this argument when we remember that ideas and impressions are representations, i.e., the artificial signs of language or the natural ones of perception. Signs are not the things represented, so that nothing whatever is proved about the separability of things signified by the separability of their signs. Hume's argument never touches the principle of sufficient reason.

The more important objection is that we cannot prove this principle's validity without assuming it: It is, we say, a contradiction that something exist or have some particular character in the absence of sufficient conditions. This is contradictory only if we assume that the principle does necessarily apply. Direct proof eludes us, though we have some other ways of justifying the principle.

4B. Using Sufficient Reason as a Leading Principle

One alternative accepts the implication of this failure to demonstrate the principle. Perhaps sufficient reason is not a necessary truth, though there may be some domains in which it does apply. This would make the principle a contingent truth, so that we might still use the principle effectively if we could locate these domains. This is not so dismal a result, especially as we realize that the laws of physics and Euclidean geometry also apply within limited domains. Why not continue using the principle as a directive for inquiry? Always look for conditions; persist in looking when you don't find them; but then admit that there may be no conditions in the circumstances at issue. People thinking in this way denied that there might be action at a distance. They argued for using an *a priori* but undemonstrated principle within empirical inquiry, only to be vindicated by the theory of electromagnetic fields. We may reasonably proceed in the same way, doubting the finality of current formulations in quantum theory, doubting that the singularity from which our world allegedly exploded

145

could have come from nothing, but accepting the possibility that sufficient reason may not apply in either circumstance.

Most of the interest in practice and science would be well served by this cautious approach. Even metaphysics might continue to enjoy the use of this principle in a variety of ways. For if we cannot prove that every existent and every difference is caused, e.g., as the singularity might not be, then we have still to explain the applicability of the causal principle to everything having a scale larger than the one of quantum physics. We also have to consider those other rubrics whose universal application is unquestioned, as consequences have premises, while dates and addresses presuppose the conditioning network of temporal and spatial positions. Metaphysics would continue to be energized, as science and practice are, by the numerous schemas having application within the world. We might also apply the principle, if only very cautiously, to the question of nature's own conditions; i.e., does nature have conditions apart from itself, or is it self-conditioned? Nothing in the contingent applicability of sufficient reason would discourage us from inferring to, then trying to confirm the reality of some alleged conditions for nature.

4C. An Analogy; the Principle of Non-contradiction

Metaphysics can not be satisfied by the ambiguous status of sufficient reasons. We need determine the limit of its applicability, while knowing if that limit is itself somehow conditioned, and in that way explicable. Moreover, we suspect that our inability to demonstrate the necessary truth of the principle is inconclusive evidence that the principle is not necessary. For there is another principle not directly demonstrable, though it too controls our thinking. That is the principle of non-contradiction; not both p and *not-p*. Demonstrations of this principle also fail because of presupposing it. We, nevertheless, have reasons for believing that non-contradiction is necessary, though undemonstrated, so that we rely upon it without fearing that the principle can or will have exceptions. Rehearsing these considerations helps us now.

First is a world sanitized against contradictions: nothing is both p and *not-p*. *Second* is the fact that any principle so elementary as this one cannot be demonstrated without begging the question because of assuming the principle when conducting the proof. *Third* is a response to the contention that non-contradiction is merely a syntactic rule, one that might easily be violated if we were not concerned to think coherently and communicate among ourselves. We declare this more fundamental reason for acceding to it: Non-contradiction has an ascertainable basis in something other than itself.

That other thing is the principle of identity: Everything is what it is, and not another thing.

Let us suppose that everything is constituted of its properties, whether finite or infinitely denumerable, and that properties are constitutive of each thing's identity. Contradictions are generated when we say of any thing that its properties both include and do not include some particular property or properties. The thing is just itself, as constituted of its properties. Not having one or more of them, or having other properties additional to those constituting it would make the thing other than itself. That is what contradiction requires, that a thing be constituted at the same moment by its properties, and by these same properties plus or minus one or more others. The thing would have to be both itself and not-itself. That cannot happen, because everything is constituted only of its properties, so that its identity is at every moment secure. Things do change, taking on new properties, or giving up old ones, but that is different.

Do we have a basis now for saying that the principle of non-contradiction is demonstrable? This is a decisive justification for the principle, but not a demonstration purified of its question-begging assumption. We have assumed non-contradiction even while elaborating upon its basis in the principle of identity: Something is not both constituted of its properties and not-constituted of those properties. We are no closer than before to a logically satisfactory demonstration. Still, the appeal to identity is a material claim, and it does confirm that non-contradiction is more than a grammatical rule.

Do we have as much reason for saying that the principle of sufficient reason is necessary though not demonstrable? Sufficient reason, like non-contradiction, is applicable but not demonstrable, though non-contradiction, is vastly stronger in its claim to being applicable necessarily. That is so, because we have specified its ground in the principle of identity, and because identity does seem to be unassailable. There is no comparable basis for understanding the applicability of sufficient reason; it does apply, but we don't know why.

It may be significant that the asymmetry between the two principles is balanced by this other one: The foregoing argument for the principle of non-contradiction presupposes the principle of sufficient reason. We have supposed that the validity of non-contradiction would be founded either within the principle itself or in some other thing. Not finding the basis for the principle's validity within itself, we have looked elsewhere, discovering that basis within the principle of identity and its material ground, i.e., that everything is constituted of its properties. Strangely, therefore, we agree that non-contradiction is applicable universally because necessary, though we cannot equally well confirm the necessity of the principle assumed in confirming non-contradiction's necessity. We do have an explanation for our inability to confirm the principle, if not for this anomaly. The consideration vital to non-contradiction, but missing in demonstrations of sufficient reason, is the discovery of its ground in identity. Having a comparable point of reference, we could equally well affirm the necessity of sufficient reason. Not having that ground, we cannot.

4D. An Indirect Argument for Sufficient Reason

There is one other lesson to be learned from attempted proofs for the principle of non-contradiction: Proofs for a principle itself assumed by the proof must be indirect. Aristotle's argument for non-contradiction is indirect when he tells what implications there would be for communication if the principle did not obtain. Do we get closer to establishing the principle of sufficient reason if we suppose that it does not hold? That assumption has three consequences.

First is the implication that anything could happen at any time, in any order. That should be so if there is nothing in an antecedent to constrain its successors. This is the sort of world implied when Hume supposes that all internal constraints are withdrawn from the world, leaving chaos the likely outcome. The regularities prominent in our world would have only a minuscule probability (though there is the small probability that our world is a random collection of accidents.)

A *second* implication, contrary to this first one, is that nothing should happen, because *ex hypothesi* nothing is sufficient to make it happen. Stasis, rather than chaos, should be the universal condition of things. Chaos was only the more likely outcome; order, even the order perceived all about us, was still a slight possibility. This second result is categorical, for the absence of sufficient conditions is assumed to be absolute: Where no thing is sufficient to determine some transformation of another or itself, nothing should happen. Indeed, stasis should be perpetual and universal, so that nothing should ever have happened. Nothing should exist; the universe should be a void. Our world is no more static and empty than it is chaotic. Here is a second kind of evidence for saying that we demonstrate the principle of sufficient reason by way of the *reductio* denying it.

It is too bad that this last argument does not work. The claim that stasis should be the outcome if sufficient reason does not operate is only the question-begging assertion that nothing happens if there is no antecedent sufficient condition for it. That is the question at issue: Can it happen that things come to be in the absence of conditions sufficient for generating them? One question-begging answer is that some things may not require antecedent conditions because sufficient conditions for their existence and character lie within the things themselves, as would be true of a necessarily existing God. Everything of this sort exists necessarily and forever, as none of the things in nature, not even the totality of space-time, need do. We are obliged, therefore, to consider this most perplexing issue: Might something have "come to be from nothing"?

This last phrase is the *third* implication of saying that sufficient reason does not apply necessarily: Some things have come to be in the absence of sufficient conditions. This is a claim we do not understand, though again for the question-begging reason that the principle of sufficient reason prescribes the very condition for intelligibility: Anything not satisfying it is said to be unthinkable. We concede that a principle of understanding does not validate itself as a principle of being. Still, the burden rests with those who say that something might come to be from nothing. Their very words are literal nonsense: "Coming to be" is not any sort of process; "nothing" is not a point of origin; "from" signifies no route.

It may be true that thought and language are so permeated by the idea of sufficient reason as to provide no other expressions for someone wanting to talk of unconditioned events. Anyone wanting to speak about them will have to coin a different vocabulary on the way to informing us in these respects: Does everything come to be from nothing? Or is it only some few, perhaps fundamental things of which this is true, e.g., quantum events or the singularity from which the Big Bang and our universe ensued? Is the existence of these things contingent or necessary? If necessary, they have, presumably, existed eternally. If contingent, they come to be at one moment rather than another. Why should these things have come to be at that moment rather than before or after?

These questions are problematic because of invoking the principle of sufficient reason another time. We do better to forego other questions in the same style, waiting to be instructed. I assume that the standards for that education will be very high. It will not do, for example, if we are told that the question is resolved by supposing that space and time began with the singularity from which the universe derives so that one cannot ask about conditions prevailing "before" its inception.[4] Cosmologists and some quantum physicists do talk this way, but that is not so much the expression of ideas thoroughly conceived as it is the willingness to talk about these things without regard for what is currently their unintelligibility. The language is merely figurative when we say that space-time lines converge on this singularity as on a point, e.g., as the great circles of longitude on our globe converge on points at the poles. Even granting the possibility that there might

149

be no temporal order in which this singularity is only one more moment in the sequence, we can reasonably invoke the logical "before," asking whether this singularity and the inception of time have antecedent conditions.

The willingness to ignore every question about conditions not specified within a cosmologist's or physicist's theory is one more expression of the conceptual pragmatism considered at the beginning of Chapter 1. Where an interpretation supplies our understanding of phenomena, we are excused from having to think about anything, e.g., "before" the singularity, not prefigured within the interpretation.

4E. Summary

Are we better placed now for confirming that the principle of sufficient reason is necessarily applicable within the world? We are not. Sufficient reason does not have support of the kind available to the principle of non-contradiction, namely, a ground in identity. We do have indirect evidence for the principle, including its use in establishing the principle of non-contradiction, and the consequences of denying sufficient reason's applicability. We are no closer to demonstrating this principle's necessary applicability. Having that missing ground and demonstration would be enormously useful, as when we argue that nature is either self-conditioned or conditioned by something beyond itself, or as we challenge the usually thoughtless claims that "something comes from nothing." Not having either ground or demonstration, we go on as before. We use the original or reformulated principle of sufficient reason as a leading principle. We look for and usually find conditions, or we insist that they may be present, though undiscovered. We agree that there may be some other way for understanding nature, as there may be no conditions for some things, either in themselves or other things. This may be no contradiction, hence a possibility. We shall have to be better instructed than we are at present to understand it.

5. A Conflict Between Metaphysics and Science

In the meantime, we continue to use sufficient reason, in its original or reformulated version, as the generator of schemas applying to the various dimensions of being. There is effect and cause, part and whole, actuality and possibility, consequent and premises, particulars and universals. Formulating such schemas as these, then pursuing their implications is one principal characteristic of metaphysical thinking. We use these rubrics like slingshots to project our thinking into the heart of being. The thing to

150

which we infer abductively is often something less than obvious, though it is, we allege, fundamental because of conditioning our starting point. There are the laws constraining particulars, and perhaps the domain of possible worlds conditioning this actual world. There are also dogs biting cats, and winds blowing the roofs off houses, so that the applicability of these completeness-satisfying rubrics is continuous from ordinary or nearly everyday experience to metaphysics.

There is, however, a considerable difference regarding the use of these rubrics as between metaphysics and science. This difference explains the antipathy for saying that some part of science is metaphysical, and that metaphysics depends on science for most of its deep information about nature. There are some other reasons for mutual suspicion, between science and metaphysics, e.g., as the intuitionism of traditional metaphysics compares to the abductive arguments of science, and as philosophy resents losing its authority to science. This dispute about the rubrics appropriate to nature is more significant than either of them.

The dispute begins in questions about the provenance of these rubrics. Metaphysics invents some of them for itself, as actuality and possibility are the metaphysical refinement of a difference signified more obscurely in everyday thought and practice. Most of the other rubrics are fairly well articulated in ordinary reflection. That is true of cause and effect, part and whole, universal and particular, moral act and moral law, spatial or temporal position and the network of relative positions. Reflection turned philosophic has refined all of these rubrics before advancing a step beyond critical common sense into science, whether modern or Aristotelian. Science may amend the rubrics, as it eliminates teleology from causal explanations, but mostly, it uses these rubrics while refining and extending the maps and plans inherited from practice. Science adds some additional rubrics of its own, e.g., fields and the phenomena conditioned by them, but mostly it uses the ones inherited.

The quarrel starts here, where scientists pick and choose among the rubrics made available within practice. Precedence in discovery, even the confirmation of a rubric shown to be widely applicable, takes a backseat to the authority of scientists as they decide whether or not a rubric is useful to them. There is a use for addresses and dates seen against the backdrop of conditioning positions, for whole and part, for particular and universal, for premises and consequent, and for that refinement of causality expressed as functional relations. But there is no interest in contingency and necessity, or actuality and possibility.

No thinker does everything, so that choosing to use only a subset of the available rubrics is reasonable enough, especially if it proves sufficient for explaining natural events to the point of being able to predict them. Metaphysicians are unnerved when told that these scientific explanations are both applicable and adequate, i.e., that there is nothing left to say of nature when the rubrics important to science have been used to generate our explanations for natural phenomena. That claim is surely mistaken. The applicability of rubrics which scientists neglect is apparent in pre-scientific practice, but also in the phenomena that science itself discovers and explains, as the necessity of laws compares to the contingency of their expressions. Scientists don't deny these subtleties, but they find them trivial. Metaphysicians may reply that the modal structure of being is a categorial difference within it, hence interesting in itself. Any characterization of nature or being which ignores this aspect is inadequate because incomplete.

Our aim, as metaphysicians, is the exhaustive characterization of the categorial features constitutive of every phenomenon within nature and its conditions, if any. The difference between contingency and necessity, together with the kinds of necessity (as something necessary in itself is different from a necessary condition), are important to metaphysics if not to science. Cause and effect is important to metaphysics, as its basis in nature, possibly in the dynamics of a geometrized space-time, could not be unimportant to physics. Fact and value are important to metaphysics, as we discover the basis in fact for the consequential values that things have for one another. Scientists might be unconcerned, though ecologists and atomic physicists do care about the relation. Let it be true, therefore, that scientists discount all but a few of the completeness-satisfying rubrics first discovered in the course of practice, and refined by philosophic analysis. That is no reason for believing that neglected rubrics are not applicable to nature and its conditions, or that scientific explanations generated by the applications of its small set of preferred rubrics could be adequate. We rightly demur when anyone argues that every rubric uninteresting to science is valueless in itself.

6. An Error to be Averted

There are, I shall suppose, a number of useful rubrics. We affirm them as hypotheses about significant relationships within nature, and also as leading principles for directing reflection and experiment. These are the schemas driving speculation about nature and its conditions.

There is, however, the prospect for a certain kind of mistake, one that occurs sometimes when rubrics are overlaid, one upon another. This use of rubrics is often legitimate, as we might locate phenomena in a network of spatial or temporal relations, while saying that one is cause or effect of the others. Trouble occurs, for example, as we use a rubric applicable within nature, and another that is applicable only to nature in its relation to extranatural conditions. Suppose that we have identified God as the necessary condition for the existence of our contingent world. This necessary condition may or may not be a necessary being in its own right, i.e., one whose nonexistence is a contradiction; but that is incidental here. My concern is only the anomaly resulting when we say that this necessary condition is a cause having our world as its effect. Saying this is the plausible conflation of necessary condition with cause, and of contingent world with effect, where God is alleged to be the cause without which our world would not be.

This familiar way of describing God's relation to nature is the ill-formed product of overlaying two rubrics belonging to different domains. Let us suppose, by way of explication, that the contingency-necessity rubric does apply to nature's relation to its extranatural condition. There is St. Thomas's claim that a contingent being can only come to be, and endure in being, if its existence is supported by some condition apart from itself. But then we need be careful that necessity-contingency is not assimilated to cause and effect. Remember that the cause-and-effect rubric is introduced so that we may explain the changes occurring in one or more of a set of interacting causes. Causes are physical systems having spatial, temporal, and dynamic relations to one another. We may extend this rubric's application to things not conclusively shown to be physical, as insulting speech may hurt one's feelings, but feelings are, somehow, connected to bodies so that the original locus for applications of the cause and effect rubric is present here too. We have no evidence for saying that the cause-and-effect rubric also applies to the relations of things which are not, all of them, physical agents or a mind mysteriously paired to one. God is neither a physical system nor the mind somehow connected to a body. What is more, God is independent of, and external to, the entire space-time of the nature He is credited with making. There is, accordingly, no basis for applying the rubric of cause and effect to the relation of God and nature. This implies that "God, the Maker" is a solecism, one that results from the misapplication of the cause-and-effect rubric to the relation of things alleged to exist as contingent nature and its necessary condition.

Objections will be vivid and quick. Most of them may come to this: Why deny that the cause-and-effect rubric can be extended beyond the dynamic relations within space and time to every productive relationship, hence to the one of nature and its Maker? Where possibilities are discovered and signified as we abstract from things observed, then as we vary and combine the abstracted ideas, why not allow that cause and effect might be abstracted from the context of its first confirmed applications?

The answer I propose goes as follows. We acknowledge that an idea is very often varied beyond the scope of its first confirmed applications. There is, however, the problem of controlling the variations so that we preserve whatever was significant in the original notion. In the relation of cause and effect, this core notion includes the efficacy of interacting causes, not merely their correlation, as the serrated edge of the moving knife does not merely correlate with the cut being made as the knife moves through bread. It is vital to the core notion of a causal relation that we have no idea of efficacy apart from the one of agencies accessible to one another, then interacting in space and time. Abstracting from the medium of interaction, namely space and time, on the way to describing nature as God's effect is another example of using words for their allusive power in circumstances where the things signified cannot have that relationship.

Negative theology further distorts this result. God is a cause, it says, but not a cause like any other. Nature is His effect, but not in the way that any other effect is caused. See what this implies. We have extended the application of the cause-and-effect rubric, so that we might explain nature's relation to its necessary condition, only to be told that this rubric does not apply in any way that we may ever conceive. What have we gained by exporting the cause-and-effect rubric from its original domain in nature to this extended one? Only the play of rhetorical allusion as we evoke the idea of generation while denying that God's relation to nature is anything like the one intimated by our words. This is a result slightly different from the one first alleged when I claimed that overlaying the cause-and-effect rubric on the one of necessity-contingency yields a solecism. We have a solecism extenuated by the possibility, so far unconfirmed and not meaningfully formulated, that this cause-and-effect rubric might have application beyond the domain of physical systems interacting in space and time.

This conclusion should ripple through our every claim about God's efficacy. We may, for example, have been tempted to agree that our world is the instantiation of the many possible worlds, then to say that God chooses among the possible worlds before "actualizing" or "instantiating" this world of ours. This is causal talk, implying again that cause and effect has application beyond nature to nature's relation with one of its allegedly necessary conditions. But this is metaphor only, with the words suggesting a relation that is, according to negative theology, never intended literally. The idea of possible worlds instantiated by a God is devoid of literal sense, for we have no idea of God or of his manner of operation. Instantiation

154

is left as it was, i.e., as signifying nothing additional to the fact that a possibility is actual.

This extended example should not obscure the larger point: The overlaying of completeness-satisfying rubrics may produce anomalies having no referent, if one of the rubrics is applicable within nature, while the other one is applicable to nature and to one or another of its alleged conditions. We expect this result, more generally, wherever a rubric applicable within one domain is imported into some domain where it does not apply, then overlaid on a rubric having application there. The domain appropriate to the rubric of premises and consequent is, for example, distinct from the domain of universals and particulars, so that the relation of premises and consequent cannot be mapped onto the relation of natural laws and their particular instances, or onto the relation of Plato's Forms and their instances. We end this part by remarking on the contrary error: It supposes that a rubric is not applicable within some domain after falsely reifying that domain in order to make it exempt from this and other rubrics, as facts and values are two aspects of one domain, not two distinct and mutually inaccessible domains. Rubrics appropriate to one may very well be appropriate to the other.

7. Conclusion

The previous section only slightly reduces the power of all our thinking, whether practical, scientific, or metaphysical, as completeness-satisfying rubrics direct it. Individual rubrics are vastly effective as directives for inquiry. We may discover new rubrics and, subject to the restrictions just described, new opportunities for applying previously discovered rubrics to domains where they have not previously been tested. The principle of sufficient reason, in both its original and its reformulated version, is neutral regarding these initiatives, though it supplies the leverage for moving beyond anything specified to its condition. We are the ones responsible for imagining new domains in which the principle might apply, then for characterizing the things present there in a way appropriate to describing their condition, e.g., calling children "effects" before looking for their causes. Sufficient reason propels us beyond the current observables, but also beyond nature to its conditions. Here, especially, we have to be careful that this is not a trajectory into limbo.

That is no threat if speculation is everywhere encouraged, but always conducted so that no hypothesis is credible if it is not testable. For if it were confirmed that the principle of sufficient reason is true necessarily, hence throughout being, it would not follow that any one of its particular, more determinate expressions is necessary. Where some are not, each of the others is always on trial, having to prove both its applicability and its scope. Nothing justifies us if we assume dogmatically that one of our rubrics applies everywhere to everything. The contrary is true: None of them has assured application. All of them are used hypothetically and testably.

5

Ontology

Every method of inquiry postulates the domain of things to which it applies. The sorts of things comprising this domain are the method's ontology. This chapter describes the signs, possibles, and actuals of hypothetical method's ontology. It collects the arguments and claims made already in Chapters 1 and 3, while extending and justifying them.

My characterization of hypothetical method emphasizes its ontological commitments. One might describe the method's procedures without this emphasis, as it may still be our inclination to say, after finishing this chapter, that talk of the possibilities signified by our words is "just a way of speaking." I mean to prove that this attitude is an evasion. Averting or denying the question will not save hypothetical method from having an ontology. We do better to consider the matter directly.

1. Thoughts or Sentences Representing Possible, Sometimes Actual, States of Affairs

Hypothetical method prescribes that we conjecture about matters of fact, using well-formed thoughts or sentences to represent possible states of affairs. "It squeaks if stretched" is one hypothesis. "Fred is bluffing" and "Everyone knows it" are two more. "I believe that" might be a declaration rather than a hypothesis, but there are some contexts where this too is hypothetical, e.g., as when I try to identify the things I do believe. The diversity of these examples shows that grammatical form is not the consideration determining that a sentence is used hypothetically. Thoughts and sentences qualify as hypotheses, whatever their grammatical form, where they signify possible states of affairs, and where the tacit question is, Is the signified possible instantiated? We say that this is yellow, but is it? That may or may not be so. Still, the hypothetical method would be only the hypothetical attitude if it carried no farther than our recognition that every claim about contingencies is fallible. Hypothesis becomes a method as rules for making hypotheses are joined to the procedures for confirming, rejecting, or revising them.

2. A Two-part Ontology

Every sort of thing not falling within a method's ontology must elude us as we try to use the method for specifying it. This prospect is dismaying to metaphysicians, because we don't want a method that excludes us from any aspect of being. Does the hypothetical method guarantee that we shall have this universal access? It does, because of having a two-part ontology: one part provides for hypotheses, the other for their objects.

2A. *Is Our Access to the World Mediated or Unmediated?*

Hypothetical method provides mediated access to the world, i.e., an access mediated by thoughts and words construed as signs. Compare intuitionism. It promises that we shall have immediate access to all the matters known, but only as they are set directly before our inspecting minds. Plato's Forms are said to be like that. So are Descartes' *cogito*, Hume's impressions, the schematized experiences described by Kant, all the uses of ordinary language, Carnap's semantic constructions, and Husserl's ideas. Notice that restricted access is the price of unmediated access. I mean that intuitionists do not acknowledge anything as real if it cannot be inspected. A great many things that might be counted as real are missing, therefore, from the intuitionist catalogue, as configurations of matter, eternal possiblities, and force fields are purged from it. Hypothetical method is superior to intuitionism because of giving us access to all these things; though it displays a contrary fault: Unrestricted access goes with mediated access, i.e., with signs.

Which is preferable: unmediated access to a restricted reality, or mediated access to an unrestricted one? Intuitionists reject mediation because of fearing that we shall too often be mistaken about reality, with skepticism as the consequence. It is better, they suppose, that reality be reduced to the things for which we have unimpeachable evidence, because they are directly inspected. Direct inspection is a myth, while error is tolerable if we have procedures for making and testing cogent hypotheses. Unrestricted but mediated access is, therefore, our only choice.

Mediated access to everything does not imply that we do or could have evidence of all the matters of fact in every sector of reality. We might lack the inferential or perceptual powers for learning about them. That would deprive us of the information required for representing them. Still, we are not precluded from knowing any thing merely because of having a method that will not let us consider it.

2B. *Making and Using Hypotheses*

What resources do we have for signifying all the many things that might be represented? Principally the words and thoughts, hence the marks, sounds, and brain events comprising our hypotheses. These are the things construed as signs having referents distinct from themselves. The only relevant consideration just now is the use made of these things. It is incidental that their substantial nature is material or angelic. The one essential point is our use of signs having possible differences or relations as their objects.

The only limits on our power for representing these things are three, sometimes linked considerations: (1) We may lack information about them, even to the point of being incapable of getting that information, as mentioned above; (2) Our imaginations may be too feeble for extrapolating from the information we do have; (3) We have a limited vocabulary of words and grammatical forms for representing things. The first point would seem to be an absolute limit upon our ability to represent one or more domains of being, though we might hope to discover an inferential basis for claims about them. The other two limits are not so rigid. We reshape them whenever inquiry and exfoliating language reach beyond some earlier development to signify differences that were previously unsuspected. This often happens in mathematics, but also wherever dramatic changes provoke the creation of new verbal and conceptual resources.

We are familiar with new words, but unfamiliar with the strategies appropriate to inventing new ways for combining them. These strategies extend the domain of differences and relations representable by hypotheses. Examples of new syntactic forms are hard to find in ordinary language, but they are easily discovered if we consider improved languages. The notion of a mathematical function is one conspicuous example. We can use ordinary language for saying that one quantity varies systematically with changes in a different quantity, but we rely on mathematics for the information that this relation can be expressed as a complete syntactic form. Someone whose notion of reality was founded only in the scrutiny of ordinary language syntax, with its subject-predicate forms, might think himself vastly enriched by having this alternative construction for representing possible states of affairs.

It is these words and grammatical forms, whether new or old, that comprise the mediating sector of hypothetical method's ontology. The complex signs representing possible states of affairs are their product. Using these signs liberates us from the requirement that we attend only to the things set directly before our minds. But signs are only the vehicles of our thinking. The proper objects of thought are the things signified. They lie elsewhere.

3. Actuality and Possibility

Marks, sounds, mental events, and the further activities required for construing these things as signs are actual states of affairs. Each of them is an array of properties configured in space and time, or more accurately space-time. The objects of our signs are possible states of affairs. When these possibles are instantiated, the things signified are actualities, meaning again properties configured in space and time. Where the first part of hypothetical method's ontology is comprised of actualities, i.e., words, thoughts, and the acts construing them, the second part is comprised of possibilities and actualities. This pattern of actualities, possibilities and actualities sets the problem for exposition: What is signified by *actuality* and *possibility*?

3A. Actuality

Actuality is relatively straightforward. Properties configured in space and time include mass, charge, spin, and all the "emergent" properties resulting from the aggregation or configuration of these properties, as voice and a capacity for walking result from assembling the parts of a body. Actualities include, therefore, the things normally counted as physical together with the assemblies of things transformed by their interactions (i.e., events), and the dynamic, geometrized space-time where differentiated things and events are generated and sustained. All of this needs exposition, as we need to explain the relation of space, time, and motion, the character of mutually transforming interactions among causes, and the immanent laws constraining these interactions. But none of this, however contentious, compares to the difficulty of confirming, or even making it plausible to say that the objects of our signs are, in the first instance, possible states of affairs.

160

3B. Eternal Possibilities

How shall we appraise the argument, detailed in Chapter 1, that whatever is not a contradiction is a possibility, so that anything not a contradiction is, by the principle of excluded middle, necessarily, hence eternally, a possibility? This sanctioning formula is the *principle of plenitude*, with its name implying that there are an infinity of possibles satisfying the principle. Plenitude, itself, begins as a tautology: Whatever is not a contradiction is not a contradiction, where *possibility* is made to substitute for the second appearance of *not a contradiction*. These exclusively logical considerations justify the familiar saying that the possibilities sanctioned by this principle are logical possibilities; they earn the status of possibles in only the respect that they embody no contradiction. Yet, this cannot be all that there is to say of these possibles, for it is something having a distinguishable character in its own right that embodies no contradiction. Casting about for candidates among the "somethings" that might qualify for this role, I have suggested that they are properties. Why make this suggestion? Because properties seem to be the elementary constituents of which other things are made, and the attributes of things comprised of their properties (e.g. a fast car). Where properties are the possibles, every thing constituted of them is also possible. It is true of these things too that their possibility is entailed by the fact that they do not embody contradictions.

This argument is hard to fault given the modest resources on which it depends. The original tautology would seem to be unexceptionable. Substituting *possibility* for *not a contradiction* is also benign where these two are assumed to be synonymous. Using the principle of excluded middle for inferring that something not contradictory is, necessarily, a possibility would be dubious within three-valued logics. But there is no apparent third value here, as there is a third value when neither of two contrary predictions about the future is either true or false in advance of the time when the event does occur. Saying that something is neither a contradiction nor a possibility leaves us pawing the air waiting for an explication of that missing third value. There does not seem to be any third thing it might be, so that invoking the principle of excluded middle in this case seems to be unexceptionable. The one real point of vulnerability is my suggestion that the "whatever" or "somethings" not contradictory, hence possible, are properties. This substantive claim is independent of the logic of the argument, even granting that it helps to drive the subsequent use that is made of it.

What of *possibility* itself? Isn't this the dangerous word? *Possibility* is uncontroversial if we introduce it merely as a synonym for *not a contradiction*.

Nor is anything malign interpolated if we understand *possibility* as signifying that which can be. For *contradiction* may already be the synonym for *that which cannot be* so that noncontradiction is just that which can be, i.e., that which is possible.

Possibility becomes seriously problematic only as one argues, as I believe we should, that this word requires a more extended interpretation. What status is claimed for the properties, or other things, described as possibles, especially when there are no instances of these things in space-time? What of the many worlds, each having a set of physical laws as its signature, though none of those laws can be expressed in our world because of being contraries to laws operating here, e.g., as the contraries of $F = MA$ are $F = MA^2$, $F = MA^3$ . . . $F = MA^n$? These other worlds are possible, but what could *possibility* signify in them?

Here is the place where my claims about hypothetical method's ontology are too rich for many tastes. I interpret possibility as a mode of being, i.e., as the manner in which all the logical possibles exist. It is, I suggest, determinability that characterizes this mode of being. All possibles are numerically determinable, as the possibility for a particular shade of blue is multiply instantiable. Possibilities differ, however, as regards qualitative determinability. Some are qualitatively determinate, as there is a possibility for every shade of blue. Others are qualitatively determinable, as color, sound, and shape are generic possibilities. Actuals, by comparison, are particulars in space-time. Each of them is a network of instantiated possibles, and each one is or is not the instantiation of every possible property, e.g., as one may be a specific shade of pink, and no shade of blue.[1]

Joining these points, we get this summary claim: Logical possibilities sanctioned by the principle of plenitude are also to be described as properties existing as possibles. Possibility is the mode of being counterpart to actuality.[2] The determinability of the one is complementary to determination in the other.

3C. *A Priori Demonstrations of Existence*

How much credit should we give to a hypothesis about the world when its claims are driven by an *a priori* argument, especially when we don't like the entities it postulates? The second part of the question is not so baffling. Physicalists and phenomenalists share a prejudice against anything they cannot perceive. Their discomfort in the presence of claims about entities or classes of entities unperceivable is predictable, but not persuasive as a reason for rejecting those claims. The other part of the question is more serious: Why believe any claim about the world when argument is its only basis? We are reminded that *a priori*, ontological arguments are always dubious. The *a priori* part of my argument is the one concluding that logical possibilities exist necessarily, hence eternally. The choice is only between something that is either a contradiction or a possibility, where anything not internally contradictory is forever possible. Does this argument establish that anything exists?

That it does not is plainer when the argument is restated in this conditional way: Were there to be anything, and were that thing not a contradiction, then it would be a possibility. The intrusion of this conditional phrase, "were there to be anything," makes the point that plenitude by itself, i.e., either a contradiction or a possibility, does not establish that anything exists to satisfy the alternation.

This cannot be the end of the matter. Granting that the principle of plenitude does not generate existences or guarantee that anything does exist, we ask this other question: Is there evidence, independent of the principle, that there are some things existing? Those things, in a world where contradiction and possibility are mutually exclusive and exhaustive, would be one or the other. Not being contradictions, as they could not be as otherwise they would not exist in any way, they must be possibilities. Are there any of these entities to which the principle might apply? There are, of course, all the contingently existing things perceived. Here, then, are some things satisfying the alternation. These are things existing necessarily as possibles because of embodying no contradictions.

Should we also infer that some head of cabbage exists necessarily because of not being contradictory? We do not say this, and we are not encouraged to say it, because the principle of plenitude affirms only that it is possibles which stand in alternation to contradiction: either a contradiction or a possibility. It does not follow that the instantiation of any possible is necessary. We do, nevertheless, supplement the *a priori* argument with empirical claims about matters of fact. Otherwise we have no reason for saying that the *a priori* conclusion has application to our actual world. The evidence of these instantiated possibles is decisive for the argument because of confirming that there is a domain of existents to which the argument applies.

The scope of its applicability is more apparent when we consider the time when contingent things did not exist. What were they then? Nothing at all, you reply, or at most, possibilities. We accept this last concession most carefully, saying that these contingent things existed merely as that which could be. Consider now the domain of things which can be, but are not. Does it include only the things that come to be? No, it includes the infinity of can be's which are not now or ever, in addition to that smaller set of can be's which have or will some time come to be. Here is a domain of existents, the domain of logical possibilities, to which the principle of plenitude applies. The *a priori* argument has not generated these possibles. It merely discloses their limiting condition; namely, that they are set in opposition to contradiction, as whatever is not a contradiction is a possibility.

This result is prior to, and independent of, the further claim that logical possibilities are properties or complexes of them having possibility as their mode of being, as being noncontradictory is not the same as being a numerically and qualitatively determinable property. This further part of the ontological claim is the result of an abduction: Granting the logical possibles, we ask about the mode of their being. This is the question to which possibility, described now as the mode of qualitative and numerical determinability, is an answer. This is a reasonable, not a gratuitous proposal when we have acknowledged that the status of logical possibilities is more than a quibble. None of the past and none of the future, relativized or not, is actual. Where nothing is actual if it is not possible, we may worry about having a future if its possibilities do not already have some status in being.

4. Alternative Ways of Accounting for Possibility

Arguments alone will not convince us that properties exist as possibilities so long as we believe that possibility might be provided for in some other, more ontologically economical way. Here are two other views of it. Each one explicates the claim that signs represent possibilities, and each averts our having to say that possibility is a mode of being.

4A. *Material Possibility*

One suggestion is that the possibilities signified by our thoughts and words are material possibilities for events that would occur if all their generative conditions were in place. Saying that rain is possible, we mean that one or more of its material conditions are satisfied. Material possibility is leaner than eternal possibility, because it saves us from the array of logical possibles while committing us to nothing richer than the material circumstances current in our world. It does require that we acknowledge the dispositions of things, as air must be disposed to gathering moisture if rain is to fall. Still, dispositions may have a strictly material basis, as a key can open a lock because of their complementary shapes. Material possibility is, therefore, much less speculative, even as we allow for dispositions, than the "slum of possibles."[3] Why not say that the possibilities acknowledged by the principle of plenitude, and required for representation are only these material ones?

This does seem to be an adequate account for most of the possibles we want to represent, especially as they concern events that are realizable in the evolution of our circumstances. Possibilities for making dinner or winning the *Tour de France* might seem to be material only. There are, however, more difficult examples. Consider Mozart's one hundredth symphony. This is one of the many Mozart never wrote, but we may hypothesize what is might have been had he lived to write it. There will likely be many hypotheses, each one extrapolating from the music Mozart did compose to changes in the form of the music he would have written. Each of the many hypotheses represents a possibility, but does any of them represent a material possibility? How could that be so when all the material circumstances for realizing the possibility, Mozart especially, are defunct. Suppose, however, that Mozart's piano or any other one survives, for then it seems that every possible combination of notes playable on its keys survives to be composed and played. Isn't it true that music of Mozart's kind is only a configuration of notes, so that the instrument for combining them is the sufficient ground for the material possibility at issue? Indeed, any pencil and paper might be sufficient to justify our saying that material conditions for this uncompleted work do exist. This is plausible only as we forget that Mozart's distinguishing configurations of notes were possible before pianos, claviers, or pencils were invented. They were possible, in some respect, before that singularity from which our universe is alleged to have exploded. We should be skeptical, that material possibility could ever be, or have been the basis for eternal possibilities. Still, we may ignore this point while continuing to propose that we provide for eternal possibles by way of the material ones. Perhaps we can do that by saying that some event or outcome is materially possible if one or more of its material conditions ever did exist. Mozart's unwritten music is therefore materially possible because he once lived. Material possibilities still look safe as the referents for our hypotheses, as talk about Mozart's unwritten music is just talk about him and the work he might have done.

This next example confirms that this strategy fails. Imagine a world whose space-time has a geometry different from the one of our world. This is an example of worlds whose laws of motion are different from those of our world. We might supply detailed descriptions of events in that other world, and also the laws they satisfy, but neither those events, or that world is a material possibility. It does not exist; there are no material conditions from which the events we describe could be generated. We might propose to account for their material possibility by describing them as extrapolations from processes in our world, as we might reasonably say that our understanding of that other world is predicated upon our understanding of this, our actual world. But this claim is a *non sequitur*, for material possibility is founded in the material conditions presupposed if events are to occur, not in our analogical thinking, or in extrapolations from our understanding of one situation to our speculations about a different one. There is a still more decisive point. The possibility for a world having laws different from our own could not be a material possibility originating in our world, for the reason that the two worlds are contraries: One cannot get from here to there by any imagined extrapolation.

Is this really so? Can't we justify talking about an infinity of possible worlds by saying that each of them might evolve from the current circumstances of our world? Everyone endorsing this inference supposes that all material possibilities are founded in every current situation. Thinking of a beloved child while imagining that he or she might yet be President, we could as plausibly look at any doorknob and think the same thing. This is Hume's view. He has mistaken a fact about the association of ideas, i.e., that any one may be the sign of any other, for an analysis of cause and effect. There is no evidence that nature is as loosely bound as words and ideas, and considerable evidence that it is not. There is, furthermore, no evidence for the presence in our world of material conditions that would qualify it for evolving into any and every one of those contrary worlds which are possible. Their possibility cannot, therefore, be explicated as another expression of material possibility. We need some different account of possibility if we are not to lapse again into saying, as I believe we should, that properties and complexes of properties, e.g., these possible worlds, exist as possibilities.

4B. Possibilities "Expressed" by Thought or Language

The alternative way of accounting for possibles identifies them with the possibilities "expressed" by our thoughts and words. Is this an adequate interpretation for the more literal claim that possibilities are represented?

Saying that something is admired or deplored, wanted or not, we express our feelings about it. Adding the verbal expressions for doubt, surprise, sensibility, courage, cynicism, and duplicity, we confirm that language is often used expressively. This much is beyond argument, for words no less than one's voice and eyes and the slope of one's shoulders express what we think and feel. These expressions of feelings and attitudes are not, however, the ones thought germane to the idea that possibilities are merely a conceptual or verbal expression. This is a different notion going by the same name. In the one case, feeling is shown, sometimes for the purpose of evoking other people's feelings. In the case at hand, possibilities are expressed by telling a coherent story. "Consider the possibilities," we say, before listing

166

them, or we listen to a proposal of some kind, before deciding that this is or is not a possibility interesting to us. The words, in either case, are a kind of tableau. Reading or listening to them, we imagine ourselves seeing the possibility through the transparency of the words expressing it.

The strength of this idea originates in a delusory affect, as though words and thoughts were animated from within by the possibilities they signify. We get a similar experience watching a motion picutre, as images on the screen seem to come alive. But we ignore in the first case and sometimes choose to forget in the other one that words and images express only as much as we or someone else puts into them. Thought and words are mental activities, marks, and sounds. If they mean anything it is only because of something that we have done to them.

The one pertinent thing we do is construe these thoughts and words as signs. They come to have intentional meaning. Reading the description of dirty fog swirling over the roofs of a Victorian factory town, we may have the feeling of a door opened onto a possibility hitherto unimagined, though the possible is made accessible to us only as we construe the words. Could this be the clue to acknowledging possibilities without having to agree that possibility is a mode of being? Why not say that the phenomenon naively regarded as the "expressing" of possibilities is only the fact that thoughts and words acquire intentional meaning as they are construed?

The power of this suggestion has sources in the ontological economy it promises, and in its assumption about mind and mental activity. We are encouraged to suppose that the act of construing thoughts and words is the intentional act of focusing upon a subject matter. Where construal occurs, the act would be complex: We would entertain a word, for example, thereby reading into it a sense postulated as its referent. The word would have occasioned this interpretation, having as it does a standard construal; it would have provided the window or screen through which the postulated sense is thought and entertained. Intentional meaning would be complementary to intentional objects. Mind would have set this intentional object before itself merely by construing the word.

We have Plato, Descartes, Brentano, Husserl, Frege, and Meinong to instruct us in this view. We also have their warning that the possibilities discovered within thought have an objectivity surpassing the manner of their discovery within our minds. This is to be "logic," not psychology.

It is too bad that the idea of intentional meaning is so firmly captured and distorted by the intuitionist model animating this tradition. Its idea of mind has become a paradigm for philosophic self-understanding, so that we turn upon ourselves finding safety, freedom, and power within the theatre that mind so easily supposes itself to be. Here is a place of near self-sufficiency where beams of mental light are directed upon whatever object we care to introduce. This is the crucible where encircling self-consciousness sustains mind's boundary while mind's luminosity guarantees that everything within it shall be visible to a comprehensive self-inspection.

This baroque idea of mind is the centerpiece of intuitionist method's psychocentric ontology. In Plato, *nous* is only co-equal with the Forms. His modern successors are Cartesians. They struggle to defend themselves from psychologism and the charge that what they describe as intentional objects are merely the posits of intentional activity (though chilliagon is a possibility not depending upon our thinking it for its status as a possible). This realization is presumably the reason for claiming a logical, as against a merely psychological, status for mind's intentional objects. Still, the idea of mind as a theatre comprised of the beams directed onto stage or screen is only the contrivance of intuitionist hyperbole. Behaviorism clears the air by scrapping this introspectionist enterprise, with all its acts and objects, but this solution is expensive in its own way, as we lose all the functions crucial for an active, understanding mind, and a cogent central-state psychology. Closing windows at the first sight of rain is an exhibition of intelligent, purposive activity, though citing this behavior is not also a specification of all the relevant mental activities.

Even a central-state psychology can be used to promote the idea that possibilities are merely "expressed" by thought or language. So, the possibility for red is established by associating *red* with the thoughts, words, and behaviors terminating in a red percept. Association, hence construal, is to justify our saying that intentional meaning, in the associationist guise here claimed for it, is the sufficient basis for invoking or introducing possibilities. This too is unsatisfactory as an account of possibility, when only a small subset of logical possibles is expressible by way of these associative networks. We might appeal to languages and networks to come, but that is question-begging when the principle of plenitude sanctions these logical possibles already, and when the promise of a comprehensive set of associatives networks is unfulfillable, i.e., there are an infinity of logical possibilities.

Notice something familiar about these reductionist strategies: They satisfy the intuitionist premise that nothing is real if it cannot be translated into something set before, or in this case set within, our minds. I do not mean that associationism is an intuitionist notion, only that the attempt to provide for possibilities with merely intra-psychic resources is another expression of the intuitionist motive. We should renounce that motive, as we also declare that this account of possibilities is deficient because of having nothing to say about most of them. And anyway, is it really plausible that the logical possibility for red should be founded only in our being able to associate 'red' with other words, behaviors, and percepts? That is merely a confusion, and not by any means a way of accounting for the logical possibility.

4C. Two Questions about Possibility

Neither of these options, not material possibilities and not the idea that possibility is expressed by our thoughts and words, saves us from logical possibilities. Two questions about them require attention. What is the relation between material and logical, or eternal, possibility? How should we appraise the claim that possibility is the mode of being for those properties and complexes of properties known as logical possibilities?

4Ci. The relation of material to eternal possibilities

The distinction between material and eternal possibilities is easily drawn. Eternal, because logical, possibilities include every difference and complex of differences embodying no contradiction. Material possibilities are those eternal possibles for which one or more material conditions are in place. Superluminary velocities are logically possible, though they are not materially possible, we currently believe, in our world. Riding a bicycle is eternally and materially possible. Every material possibility presupposes a logical possibility, though not the converse.

I suggested earlier in this chapter that we might reasonably worry about having a future if unrealized possibilities do not have some status in being. This is true, but inadequate because of failing to distinguish between these two kinds of possibility. On one side are eternal possibilities. Everything that is possible in this respect is instantiable in some possible world. But then it is also true that the future is vastly more limited than would be so if Hume were correct in saying that anything can follow anything else. For then each of the logical possibilities would be as likely as any other to occur in the future. Hume is mistaken if the possibilities for the future are limited to material possibilities founded at any moment in prevailing material circumstances, as there is no material possibility for hens' teeth. Anything that does happen is the realization of some previous, though always changing, set of material possibilities, so that nothing can happen, assuming it to be a logical possibility, if there is not a material possibility, i.e., one or more causal conditions, in place.

Should we say that the discovery of insulin was materially possible from the inception of the singularity from which our universe is said to derive? Isn't it true that material conditions were successively transformed up to the moment when the discovery was made? We probably don't want to speak in this way, correct though it is, because the transformations required for getting from one stage of development to a remote one are complex and often unspecifiable. We can say that material conditions for winning the Kentucky Derby in 2001 are already in place, though none of the things needed then, including the horse, are yet available.

4Cii. Possibility as a mode of being

Material possibilities exist by way of those material conditions whose transformations or interactions would have the possible events as their outcomes. Hearing the wind is a material possibility because, among other conditions satisfied, it is just now blowing. Logical possibilities also require an explication of their status.

Calling them "logical" rather than "eternal" invites a particular thrust to the assault upon them. We may be tempted to say that logic is itself merely a set of rules, where anything depending on them for its existence is easily accounted for in whatever way we provide for rules. If the rules are syntactic in the way that logic is often said to be, then the product of their applications will be ordered marks or sounds. Perhaps logical possibilities are just the ordered marks and sounds generated by the applications of these rules. There should be nothing ontologically problematic in this.

Completing this program requires a convincing argument for the claim that the principles of plenitude, non-contradiction, and identity are, all of them, merely syntactic conventions. Is that an apt description for the principle of identity, i.e., everything is what it is and not another thing because of being constituted of its properties? Its domain includes every state of affairs, not only the orderings of words. One must have a very extended notion of syntax before calling this principle syntactic. Here, where identity is more than a syntactic rule, contradiction is also something more. Both of them are least conditions that must be satisfied if a thing is to have any character whatever. Now consider the principle of plenitude. We express it by substituting the word *possibility* for the phrase *not a contradiction* in the tautology, 'Whatever is not a contradiction is not a contradiction'. The resulting claim is not so arid as this beginning suggests, for the sentence, 'Whatever is not a contradiction is a possibility' is also expressible in these equivalent ways: 'Either a contradiction or a possibility' and 'Either something that cannot be or something that can be'. These versions of plenitude derive from the two previous and substantive principles, as contradiction derives from identity and plenitude from contradiction, possibilities being all that is left over when contradictions are barred.

Are there any things not precluded by the absolute prohibition against contradictions? We have seen that there are, as every actual state of affairs is evidence of them. These things are possible, because of embodying no contradiction before they are actual, so that they are included within the domain of the many differences which are possible because of not being contradictory. These are the logical, eternal possibilities. It is their status in being that concerns us now.

Acknowledging these logical possibilities, then claiming a distinctive place for them within being provoked the two arguments considered above and rejected: Eternal possibilities cannot be provided for as material possibles, or within a theory of linguistic expression or association. There remains the proposal that possibility is itself a mode of being, i.e., that properties which embody no contradiction exist, in the first instance, as possibles. They are distinguished as possibles by the fact of being numerically and, sometimes, qualitatively determinable. Possibility, this implies, is a counterpart mode of existence, one that is prior to determinate actuality, as nothing can be actual if it is not first determinable and possible.

4Ciii. Summary

Hypothesizing about possible states of affairs has seemed innocent enough. Someone using the hypothetical method without regard for its ontology might be surprised that his method presupposes a theory of being. Will anyone repudiate the method if we determine that it presupposes the two-part ontology described here? I doubt they will, especially if it is true that intuitionism is the only alternative to making and testing hypotheses about possible states of affairs. There will, perhaps, be an inclination to ignore hypothetical method's ontological presuppositions, or to suppose that careful thought will save us from having to agree that logical possibilities are properties existing as possibles. I expect that a review of the alternatives will discover only the ones considered here and rejected. Possibility and possibilities will not easily go away.

5. Some Problematic Possibilities

This concern for ontology is not quite done, for there are three more issues to which hypothetical method draws our attention. All of them are apparent on the surface of the hypotheses themselves; some are negative, others are conjunctive or disjunctive, many are general. Does it follow from the truth of these hypotheses that there are negative, conjunctive, disjunctive, and general facts?

5A. Negative Facts

We get negative facts by way of sentences such as 'Jack is gone' when he is and 'Phlogiston is not the product of combustion': Does it follow that these negative facts exist, in some way having parity with the existence of positive facts, i.e., that New York has five boroughs? If we decide the issue merely be regarding the facts represented by our true sentences, we shall have no choice: There will be positive facts and negative ones too.

This implication, is undesirable when it is affirmed already that actuality is the instantiation and configuration of properties in space and time, as mass is instantiated there. This way of describing actuality restricts it to those things present, not missing, so that there is no provision so far for negative facts. How shall we introduce them? We might do that by extending our notion of actuality. An actual state of affairs, we might suggest, is constituted of all the properties instantiated and configured there, but also by its exclusion of the infinitely many uninstantiated properties and configurations. This proposal implies that every apparently simple state of affairs, e.g., the clock on my wall, is indescribably more complicated than it seems. Certainly, the physical fact is complicated, but is it complicated in the way just described?

There is a way of averting this outcome. It allows us to retain the previous account of actuality, i.e., of properties instantiated and configured in space and time, while also providing for negative facts. Positive facts are primary we say; but then we also remark that things significant in one way or another are absent. An earring is missing; it is not included among the possibles instantiated here. That too is a fact. We lose nothing except the primacy of negative facts.

5B. Conjunctive and Disjunctive Facts

Conjunctive and disjunctive facts are partly but not altogether explicable by way of the conditions for actuality. There are, for example, the conjunctions and disjunctions founded in the character of space and time. Saying 'This and that' and 'This or that', we may be representing the spatial or temporal contiguity of things, or the fact that two houses of equal bulk are precluded from occupying the same plot of ground at the same time. There are also those forks in the road where alternative paths are contraries. Change is like that, as it goes in one way or another, not in two or more of them at once, as war and peace are mostly contrary. All of this is plain enough to anyone surveying actual states of affairs.

There is another confirming point: The possibilities signified by our

words, then sometimes instantiated, are related as conjuncts and also sometimes as disjuncts. Possibilities are conjunctive in a respect satisfying the principle of plenitude. They are, at once, situated in Wittgenstein's "logical
space". There are also those disjunctive relations occurring among them
when lower-order possibilities are related to one another as the determinations of higher-order possibles. Color, for example, is higher-order relative
to red, yellow, and blue. But then color as it receives lower-order expression, still in possibility, is either red, or yellow, or blue. This, in actuality,
is the fact that nothing is red, yellow, and blue all over at the same time.
The lower-order determinations of a higher-order property are, this implies, contraries. A disjunctive hypothesis, e.g., 'His shirt may be all red,
all yellow, or all blue, but not all three at once' expresses this disjunctive
relation among possibles. Conjunctive and disjunctive facts are, therefore,
as fundamental to possibility as they are to actuality.

5C. General Facts

What should be our policy regarding general facts? Here to start are
five kinds of generality: (1) Distributive generality, e.g., 'Any dog'; (2) Statistical generality, e.g., 'The ordinary man'; 'Three percent of the time'; (3) A
class of things or events treated as a particular, e.g., 'America, the beautiful';
(4) Citation of a class property, e.g., 'Knowing how is different from knowing that'; (5) Normative generality, e.g., '$F = MA$'.

Distributive generalities are the nominalist paradigm for analyzing
generality; they are summary claims about one or many particulars. Statistical generalities of the two kinds illustrated, statistical averages and frequen-
cies, are not at issue. Aggregates treated as particulars, e.g., America, are
also incidental here. These two can be dismissed, because statistical generalities have particulars as their domains, while aggregates are sometimes properly treated as individuals. More problematic for us are class properties and
normative generalities. Neither of them seems to be analyzable as a merely
rhetorical form disguising a distributive generality. Claims invoking them
are reports about *intensions* or *kinds*. Generalities of the one sort mention,
characterize or compare class properties; normative claims assert that these
properties have a constraining force upon the particulars in which they are
realized.

5Ci. Class properties

Characterizations or comparisons of class properties might not seem
to be generalities, because class properties, like aggregates, might seem to
count as particulars. This is so in the limited sense that these properties are

subjects of discourse; it is false, however, in the light of our assumption about actualities. Particulars are individuals having addresses and dates in space and time, as America is a particular because of being an aggregate having an extended position in space and time. Knowing how and knowing that are not particulars. These are specific but determinable properties having many different possible expressions. They are generals, as claims about them are general because of applying to their infinitely many possible instances.

Could we, nevertheless, replace the generalities about these class properties with distributive generalities about their instances? Every claim about knowing how would then reduce to the infinitely lengthy description of individuals knowing how to do some thing. Similarly with knowing that, so that the difference between the two would be a particular difference specified throughout the ranges of their applications. The length of these analyses would make it impractical to use the replacements, but there would be replacements, so that our preference for the generalities could only be justified by convenience.

The weakness of this extensionalist program is its requirement that the class property be traced through the infinity of its instances. A finite task, i.e., specifying the class property, has become an infinite one. Why should this be counted an advantage? The class property would be exhibited by each of its instances; but why suppose that the property must be explicated by way of its instances, then identified with them? It is not that we cannot specify the property without referring to them, for we can signify it even where the property has no single instance, e.g., as there are no unicorns. The reason for this extensionalist analysis is our dread that the property might be regarded as having a status independent of its instances. What sort of being could it have when the only actualities are datable, addressable particulars?

The principle of plenitude is relevant here. It acknowledges as possible every property embodying no contradiction, irrespective of its degree of determinability. Knowing how and knowing that are determinable in the respect that there are any number of different things to be known in one way or the other. Knowing that one has shoes and knowing how to tie them are, this implies, no more or less logical possibilities than are the determinables, knowing that and knowing how. Possibles having these several degrees of determinability would seem to be ordered hierarchically among themselves, so that determinables are higher-order relative to their lower-order, more determinate expressions. Instantiated possibilities always have some lowest-order, qualitatively determinate property or properties, e.g., a particular shade of pink, as their manifest property, though an entire hierarchy of differentiated determinables is instantiated within each par-

174

ticular, e.g., as a paint chip instantiates both color and some particular shade of it.

Suppose now that there are determinable properties, i.e., intensions, existing as possibles, so that the generality of claims about them does not reduce to distributive generalities. Does this prove too much because of implying that these determinable properties are individuals of a sort? Let us agree that there are two kinds of particulars, i.e., datable, addressable actuals, and these possibles. The possibles are numerically and sometimes qualitatively determinable (e.g., as a particular shade of color is numerically determinable but qualitatively determinate, though color is determinable in both respects); hence they are class properties. We may regard them alternately as generals and as particulars, so that reference to a class property may signify either the class of its instances or the property.

5Cii. *Normative generalities*

Still to consider are the normative generalities, where 'F = MA' is the suggested example. Never mind that this law sentence has been replaced after having been shown to be only the approximation, under restricted conditions, of a different law sentence. More relevant here is, first, the use of generalities like this one, and, second, the basis for this use among the possibles.

The use concerning us is half-implied by the old dispute regarding the status of such sentences as 'F = MA': Are they definitions? This query obliquely suggests their normative use, as we suppose that every motion must satisfy them. Prescriptive force, this implies, is a disguised way of saying that we will not acknowledge any event not satisfying our stipulations. Prescriptivist intuitionists make this very asssumption when they say that anything failing to satisfy our interpretations is unintelligible. Their view is mistaken if the world is intelligible in itself because of instantiating a possible world having an intrinsic form of its own. No hypothesis dictates to that instantiated possible world, i.e., our actual world, what its form shall be, so that refusing to acknowledge states of affairs not satisfying our hypotheses mixes affrontery and conceit. We need a better explanation for the normative character ascribed to generalizations such as 'F = MA'.

Two considerations are jointly sufficient to explain it. One is epistemic and pragmatic: having a well-confirmed hypotheses, e.g., one such as 'F = MA', we expect that everything will conform to it. Knowing that we might be mistaken, we persist in using the law until the evidence deters us. The other consideration is ontological: We suspect that the forms embodied within nature contrain the changes occurring there. By "we," I mean everyone who hasn't read Hume, and those others who believe that nothing in Hume's arguments entails his inference that anything may follow anything else. If ideas and impressions can succeed one another in that way, even being imagined as having no antecedents or successors, this tells us nothing whatever about nature. For, *yes*, it is not contradictory that events be conceived in this way; but, *no*, the principle of non-contradiction is not the one operative physical law in our world. Other laws operating within and upon the events occurring here are also constraining. 'F=MA' was long thought to be one of them. If it is not, because some other law sentence seems to be a better representation of that internal constraint, then we easily accept this change in our thinking. But this is a move from one representation of nature's internally constraining form to a different specification of it. This new law sentence is also used normatively, and with more confidence than the one replaced, because we believe the constraining form is now more accurately identified.

There is one last question to answer. Consider these normative forms: What status do they have in possibility and actuality? As possibles, these are the higher-order determinable properties sanctioned by the principle of plenitude. F=MA is a possibility of that sort. Every higher-order determinable within the domain of possibles is normative as it imposes a certain least demand upon all of its lower-order, more determinate expressions. Color, sound, and shape are, in this respect, like F=MA. Where, however, is the place for these higher-order determinables in actuality? They are present there wherever possibilities are instantiated, as the determinable laws of physics are realized in every motion and as color is present in every instantiation of red, yellow, and blue. Where possibility as a mode of being justifies our saying that logical possibilities exist *ante rem*, hence whether or not the possibles are instantiated, determinable constraining forms are present within nature *in rebus*, i.e., in the things expressing their constraint.

6. Conclusion

The ontology of possibilities and actualities, of intensions and individuals, universals and particulars is daunting in itself, and a sure deterrent to everyone who supposes that method might be ontologically naive. The arguments and proposals of this chapter supply an ontological backing for the hypothetical method when, as I believe, the use of that method presupposes this ontology, or one very much like it. We are right to purge our claims about reality of every theoretical excrescence; people finding these claims excessive are justified in wanting to cut away the dross. They will need to do better than suppose that all the familiar reductions of possibility, i.e., to material possibilities or expressive language, can suffice. A more likely result is the one of neglecting the ontological question because of not liking this solution. We can use the hypothetical method, even in metaphysics, without bothering to consider its ontological presuppositions. If those assumptions are unthinkable, because our phenomenalism or physicalism will not let us consider them, then this self-enforced oblivion seems the safer way. Though hypothetical method does have presuppositions. They do not go away just because we choose to ignore them.

Suppose, however, that this method's ontological assumptions are acknowledged, and that we find them to be as they are characterized here. We discover this convergence, mentioned before in Chapter 1.

There are two requirements upon our ontology. We are to identify the extraconceptual and extralinguistic referents making our thoughts and words meaningful, and to tell if nature is self-sufficient, or conditioned by something distinct from itself? Properties existing as possibles are a solution to both questions. They are the senses of our thoughts and words, while every property and complex of properties in space-time is the instantiation of these same possibilities. The referents for our thoughts and words are also, this says, the extranatural conditions for actuality, as nothing is not actual if it is not first possible.

This ontology is an aswer to Kant's assumption, in the Transcendental Dialectic of the First Critique, that thought can never exceed the domain of experience, meaning sensory data schematized. Kant has supposed that ideas are rules for organizing sensory data, not the representations of things existing apart from themselves. The ontology of possibilities is, by comparison, an opportunity for reaffirming the older notion that thoughts and words *represent* matters distinct from themselves. We surpass schematized sensory data, representing something whose existence is independent of our thinking it, merely by signifying a possibility. We say, for example, that there are properties existing as possibles, meaning nothing we have schematized and nothing that we do or could perceive. Here is a specifiable reality beyond the forms of intuition and their sensory contents. We no longer require that thought and language be world-makers. We say, instead, that the existence and character of things are independent of the ways we think and talk about them, though these possibilities and possibles instantiated are accessible to thought and language because of being representable.

6

Hypothesizing Mind

1. Inferring From Mind's Activities to Its Character

Every way of thinking presupposes a mind empowered for thinking that way, as activity requires an agent. Not surprising, you say; and not different from inferring opium's dormitive powers from the evidence of the man who sleeps after taking it. I suggest that inferences from an activity to its agent may supply important information about both of them. This is apparent when the chemical analysis of opium and the identification of receptors in the brain explain some of opium's effects. The inferences are equally potent when we note that mind's use of the hypothetical method is significant in two ways: first, as we discover the objectives served by this way of thinking; second, as we identify mind's structures, and the activities it performs as hypotheses are formulated, tested, and revised. The circle of our reasoning is small but cogent; mind's activity is the principal clue to its character as an agent, while mind's character is decisive for its behaviors.

Philosophers have too often assumed that our choice of method is exclusively pragmatic, i.e., that we might adopt whatever method best serves the purpose of truth or effective action. There were, otherwise, thought to be no constraints. We have supposed that method is independent of our nature; or that nature is so ample and determinable as to be consistent with a great variety of methods. This view is mistaken if method is the expression of what we are, and cannot otherwise be. Intuitionists have understood this point, and they have argued or assumed that their method is the exercise of powers essential to our being as thinkers and knowers. But then intuitionists have relied upon the metaphor of the mind's eye for interpreting their claims about the inspectability of everything construed by, or given to our minds. That claim misdescribes our thinking. More, it is too flagrantly at odds with even a rudimentary physiology. Accordingly, we cannot pretend that method is a matter of choice, where every choice says nothing definitive about our nature; but then, we cannot be intuitionists.

The better alternative says that hypothesis is our method. We never did have a choice. It is our nature to generalize from current information, or to argue abductively from information about some matter of fact to its conditions. These are the procedures for creating testable hypotheses, and the plans useful for dealing with some real or imagined state of affairs. Elaborating upon these activities, on the way to describing the hypothesizer, is my purpose in this chapter. The overall problem, I shall say, is the one of diminishing our vulnerability by securing and satisfying ourselves within the world. Hypothesizing mind is the equilibrating activity of body as we engage one another and other things in ways having these effects.

Where shall be begin? Not yet with a description of the activities and faculties required for hypothesizing. That would be too much like explaining the migration of birds by describing the flapping of wings. We want a larger context, one that includes the objectives served by our hypothesizing. We describe that context from its inception in the following way.

2. Vulnerability and Security

Human life is two-faced. On one side is the continuing pursuit and enjoyment of security amidst the uncertainty of our chronic vulnerability. The other side is the pleasure of vulnerability, a pleasure enjoyed most when it is bounded by assured securities. We act, from earliest childhood, to find or make situations where we shall be secure. Security, and the feeling of it, are for us the greater part of well-being. We sometimes find that security as infants, nurtured and loved. When the support cracks, however temporarily, or when moving beyond the support of those securing circumstances, we rediscover the original vulnerability or a different one. We remember, even as we work to secure ourselves, that vulnerability was also good: first, as we were passive and needy having others to care for us; later, as we tired of routine, wanting to risk danger without destroying the cords that secure and finally save us. Somewhere between these extremes, each of us finds a balance.

The sources of vulnerability are various but familiar. We risk injury, pain, embarrassment, frustration, rejection, isolation, hunger, and death.

180

Threats unknown to us make no difference to our behavior, but we do know of these risks, and we learn from infancy to act in ways that will secure us against them. Where loneliness is the source of our pain we learn to make and keep friends. Fearing illness, we invent medical science. Vulnerability is reduced for each of these threats by behaviors performed under the direction of plans. We take the measure of our circumstances while acting to change them in ways that will secure us.

3. Sources of Our Vulnerability

There are, generically, four different sources of our vulnerability: biological, social, developmental, and situational. Biological risks include deprivation, injury and death. Social risks include damage to our self-esteem, and damage to the interpersonal relations on which we depend for both identity and the satisfaction of biological needs and social responsibilities. Losing one's job is a social risk, with consequences for all shades of our well-being. Developmental risks are the ones incurred as we learn the skills required for some age- or gender-appropriate task. That might be learning to summon help by crying, to negotiate pregnancy and bonding with one's child, or more generally to live as an adult with responsibilities for oneself, one's family, associates and friends. Situational risks may be characteristic of one's place, or accidental; coal mining is always risky, being hit by a meteorite is only accidental.

These four are not perfectly distinct from one another, as development has both biological and social bases. Each of the four kinds of vulnerability applies within the other three domains, so that a child learning to walk who hurts a leg when falling on a slippery floor only to be ridiculed suffers in all four ways.

4. Plan-directed Activity as a Security-enhancing Response to Vulnerability

Each of us lives always in a minefield of vulnerabilities. We make our way through these risks because the physical world is often benign, because heredity has made us effective in surviving them, and because we have cultures that extend us the protections learned over millennia of trying various strategies for surviving these obstacles. We do not often notice that the artifacts of a culture, e.g., knives and forks, are the result of hypotheses about the instruments sustaining life. Certainly the cutlery displayed in the Louvre hardly suggests vulnerability; but that is the strength of our learned forgetfulness. The vulnerability was and is real, whether or not we choose to ignore it.

How should we understand the first realizations of this vulnerability, and the first tentative responses to it? It is too late to do better than speculate about our primal ancestors; but we do have about us the infants who must learn to secure themselves. What do they do?

It seems likely that the first plans are made as we act to reduce a discomfort. We are cold, and desire warmth; hungry, we want feeding. These inclinations might be instinctual only, or instinctual with an overlay of experience, as we learn to move from warmth to cold, or remember being fed when hungry. An infant might be several weeks old before being able to use these learned associations, so that he or she smiles or cries in order to get the previously associated result. That behavior is only proto-abductive. Nothing so articulate as a consciously formulated hypothesis or plan is required, though there is a tentative, searching quality to the child's behavior. He cries from discomfort, but also to summon help. He experiments with different sorts of cries, waiting to see what help comes, and how long it takes to arrive. He sometimes anticipates the behaviors of those who come to him; and at that moment he is satisfied by having his hypotheses confirmed. These are the first occasions, occurring before a baby is two months old, when hypotheses are used to produce a desired result. The child has learned that his own behavior may secure his well-being.

Someone in trouble thinks first of what he or she wants to preserve or the least he needs, then abductively of the conditions for keeping or having it. With age and experience, he surveys a number of these options, calculating the likely success of alternative behaviors before choosing among them. He might also choose to do nothing, if all the plans are more expensive in effort or resources than he can afford; or if it seems likely that none of them will produce a better result than the one obtaining. Doing nothing, he waits, as all of us can only wait for the weather to change.

This acquiesence in circumstances we cannot control is odd in one respect. We have been encouraged, for millennia, by the experience of making the differences that reduce our vulnerability while creating environments enjoyed for themselves as much as we enjoy the security they provide. If long ago, our ancestors were only reactive, planning a response only as circumstances threatened to overwhelm them, if we were ourselves that way as children, we have by now learned to plan more systematically, as farmers buy seeds and mulch for next year because of knowing that these are conditions for a next crop. It is the aggregate of these myriad, successful abductions and plans that creates the thick tissue of practice and habit securing us. Cities, farms, factories, ships, and mines are merely the artifacts created and used by the behaviors sponsored by these plans.

5. Submission and Control, Dependence and Self-sufficiency

One might suppose that the difference or distance between vulnerability and security is usually plain, so that we have only to avoid the one while striving for the other. This is too simple. We respond to trouble and risk in ways that may be represented as two axes, each one defined by the contraries at its ends. There are many different styles of behavior as each of us learns to position himself or herself along these axes.

One axis is defined by submission or control, the other by dependence and self-sufficiency. These two are not the same. One submits, for example, to desert heat, accommodating to it by working early in the morning and late in the afternoon, or we control the work situation by building air-conditioned factories, using them all day. Submission and control are mostly exclusive of one another, as regards any particular activity or kind of activity. Dependency and self-sufficiency are not mutually exclusive. There is a middleground between them in reciprocity, as husband and wife may be mutually dependent but also self-sufficient. One may, furthermore, be more or less dependent, and conversely more or less self-sufficient, as children learning to feed themselves also like being fed. But again, we see the independence of these two contraries from the ones of submission and control. The child learning to be self-sufficient does not also get to prescribe the manner of his eating. He submits to the cultural norm, using a spoon or his hands.

Every provocation to abductive thinking and planning is determinable with respect to these two axes. We may respond to it from a posture expressing any of the range of solutions on either axis. Plans, too, may vary because of requiring that we be more submissive or more controlling, more dependent or more self-sufficient, than differing individuals care to be. These two axes are measures of difference among us, and dimensions of our freedom for choosing to act in one or another of these ways. Do we value self-sufficiency or dependence, submission or control? The answers are determining as we invent and act upon plans calculated to secure us while having one effect or the other.

6. Provocations to Thought and Action

Why does someone work to secure himself in one or the other of the ways anticipated by these axes? If we might secure ourselves in either way, why prefer one of them? We get an answer by considering the circumstances where hypothesis and action are required. There are, principally, five security-threatening provocations to thought and action.

1. Current circumstances are threatening, e.g., one is hungry, or lightning flashes all about.
2. Previously stable conditions have changed, as the Sahara turned dry, and Germany elected the National Socialists.
3. One's understanding of a situation changes: What looked safe or threatening no longer seems to be so. The dog baring its teeth now seems benign.
4. One's values change. Something that seemed threatening has become inviting. The self-sufficiency or dependence that secured us is no longer pleasing.
5. Development, from infancy through adulthood, engages us in a succession of circumstances, changes, and challenges for which we are underprepared or unprepared.

We may respond to each of these provocations in a halting way, uncertain whether self-sufficiency and control, or dependence and submission is the better policy. But there is a result as we behave the one way or the other. The danger to us is reduced or increased. Security is enhanced or not. We may stumble for a time, not yet having a fixed style of response, still we try various possibilities until the aggregate of punishments or rewards confirms a particular style within us. A baby always slapped when he cries learns not to cry. He avoids trouble by learning control.

Probably all five of these considerations have a significant effect in determining the style of our individual responses to vulnerability. But one of the five, development, is more important than the others. What is encouraged and rewarded, or discouraged and punished, as a child grows to adulthood? Is it dependence or self-sufficiency? Submission or control? Is he or she caressed and fed, ignored, or abused? Is the child responsive and alert, apathetic, or anxious to the point of recoiling when touched? Does he enjoy taking initiatives, or wait suspiciously as if to defend himself against those who act upon him? There is, to be sure, a strong dose of biological determinism in the answers, as shyness seems to be inherited. It is true, nevertheless, that the biological inheritance is determinable and plastic, so that the whole warp and balance of every child-become-adult is decided by the encouragements and deprivations in each child's developmental history.

The treatment received by individual children is not independent of physical and social circumstances, as a farmer's children see their father regularly and a fisherman's children do not, as discipline among us is rigid or loose, as life is more or less stable, as we are rich or poor. The mix of these factors in a particular family, province, or town sets the tone for child-rearing there, so that children sharing this setting are in general subject to treatment that encourages deference or self-assertion, anxiety or assurance.

Some stages of this developmental history succeed the prior ones as though switched on by maturing affective and cognitive abilities. This implies, as does happen, that faults in development are sometimes the result of an impaired nervous system; we talk if there is no lesion in the speech area. An exaggerated social determinism might imply the same "natural" course of development for social and economic skills, as we grow into adulthood and a job, unless there is no work available. There is, however, more variation among us than these situational and biological determinants would seem to imply. For they are never sufficient in themselves to decide what anyone shall do in a particular situation. There is usually a great similarity in the solutions devised by people of similar background facing similar difficulties. Nevertheless, each of us will have experienced the risks, then the confirmations and deterrents differently, so that each of us is ready to confront any future challenge to his or security in ways that may deviate considerably from these socially determined or biologically "natural" developments. What is more, a common outcome, e.g., two of us doing the same work, may disguise radically different histories and solutions as each of us has contrived a balance unique to himself.

7. Constraining Values and Ideals

Let us suppose that physical circumstances, e.g., living in a city or a village, together with a particular biological inheritance and the tradition of accepted social behavior among us, have fixed the more or less rigid limits within which development occurs. These established forms join with the situational accidents in every life to shape and direct a child's own responses and initiatives. He or she learns a style of life-securing, vulnerability-testing behavior. That style is submissive or controlling, more or less dependent or self-directing in each of the sectors where security-enhancing or risk-taking behavior is required or encouraged. The child acquires, like a fingerprint, his distinguishing mix of *constraining values*. They operate within him to restrict the variety of entertainable plans, as someone who has learned to be submissive cannot imagine making and acting upon choices that would make him responsible and controlling. This sensitivity to constraining values is apparent in our aversion to whatever behaviors exceed the degree of change tolerable within us. When stretched too far in one direction, we compensate on another side, as a sailboat can lean into the wind if its crew will hang from the rail on the other side.

The overall cast or preponderance of constraining values seems rigid in adults, and even, fairly early, in children. But there are some or many sectors in most lives where the constraining values differ from the ones obtaining in other sectors. The balance of constraining values in each of us is, therefore, a distribution of varying determinations in a kind of multidimensional space. Every plan on which we act expresses the relations among several at least of these mutually affecting sectors. One expects and finds a law of mass effect, where deviant sectors are altered in the direction of the mean. Where this happens, we become ever more predictable and fixed in our ways. Yet, every plan enacted may alter the character of constraining values throughout the sectors engaged by it, because we may be thwarted or rewarded in ways unanticipated. This has the effect of altering, consciously or not, the character or balance of constraining values within us. That slow change may also occur if we dare to be vulnerable in one respect, even extending our previous limits, while securing ourselves, perhaps by repetitions of safe, familiar behaviors, in other ones. But then we do gradually change our constraining values, and thereby our responses to the shifting grounds of vulnerability and security.

Constraining values are a limit on the choice of plans. They have their complement in the values directing our behaviors to particular objectives. There are two sorts of directing values: the particular ends of our various desires, as drinking is a value and end to a thirsty man; and ideal values, truth and beauty being two examples. Ends have typically a biological and social origin. Ideals too are socially prescribed, though reflection upon the effects of plans enacted may suggest previously unimagined ends and ideals. Justice is probably a value of that sort.

Plans are formulated, and actions performed so that ends may be achieved, all within the limits set by constraining values. A useful risk is taken, or security is enhanced. Ideal values are more equivocal; they may serve either as objectives or as constraining values. So, truth-telling is constraining because of making us more secure by reducing confusion, though truth is also an ideal to be realized, as knowledge is an end in-itself. Can these ideal values also be rationalized for their instrumental value in securing us from risk? They do have that support, as knowing where we are in the world and being fairly treated there reduce our vulnerability. Still, this instrumental value is surely no more than a fraction of the motive for them, as we may press for the redistribution of wealth or oppor-

186

tunities even while knowing that this will have the effect of making some people more vulnerable.

Here is a place, in the justification and pursuit of ideal values, where we escape the pedestrian but prudent concern for our vulnerability. We are not surprised that constraining values very often prevent us from acting to achieve our ideals. Knowledge may seem to be a useless indulgence or dangerous; justice may be too expensive. Perhaps the good, the true, and the beautiful are so often thought to be subversive because of threatening the current balance of constraining values, hence our developmental experience of safety and risk.

8. Cognitive-affective Balance

The balance of constraining values in the many sectors of our learned behaviors has these two constituents, one affective, the other cognitive. The cognitive-affective balance within us is the product of our development, and the measure of our constraining values.

Our feeling of exhilaration and confidence, anxiety and obsequy vary among the sectors of our learning. Someone who is anxious doing one thing is confident when doing something else. There is, however, a dominant affective tone to one's life, as security or vulnerability and our individual realization of this dominance determines the global affective quality of our lives. Sometimes the feeling is out of character with our facility for securing ourselves. Someone is confident, because of reassuring experiences, e.g., he is often praised, though he is incompetent. More often, the feeling is appropriate to our abilities for making and fulfilling plans, as we are anxious because of feeling and being clumsy. These feelings of generalized well-being or dread are different from such feelings as hunger and pain. Hunger and pain are more directly engaged in the particularities of life. They are, moreover, the immediate provocations to action, as someone touching a stove may not realize it until he feels the pain. Feelings of the other sort are more typically the products of reflection; we come to have them because of having failed or succeeded in accomplishing our aims. This is the reason for the self-appraisal so often apparent within them: We are self-condemning in our anxiety, or self-congratulating in our well-being.

The cognitive-affective balance, may be dominated by feeling. It is, nevertheless, founded in the successive recognitions and appraisals of whatever states we have achieved in our developmental history, as we are properly anxious if security has eluded us. Parents didn't reassure us; circumstances defeated us; we live at risk, and we know it. This is not, of course, the sober reflection that all of us are always at risk, but only the personal realization that we lack the means for stabilizing ourselves when too many things threaten to hurt us. The feeling may of course be exaggerated or inappropriate, as someone frustrated in one sector of his life may forget for a time his success in the other ones. Exaggerated or not, feeling is consequent upon the understanding, accurate or not, of our situation.

That feeling may also be cognitive in this other, more distinctively philosophic way. Our solutions for the alternatives of self-sufficiency and dependence, self-control and submission are the particular and concrete solutions for the pervasive opposition of vulnerability and security. Having achieved resolutions for that tension in many sectors, we might forever ignore it. Life might go on, unreflectively, in circumstances supporting this learned style of accommodation. Yet, submission and control, dependence and self-direction are only the forms within which that other, more elementary opposition expresses itself. The fluid, shifting, seismic quality of this more elementary fact makes it difficult to say that any particular developmental result is more than contingent and fragile. Someone who realizes that this is so – Sartre, for example – might find his life suffused by a global, intellectual anxiety. It might endure alongside, while hardly affecting, his confidence and well-being, or it might reinforce the real fright learned over the course of failed initiatives. The one result might express itself as irony, the other as a deep and withering depression. Most people can do without this further twist of self-reflection. Some others are peculiar for having noticed that every developmental result, however secure, is an island in the dark.

Let us suppose that one's cognitive-affective balance is not cosmically ironic or depressed, or pathological either; i.e., it is not significantly inappropriate to the person's circumstances or experiences. Where does a "healthy" balance and conduct fall between the extremes of self-sufficiency and dependence, self-directedness and submission? There is no single answer, first, because there is a wide range of affectively tolerable balances; second, because there is considerable latitude in the variety of socially acceptable behaviors; third, because physical reality rewards by securing us for a variety of behaviors. Most of us find a sustainable accommodation, meaning one that allows expression for our ideals, desires, and normal requirements while acknowledging both the physical reality, and our obligations to other people, laws and customs.

Accommodate and *adapt* are not words that should have turned a Nietzsche to loathing. Even a Picasso or Michelangelo is adaptive: Who knew better than either of them about the physical limits of metal, plaster, paint, and canvas? Adaptation implies our accommodation to the real shape and resistances of things, together with the initiatives directing us as we find our own particular way of relating to them. A healthy resolution to the problem of securing ourselves in the midst of vulnerability requires, therefore, a combination of self-sufficiency and submission. Both sides are apparent when the plans we formulate are used in conjunction with maps representing the terrain where the plans are to be enacted. We have to know where we are, while constrained by the fact of being there, as we do the thing desired. Where social rules have been learned, and our maps are formulated, tested, and revised, we are healthy (in this restricted sense) if we act with others or alone to create a stable, life-enhancing place for them and ourselves.

9. Selfhood

Selfhood has its origin in behaviors that are directive, adaptive, and revised in light of our interests and the realities about us. It presupposes these realities, as we learn to be selves in a community of other, already established selves. Those other people are never sufficient, however, for creating a self distinct from themselves. Each of us is self-crystallizing. Selfhood comes in the midst of other selves, as a child achieves it in the midst of his or her family; but always selfhood is a distinct achievement, one that is no way reducible to their effect. Each of us has a force of his or her own. Lacking the instincts that might secure us in the world, and without the barnacle's good luck in having currents to bring the required things our way, we have to move about for the information that can be read to disclose our place in the world, for the nourishment and other things which sustain us, and for the company of other people. Selfhood emerges in the act of making, acting upon, and revising hypotheses about these vital concerns. Selfhood is, therefore, the achievement of a body which thinks abductively as it creates a network of securing habits and relations for itself all the while resolving the opposed requirements of submission and control, dependence and self-sufficiency. Selfhood is the consequence of development, and a condition for the intelligent control directing our further development. This is the learned gyroscope within us, the condition for our sustainable accommodation to, and equilibrium within, the world.

We move in the way of beginners on skates. Development prescribes the direction in which to circle the rink, but all of us move as much laterally as we do straight ahead. We try our own solutions to successive obstacles, finding a balance that is appropriate to our situations, one that feels tolerable to us. Some of us slip a lot at the beginning but rarely fall; others fall often. There are standards of achievement, but no fixed "natural" ideal. There are many variations of facility and style. Those who do not fall, and those who get up to skate again learn to enjoy skating. They go faster; they compete with, and like the company of those who are like them. The others go slower, some moving as slowly as they need do to stay on their feet. Some who fall stay down, feeling wet and cold but not wanting to risk getting up to fall again. How shall we stand on ice, stiff-legged, or knees bent? How close should our feet be to one another? Should we look at our feet, or the ice ahead? Every voluntary movement is directed by a tentative estimate of what might be done most effectively. We watch the better skaters for clues. How do they do it so well, we want to know? We try controlling our own feet to mimic them. With abduction as our method, selfhood is the learned power for directing its applications.

9A. The Factors Constitutive of Selfhood

Seven of the factors responsible for selfhood are apparent or implied in this example.

9Ai. Testing the world by acting on plans

Wants and needs require that we test the world by acting on our plans. If the first plans are based on learned associations, as between crying and being fed, then effective behavior begins as we do the one thing to get the other. This facility for making and acting upon plans is the engine propelling us.

9Aii. Monitoring the consequences of action

We appraise the effects of our own behaviors. This is critical, for any plan may be wildly inappropriate, needing replacement or revision if we are to achieve the desired result. Monitoring the consequences of action supplies the information required before we can safely repeat the behavior or alter it.

9Aiii. Constraining values

Variations in the sense of our vulnerability, e.g., being more or less hungry and uncomfortable, reinforces or reduces the force of whatever constraining values we have already acquired along the axes of submission and control, self-sufficiency and dependence. The values are plastic and determinable early in our lives, when innate inclination or chance first prompts us to locate ourselves at some particular place along these axes. Later, when initiatives succeed or not, certain expectations and defenses have been established. These are the learned values limiting future initiatives.

9Aiv. *Physical constitution*

There is each person's physical nature. A weak baby, born prematurely, may become a vital child; our real strengths are determinable and disguised at birth. But there are real differences of strength, curiosity, reactivity, and affectivity among infants. There are also differences in mental ability and physical beauty. These differences have a significant effect on both our abilities for initiating action and other people's responses to us, as handsome babies may get more attention. These differences have a vast effect later on, as when plans are more or less well made, and other people are more or less receptive to us.

9Av. *Socially determined ideas of self*

There are ideas of selfhood learned from the society in which we are born and grow. The paradigms are enforced as we coo at little girls or treat boys more roughly. Girls and boys quickly learn the lesson so that the cognitive-affective balance within each child likely falls into one or the other of these two gender-correlated styles of organization. There are many of these socially determined roles to be learned, roles for work, citizenship, dress, even the degree to which introspection, intellect, and activity are encouraged. Are we to be married or single, socially mobile or loyal to the ways of family, class, or neighborhood? All the ways of recognizing and appraising ourselves are powerfully shaped by these learned expectations.

What makes us good, Socrates asks? The laws, Meletus answers.[1] Laws, including all the practices of a culture, make us uniform and predictable. They give us identity, making us recognizable to other people and ourselves. Conformity to them establishes our membership in a community, thereby promoting our interest in all the activities pursued by community members for their mutual advantage. These behaviors enhance our security, as when cooperation under laws makes us interdependent and mutually securing. It is most important, therefore, that we learn to formulate our plans in ways that cohere with these mutually securing laws and practices. This does raise a problem that is never more than crudely solved: how to be socialized and autonomous, how to share in group identity while having an identity of one's own. We do not want an accommodation reduced to submission, though the requirements of security might seem to imply a diminished autonomy.

9Avi. *A unique developmental history*

Physical and social circumstances are the context for individual developmental histories. Having a particular physical character while living in particular physical and social circumstances determines much of what we are, but not all of it, because we shall have taken myriad initiatives of our own, and because the deterrence or reinforcement resulting from them will have produced both our constraining values and our cognitive-affective balance. This, more substantially, is who we are.

9Avii. Self-image

There is, finally, self-image: that representation of one's body, values, and situation which is acquired as we monitor our own behavior and regard its effects on other people and things. Self-image is not altogether or even significantly an image. Part of it is a learned facility for recognizing ourselves, as someone may be surprised by the face he sees in the mirror after shaving a long-worn beard. There may be, in addition, some visual-like images that one can summon of oneself. These images may be very important to us, as we may be more or less secure because of having an idea of ourselves as too fat or too thin. Yet, even these "ideas" may not be images. Self-image is more fundamentally a set of hypotheses about one's body, character, and place in the world. These are hypotheses about the kinds of things one can do, based partly on memories of things one has done. They include extrapolations to behaviors that we would have ourselves do, so that self-image expresses a determination to behave in the future in ways that satisfy a standard we have fixed for ourselves. Self-image becomes, thereby, an additional constraining value, as *brutta figura* signifies all the things that would embarrass us. This concern for appearances does not imply that everyone is determined only to do well. People having a favorable self-image have the evidence of their own past competence to reassure them as they begin some new initiative. Someone having an unflattering self-image may do as badly as he expects to do. Why is the self-image good or bad? Because we find ourselves capable or not of securing ourselves over the spectrum of activities that are urgent or significant for us. Self-image is therefore three things: the product of our developmental history, a decisive variable for determining future behavior, and the expression of our self-appraisal.

9Aviii. Summary

Stepping back from these several points to consider them at once, we see that the seven factors are interdependent. Even circumstances and biology are not altogether independent of what we become, as each of us may turn upon and alter them. Selfhood is this idiosyncratic but multifaced power for securing oneself. As sharks drown if they stop swimming, so do we perish if we do not acquire the set of learned habits for making the plans which engage us effectively within the world. Selfhood is the shape and power for directing that accommodation to the world about us.

9B. Some Consequences

This notion of selfhood has several implications. Five of them are worth remarking here, namely, the consequences for will, self-regulation, interdependence, morality, and two notions of the ego.

9Bi. Will

There might sometimes be reason for speaking of particular acts of will, as one decides to raise a hand. There is also will as each person's distinguishing and more or less vigorous way of establishing control, of self and other things, in problematic circumstances. Will of this sort is the more or less steady wind energizing us as we engage ourselves in the world. Nothing mysterious is implied by this energy; this is the robust demeanor of an animal that is more or less effective and self-convinced as it responds to the threats and opportunities about it. The will that Schopenhauer and Nietzsche described may be no more than this. Even William James's "Will to Believe" may be a learned response to vulnerability, as a firm belief, with or without confirming evidence, is a plan for coping in a world that otherwise scares us.

Will, as just described, is the expression of two things: There is our native mobility and impulse to action, and the cognitive-affective balance within us as it expresses the record of our past successes and failures. The latter consideration is decisive, for people of little will are usually not less physically vital than those having a lot of it. The difference is more often the innervating or enervating record of achieving well-being through action. A different notion, i.e., that of will as initiative, is also relevant now: Do we have the will to try something new? Here too, the decisive factor is the cognitive-affective balance: Do we try new things out of the conviction, founded in past experience and the security expressed in our current balance, that we can do them successfully? People having that conviction have "will." The rest of us have less of it.

9Bii. Self-regulation

Self-regulation is apparent from infancy, when our plans are enacted and revised, because of failing to achieve the result desired. We also turn upon ourselves, appraising and revising the cognitive-affective balance within us. This sometimes happens in the midst of using a plan, and certainly it happens afterwards, as we reflect upon the information or values that encouraged us to act as we did. The information is relatively easy to change;

the values are more recalcitrant because of having been learned as part of our developmental history, and because they have seemed to us the most effective values for defending us from vulnerability.

It is hard to unlearn the values that save us from failure, or the ones that seem to have made us effective, though these values are changed, without self-regulation, if once effective behaviors are frustrated, or if initiatives once thwarted are tried successfully again. Self-regulation asserts itself as we change our values because of having thought about them while feeling some of the anxiety or elation they provoke. Psychotherapies enabling us to relive both the feelings caused by vulnerability and the experiences that fixed our constraining values may help us to alter the values. Still, these therapies are no substitute for the developmental histories that would have made us effective at making and using plans in all the sectors vital to our particular lives. They only help us to liberate ourselves from an overwhelming sense of vulnerability or grandiosity, and from the ineffective and ossified values that make us feel and act these ways.

9Biii. Interdependence

Interdependence is crucial to everyone when each of us needs the help of others. This way of making the point is misleading, however, because of making it seem that interdependence is only a pragmatic choice. Interdependence is much more than that when our developmental history is shaped by the community's notion of an acceptable self, and when it happens, still more fundamentally, that the first interpretable evidence of who we are and of who we are to be is supplied by the adults to whom we bond. We are reminded of the baby's reliance on its mother, and of her pleasure in him or her. All our first initiatives, and the first, provisional fixing of our constraining values depends upon the baby's feelings about this reciprocity, and his interpretation of it. Interdependence, as the incorporation of one's idea of the people to whom one is bonded and one's interpretations of what they think of oneself, is crucial to selfhood. That is the respect in which there is no selfhood, or only a crippled self, in the absence of interdependence.

Interdependence become more utilitarian and more abstract as we become adults; as passengers don't bond with subway motormen. We are not more closely connected to the people driving in front of or behind us on the road, observing the traffic laws as we go. These are occasions for extending the equilibrium within our selves to our relations with other people. Having become lawmakers for ourselves, by regularizing our own behaviors in ways that enhance our security, we are expected to observe, and even to make, the rules and laws that will secure other people. Our conscious interest may be only a concern for our own safety, as traffic laws are important because of making us secure. Yet selfhood is enlarged as we come to have a stake in the well-being of others. We become guarantors of one another's well-being, as the assurance of mutual security becomes a condition for each one's own well-being. Interdependence becomes ineluctably moral.

9Biv. Morality

Morality has this double focus: concern for others, and concern for oneself.

Regard for one's own well-being is something that almost no one need be taught. We seek it by trial and error, always learning as much from failure as from success about its resonances and details. We learn that the tension between security and vulnerability is vital to our well-being, so that we monitor the balance within ourselves to discover where we are pressed too hard. Each of us then acts, or tries to act, in ways that repair the damage. Still, the instinctively learned moral imperative—seek your own well-being—is not easy to satisfy. We are too often confounded by mutually exclusive alternatives, interdependence or autonomy, by frustration when plans fail, and by depression and fear. We begin to suspect that well-being is much like health: a normative condition that is always elusive though it may be close at hand.

Where is the engine and rudder for this end-in-itself? It lies within each one's cognitive-affective balance. We secure well-being by way of the plans we make and execute, then by appraising what was done and our reasons for believing that we were right to do it. These are the ample resources of selfhood. Selfhood is both the condition for well-being, and its beneficiary. For well-being is ideally a sustainable condition, though it is not sustainable if we do not have the well-developed facility for acting in ways appropriate to the physical world, to our social circumstances, and to ourselves.

What is a morally appropriate accommodation? That may vary with time and circumstances, though always it has two parameters. First is the requirement that behavior should secure us even if we seem to test the limits of our vulnerability, as divers carry oxygen. Second is concern for those other people to whom we are reciprocally related. This consideration is the other focus for morality.

Morality of this other sort may seem to be founded in laws only, but it is not. This is an affectively engaged morality, not merely a prudent or altruistic, but remote and formal one. The vulnerability and security of others have come to be experienced as harm or safety in oneself. This engaged morality recalls us to the earliest love for a responsive and caring parent.

195

Those recognitions are incorporated into mature selfhood. They may be enacted again in our relations to spouses, children, other family members and friends. This is harder to do with nations or cities or the people with whom one shares a subway car. Morality in those contexts is not so much an extension of selfhood to caring for others as one cares for oneself, as it is the skeptical but prudent hope that the risk of personal damage is minimized if equitable laws are observed or enforced. This too expresses the power for making plans that reduce our vulnerability, and the interdependence that makes us reliant on each other's powers for self-regulation. It may become more than this: We do sometimes recover the sense of caring for strangers, for reasons stronger than prudence or law.

9Bv. Descartes and Freud

Two comparisons may help to situate the notion of selfhood proposed here.

This idea of selfhood and self-regulation borrows nothing from Descartes' self-reflecting, thinking subject. Neither consciousness nor self-consciousness is invoked to explain either the use of plans for enhancing security, or the revisions introduced as we monitor our effects on other people and things. There is nothing in this to suggest that we are not both conscious and self-conscious; we are surely both of those. These are, however, background conditions. Selfhood is not described by reference to either of them. We are not hostage, therefore, to the Cartesian idea of self-encircling, self-sustaining self-consciousness. We have no motive for confusing the Cartesian account of mind with a selfhood founded in its developmental history, and constituted at any current moment by its cognitive-affective balance. This balance is a mix of feelings, habits, information, a facility for making plans, a power for self-appraisal, and one's constraining values and aims. It is not the crucible or cockpit of inspecting mind.

My notion of selfhood also differs from one familiar reading of Freud. His notions of consciousness and the unconscious are reminiscent of Leibniz's distinction between perception and apperception in a monad.[2] Perception may be the equivalent of the Freudian unconscious or pre-conscious, where *petites perceptions* have an intensity too low for our awareness of them. But then sometimes we are aware, having consciousness or apperception of them.

Bringing the material of perception to apperception becomes the task for psychoanalysis. Yet all of the content apperceived is only a fragment of the many things vital to the adequacy of any current cognitive-affective balance. There are, for example, the all-important cognitive questions: Do we accurately represent the world, do we accurately interpret the world's responses to us; are we capable of securing ourselves there? A psychoanalysis devoted only to recalling the experiences of one's developmental history falsely implies that selfhood might be achieved in the course of hermetic meditation. This guarantees that all of the issues bearing upon reality and our reality-testing will have been ignored. For the monad cannot make itself psychically or otherwise self-sufficient. Selfhood is mutilated if it is not situated within the world whose character partly explains its development while provoking its initiatives. The selfhood achieved in the course of interpreting its own past is too much like the spider that ascends, by consuming, the filament it has spun. That vast preoccupation could never, by itself, make us competent in the way of an agent having to make its place in the world. The critical point is familiar; only the comparative use of it is relevant here.

10. The Faculties Required for Making and Testing Hypotheses

What are the faculties that mind must have, and what activities must it perform in order that equilibrium and selfhood be achieved? Given a perceiving, active body, what things must mind or brain do? This question is sure to defeat us, once we have admitted that the words of philosophical psychology are no more than placeholders for an empirically tested, cognitive psychology. We can only suggest, in the meantime, the functions those words signify. The actual structure and behaviors are only a surmise; the organizing idea is *imagination*.

10A. A Two-tiered Map

We need recall what mind is to do. Perceiving the things about us and interpreting our situation among them, we imagine what things we might do to achieve some desired result. Making and using hypotheses requires that we perform three functions: Thoughts or words are construed or made construable by locating them within associative networks; these signs are organized as hypotheses; the hypotheses are tested.

This result is contentious because we feel ourselves threatened by skepticism wherever our knowledge claims are mediated by signs. Who can be sure that things are as our signs represent them? Intuitionism requires no additional justification as it rejects the hypothetical method. Intuitionists want certainty, not speculative imagination. They gladly collapse the distinction between signs and their objects, saying that mind is directly confronted by the things themselves. Platonism and phenomenalism, both of them claiming that mind has unmediated prehension of its objects, express this intuitionist demand. There are, however, all those occasions when the

197

vehicles of thought are words, rather than the things they signify. How shall we avert skepticism, while acknowledging that words mediate between mind and the things unknown?

One alluring proposal acknowledges that words mediate between thought and its objects while affirming that words or sentences are like the things they represent. There is, for example, Wittgenstein's picture theory.[3] Words can represent and communicate, Wittgenstein said, only if we regard them as hieroglyphics, each sentence showing on its face the character of the matter represented. This view is attractive because of satisfying the intuitionist demand that the character of things be available for direct inspection, as happens if a sentence shows its form, while having the same form as the state of affairs it represents. This complex proposal mitigates the intuitionist terror that we may be cut off from the world by representations obscuring the things represented because of being unlike them.

The hypothetical method renounces Wittgenstein's hope, and this intuitionist fear. Hypotheses, it concedes, are not transparent windows onto the world. These are conventional rather than natural signs, so that sentences are usually unlike their objects in all the respects significant for whatever is affirmed of these things. There are, however, prodecures for formulating and testing hypotheses. It is these procedures, not the iconic relation of signs and referents, which establish that particular signs are relevant to, and true of the matters they represent. Still, we acknowledge that all the burden for producing and testing adequate representations falls upon our minds. Picture-like sentences are the exception, not the rule. Even they would have to be formulated and tested.

How shall we describe these minds, and their activities? These are, I suppose, mature minds, minds not necessarily adult but past the learning of language, and able to speculate beyond perception to the causes of its sensible differences. Prelinguistic children have achieved and developed their equilibrium, with their behaviors coordinated, and a self established. These children sometimes formulate hypotheses that coordinate diverse perceivings by interpreting them as effects of the same cause. They also make and execute plans. There is, however, a vast deepening of conceptual power when language is learned. This new power is a consequence of the grammatical and inferential rules that facilitate the forming and transforming of our thoughts. There is also the effect of being able to use words that signify the differences perceived, and their causes. This effect is apparent when children are better able to anticipate some of the myriad perceptual differences and constancies that were otherwise ignored, as a child who says "cup" each time when seeing a cup from differing angles is better able to see and use cups.

Children, like the rest of us, demonstrate their familiarity with the world in any of three ways: They may act effectively in the way prescribed by a plan, often a plan articulated in words, and used as a self-directive; they may use words to describe or explain their diverse perceivings; they may respond appropriately to the descriptions or commands, promises, or entreaties made by others. All of these behaviors are evidence that children, or adults, have made and confirmed one or many hypotheses about the world. Every additional hypothesis extends this person's map of the world. Mind, the hypothesizer, makes and uses this map as it establishes the self-securing equilibrium described previously in this chapter.

Each of us formulates a map having two tiers, one for the world of possibles, the other for the actual world. The first is a tier of meanings; the other is a tier of truths. Meanings are the objects intended by our thoughts and words. These objects, the senses of our worlds, are the more or less complex differences and relations existing eternally as possibilities. The truths are hypotheses. They signify those possibilities that do obtain. Accordingly, their objects are the actual states of affairs comprising our world.

Together, these tiers are the complex representations mediating our perceptual, conceptual, and behavioral interactions with the world about us. They are used whenever we think or act; first, as we project some array of signs representing the possibilities affirmed as actual, then, as we confirm that these hypotheses are true or not. Each of the tiers is extended and conserved as we learn of the world while situating ourselves within it, but each tier is also modifiable, and each one is coupled to the other.

This coupling is important in several ways. Three are conspicuous: (1) It is possibilities of the first tier that are affirmed by hypotheses of the second tier; (2) We are provoked to extend the tier of meanings in order that we may formulate more ample and accurate hypotheses about matters of fact; (3) It is the amplification of confirmed hypotheses that revises and extends the tier of meanings. All three considerations are apparent as we read any last generation of science fiction. Some of its claims are matters of fact, meaning that they express hypotheses confirmed. Other parts are embellishments of the actual with hypotheses about the merely possible. The ground for both kinds of hypotheses was laid when meanings were elaborated so that hypotheses regarding these possibilities could be formulated. Perhaps mind was provoked by some of its confirmed hypotheses to extend the network of representations in which they were embedded. Now, mind is provoked again by this patchwork of fact and fancy. Can some of the more bizarre hypotheses be confirmed? Do they suggest some places where the tier of possibilities might be extended to the point where confirmable hypotheses might be formulated? These visionary hypotheses express differences or relationships that are explicit already in the tier of possibilities, but here, as these extrapolations are made plausible by their association with confirmed hypotheses, we articulate more of the possibilities that were only implicit.

Questions about the organization of these tiers are harder to answer. The words in dictionaries and the entries in encyclopedias are organized alphabetically, but nothing as simple is appropriate to a map that is probably organized in clusters appropriate to particular interests and exigencies in the life of the person using it. This implies that all of the possibilities relevant to cooking will be represented in one cluster for a chef, while they are dispersed among diverse clusters in someone not having this special interest. There is, presumably, mutual access among the clusters, but not that focus and integration peculiar to single clusters.

The organization of hypotheses confirmed is equally clusterlike, where the internal logic of a cluster may defy more general formulation, rather as a scrap-book has a "logic" of its own. There are also some other, more general and detached principles of integration. Where the principle for organizing a scrapbook is topic-particular, there are, at the other extreme, the topic-neutral integrations of formalized, deductive systems or temporal orders. In between are those sets of hypotheses having both topic-particular and (relatively) topic-neutral principles as the basis for their organization, as different domains of physics have their signature field equations while also having the laws of motion as their common organizing principles.

We often strive to organize a set of hypotheses in a way that satisfies some independently formulable principle. The cluster of hypotheses called "physics" shows that proclivity in two ways: First, there are most general law sentences used as rules for organizing all of the other hypotheses; second, the science is organized deductively. More often, the organization of a cluster is a montage, with no independently formulable integrating principle. Most of the confirmed beliefs about our individual circumstances are a cluster of this latter sort. Their principle of integration is topic-particular and not differentiable from the montage they organize.

I speculate that the tier of meanings and the tier of truths are differentiated from the first days of life. Suppose that we are born with some schemas or heuristics for thinking about the world, but without specific innate ideas. Our first representations of the differences and relations possible in any world will be the ones produced in us as we perceive some of the instantiated possibilities comprising our world. Here is the first and only place where the tiers are co-extensive, i.e., where the tier of signs for possibles does not extend beyond the one of confirmed hypotheses about actuals. These tiers quickly deviate from one another as percepts are analyzed on the way to creating signs for possibilities not perceived. These are the analyses invoking mind's powers for abstraction, variation, combination, and comparison. We should expect the tier of meanings to be elaborated as peception provokes these analyses. The tier of signs for possibles is then quickly extended so that it reaches in many qualitative dimensions beyond the ones of hypotheses confirmed.

10B. Imagination

All of this is imagination as it formulates and embellishes the two tiers of our world-map. This is the activity generating the signs which specify possibilities, as we abstract from perceptual information before varying, combining, and contrasting these representations. We assume that imagination is subject to rules for making these extrapolations, and then to other rules for constructing, amplifying, and testing hypotheses; but then we quickly run out of things to say of it. One thing we must say is that imagining a hypothesis or plan is not the same as having images of the things they signify. Someone planning a trip to Venice might always have "before" him or her the look and feel of the Rialto Bridge; but that image is only an incitement to going there, not anything pertinent to the plan for arriving. It is not even required that the images we do have should be relevant in any way to our plans, as the plumber fixing a leak thinks of other things he would rather be doing.

What could imagination be, if not this power for visual or other mock-perceptual fantasies? All it needs to be is the act or power for combining and construing signs to the point of supplying well-formed hypotheses representing possible states of affairs. This is, at bottom, the power for disciplined association. But association is itself mysterious, for how does it happen that association produces the detailed and regimented plans directing behavior, and the hypotheses tested by experiments?

There appear to be, among others, these seven conditions for that result: (1) There is a stock of details and connections remembered; (2) Topic-particular coherence rules restrict association to signs relevant to the matter at issue; (3) Constraining values and ends extinguish associations inconsistent with themselves, perhaps by inhibiting them; (4) Topic-neutral coherence rules are indifferent to particularities of content, though they supply the inferential and syntactic forms for organizing it; (5) The probably hierarchical organization of mind disciplines the topic-particular associations performed at one order by subjecting them to the values and topic-neutral rules of some different order or orders; (6) Association-generated signs are matched against actual percepts, as we determine that the testable implications of a hypothesis are satisfied or not; (7) A still more refined topic-particular association rule is used to alter a hypothesis that has failed by some specificable degree to predict the differences actually perceived.

These seven considerations ignore the need for associating a hypothesis formulated in the "language of thought"[4] into one that is expressed in some ordinary or improved language. They also ignore a host of details pertinent, for example, to measuring the fit or discrepancy between sensory data and the sign signifying an anticipated sensory effect. These details would be supplied by a comprehensive account of the activities occurring as hypotheses are generated and tested. But it is a mistake, promoted by the idea of mind as a theatre where every mental act appears before the one authoritative spectator, if we suppose that philosophy alone might provide this account. Very little of mind shows itself for conscious discrimination. Specification of all the rest depends on hypotheses that cognitive psychologists, physiologists and engineers only begin to formulate accurately. There is no hope, therefore, of philosophy's proving its autonomy by supplying all the evidence significant for a thorough account of its own speculative activity.

11. What Metaphysics Contributes to Our Well-being

When making and testing hypotheses is the method appropriate for all our thinking about the world, the psychological and existential presuppositions for that method must be important to everyone who uses it. This is more plainly true of practice and science as we use them, sometimes clumsily, to secure ourselves in the world. Their utility, even as it mostly outweighs their danger, is obvious. The utility in metaphysics is more obscure. What does it contribute to human well-being? The answer I suggest is that metaphysics helps to locate us within the world, as knowing where we are reduces our experience of vulnerability in being here.

As infants, we are submissive and dependent, but also ignorant of the world's intrinsic limits. Those are boundaries we cannot violate at all, or violate without being harmed. This ignorance helps propel us when the enthusiasm for newly discovered strengths and freedoms blinds us to the limits. We prefer believing that the world has no form in itself, that it may be shaped and reformed to our design. Metaphysics, grounded in the hard discoveries of practice and science, scales down that euphoria by extending our information about the fixed structure of things. We learn more of our place in nature, its categorial form, and conditions. These testable, metaphysical hypotheses are an accommodation to reality. The soaring kit of philosophical imagination is restrained by the taut lines of actual fact. Though accommodation is not submission: We say as much about contingency and the susceptibility of things to our control as we do of the world's unalterable form. Metaphysics, through all of this, is rational sobriety. It promises the open-eyed realism that tells us, as practice and science also tell us, what it is and is not possible to do and be. That accommodation can only help us if we are Stoic where no difference can be made, and pragmatic where there are ways of controlling the situation and ourselves.

Metaphysics, this implies, is important information. Don't wait, says the physicalism I favor, for God's word about the moral law: We shall need to invent the laws best serving individuals and our general interest. Is there something Uncle Harry forgot to tell us before expiring? Don't waste money on the seance where he might return. Nor should we believe that causal law sentences represent items accidentally but constantly conjoined so that actions cannot be planned and carried through without the fear that the conjuncts will come unstuck. In these and numerous other respects, metaphysical claims specify the boundary conditions and constituents for the circumstances where actions are planned and performed. Ignore the limits, and you guarantee that your plans will be confounded. What exactly are the limits? They are, and will likely remain, controversial.

One view has it that metaphysics starts in wonder. More likely it beings with uncertainty, as people hovering between security and vulnerability want a more comprehensive understanding of the world in which they act and live. Metaphysics helps to resolve that uncertainty, making our behavior more appropriate and intelligent, hence more effective. Where the many parts of a metaphysical theory defy easy translation into directives for action, the whole theory should nevertheless appease the insecurity of not knowing where we stand. It is easier then to accept the fact that we who know so much of the world are important only to one another. We appease ourselves, finding security in the confirmation of our own finitude, the comfort-in-conceit of our security, the vulnerability pressing us all around.

If sobriety about the world and our place there is an accommodation to reality, what shall we say of those metaphysical theories for which accommodation is delusory? Why must accommodation imply that we come to terms with a world that is, mostly, beyond our power to shape it? Why not mount one of those epistemological creation stories where the differences and relations prescribed by the theory are projected onto sensory data, thereby creating a world as congenial as we care to make it? The answer is that the independence of most states of affairs from thought and language does not originate as the discovery or decision of metaphysical theory. This is the inference of everyone frustrated when acting on a plan, or damaged after tripping in the dark. The world does not work as we supposed, or it does work as we expected but not as we can manage, or we had no idea the furniture had been moved. Realist metaphysics comes after the time when reality and our need for accommodating to it are already acknowledged. Its theories confirm and complete an understanding that does not wait for metaphysics to direct it.

Metaphysics of this kind is the Stoic embellishment of selfhood, the final, self-reflected measure of our power as set against the rigid structures of the world in which we need act. The obligation to think metaphysically is, this implies, the instrumental one of self-recognition. This is the Socratic "Know thyself" applied in the most comprehensive way, by locating ourselves in thought as we are already located in being.

12. Conclusion

The claims of this chapter may be summarized as follows. Mind is the equilibriating activity of body as it finds its way in nature, securing while liberating itself. Body moves left or right, satisfying an organic need on one side, acquiring information or defending an interest on the other. Body is engaged on all sides, and in many domains. Equilibrium is our footing in the moving tide. This is the sustained and singular way that each of us integrates the demands and projects of his or her life, all the while looking backward and forward at the same time. Equilibrium is, therefore, never disinterested or abstract. This is the always particular, always concrete solution to conflicting interests. These conflicts sometimes exhaust or force us into a one-track, snail-like routine. More often, those who have learned to cope because of a lucky developmental history and a mostly supportive world do manage their lives. Then, equilibrium is the alternately submissive and controlling organization of our behaviors and aims. This is our cognitive-affective balance, our persisting, enmattered, and stabilizing form.

204

7

A Forced Choice

Metaphysics is often disparaged for having claimed too many different things about the world, without being able to prove any of them. One solution calls for turning our backs on all of it. My suggestion is different: Look for the deeper affinities that organize and explain the diversity of metaphysical views. This book, with *Intuition and Ideality*, is an extended exposition of one organizing difference.

Some philosophers—I have called them *intuitionists*—suppose that nothing is real if it cannot be set before our inspecting minds, though intuitionists differ among themselves about the conditions for a thing's presentation to the mind. Is it merely given to us in some way unexplained; or does mind create the things thereby set before it? This difference sets Plato and Hume on the one side, and Kant with his twentieth-century, linguistic successors on the other. Still, their difference, however profound, is a distinction within the circle of intuitionist accord. Their common antagonist is the hypothetical method. It supposes that the existence and character of things are independent of our thinking and talking about them. When these two methods are distinguished, with their ontological and psychological presuppositions exposed, we discern one aspect of the deeper order within the apparent morass of philosophic ideas. Only a few thinkers are consistently rigorous in using the hypothetical method. Some thinkers use both methods, even within the same paragraph or sentence, but most philosophers are resolutely intuitionists. Reality, for them, does not extend beyond the range of inspecting mind. They have only to ask about the character of these phenomena, e.g., are they ideas or impressions; and about their source, i.e., are they given to mind or created within it.

There is nothing within this intuitionist view to help either a drowning man or the scientist speculating about strong nuclear forces, a cure for AIDS, or the warp of space. There is nothing in it for anyone who shivers when all of reality is made to collapse into the glow of self-encircling, self-conscious mind. Hypothetical method saves us from this hermetic result, but it trades certainty regarding matters set before our minds for mediated, fallible claims about the things alleged to be represented. We are made to choose, for there is no way of having both methods at once.

1. Criteria for Deciding Between Intuition and Hypothesis

How shall we decide between these methods? What should our criteria be? I propose eight distinguishing factors, all of them characterized in ways that are favorable to hypothetical method.

1A. The Role of the Given versus Observation

Compare the role of observation within the hypothetical method to the role of the given within intuitionism. Observation produces perceptual data. The same data are claimed for the intuitionist given, though it may also include such things as Forms, conceptual systems, or the mind's self-perception. The overlap between these two is real. Still, the two methods are opposed in their ways of evaluating data even when they consider the same phenomena.

Intuitionism defers to the given as the overwhelming presence of the only reality we can know. All the differentiations and relations credited to reality are exhibited there, e.g., within sensory data, or the rules and ideas used for thinking them. Hypothesis may distract us by formulating theories which seem to refer beyond our minds and the experiences qualifying them, but these theories can only be an abstracted reformulation of the differences and relations sanctioned by our direct experience of sensory data, or the conceptualizations used for thinking them. The only purpose these hypotheses might have is the one of organizing the data, perhaps under the heading of postulated entities or structures. Those alleged entities, "atom" for example, are only shorthand descriptions for the data inspected. We err if we suppose that terms signifying the "things" postulated do actually refer to extratheoretic matters of fact. Questions about them are, as Carnap says, "external" and meaningless.[1]

Hypothesis reverses this emphasis. We are always somewhat at loss in

206

the world. Its charater is never exposed to us in an incontrovertible and final way. Perception does intimate many things about the world. Hypotheses regarding it are often confirmed. Still, understanding is teased rather than illumined by the empirical evidence available to us. There are always further questions about the realities perceived, questions unresolved by the sensory data currently available to us. That result is not surprising, when these percepts are not the things perceived, but only the natural signs of their causes. We read them as we would a text, searching for the motives and meanings of its author. Sensory data are only the provocative evidence of the world's character. We expect to subsume them under the hypotheses explaining them. These differences "given" are, therefore, the beginning of inquiry, not the end of it.

This difference between the two methods shows itself in several consequential ways.

One is a question about the order of our thinking. Which comes first, theory or observation? Intuitionism never doubts that all the differences and relations constitutive of reality are present within the given. This may be a given set before a passive mind or a given created within an active one; that difference is incidental, where confronting and inspecting the given is the overriding demand. There is little or no place in this scheme for "theory" unless we understand it as either the conceptualization used for schematizing the data now set before us (thereby creating a differentiated and organized sensory given), or as the set of descriptions formulated by mind as this given is inspected.

Plato and Descartes speak on the side of schematization: Their Forms and ideas are allegedly set before our minds before being used to differentiate and organize the more obscure sensory data. Forms and ideas are separable from one another, so that we might be said to use them one at a time. Neo-Kantians suppose, to the contrary, that sensory data are schematized by the systematically related concepts or terms of a conceptual framework. Some of them, Carnap, for example, describe the articulations and organization of their systems in advance of using them, thereby assuming that these frameworks are inspectable data in their own right. Other neo-Kantians suppose that the uses of a conceptualization are unselfconscious, e.g., trancendental or socially determined. They insist that we can only identify the framework used by searching for the evidence of it in a schematized given, e.g., language, history, social practices, or individual styles of behavior. Husserl and Austin are intuitionists of the other sort. They speak on the side of theories used only as descriptions, but they, like intuitionists of every sort, report their discoveries of ideas or linguistic uses and rules, after inspecting the given.

This sample of Intuitionist beliefs represents the bias common to all of them: Intuitionism affirms that our inspection of the given (whether presented to a passive mind or created by an active one) is first in the order of knowledge. "Theory" is either an ideational content inspected or the description of things inspected. Theory must never exceed the matters given on the way to signifying their unobserved and unobservable conditions.

Hypothetical method has a different bias, as it argues abductively from sensory data to their alleged conditions. Hypotheses are the source of predictions about other, previously unsuspected observations, so that theory now precedes observation as we search for perceptual evidence that would satisfy a hypothesis. Theory, not the things inspected, is the fulcrum for understanding.

Where do we search for phenomena, within our minds or beyond them? Here is a second consequence of this opposition.

Intuitionists sometimes agree that the perceptual given is deficient, e.g., it lacks clarity or detail They correct this deficiency by instructing us in techniques for focusing the mind's eye, or by introducing those ideas or rules that enhance the data. The difficulty is always to be solved by some act or refinement in us, never by manipulating the things existing apart from us but perceived. Descartes, for example, never doubted that his clear and distinct ideas did have these extra-mental referents, but only because of God's guarantee, not because ideas are testable hypotheses representing matters independent of mind for their existence and character. Descartes, once deprived of God's guarantee, is like the photographer who can only improve the fuzzy image in his view-finder by adjusting the lens, never by turning on a light or moving the subject.

Hypothetical method does the very thing these intuitionists would bar: It exceeds the perceptual given in three ways. *First,* hypotheses may have universal application, though the sensory data confirming them are particular and local. Descartes and Kant might seem to agree about this, since every idea or rule they would have us apply to particulars is said to apply universally. The parallel is, however, superficial. They restrict the domain of a universal's application to the arena of the inspectable given, though hypotheses apply well beyond the boundaries of inspectability, as the laws of physics do. *Second*, we hypothesize about states of affairs that are unobservable, as when technological incapacity prevented our seeing the other side of the moon. Intuitionists may respond that the moon's far side was imaginable by extrapolation from other round things, but this misses the point. Intuitionists are happy talking of the moon's hidden face only when they have an inspectable simulacrum for it. Hypothesis did not need that support to convince itself of the hidden side's reality, any more than it needs visible models of curved space. It is enough that we signify a possibility, where inspectability is not the necessary condition for either the possibility or its instantiation. *Third*, and most dramatic as a diagnostic test for the difference between these two methods, are the cases where hypotheses explain the *absence* of sensory data, e.g., the gluons binding hadrons within an atomic nucleus making them apparently inseparable, the light sucked into black holes. These are realities representable by hypotheses, though intuition could never acknowledge them. Intuition supposes that knowledge is achieved as we inspect the matters given, never because of inferring from something absent to the character of an otherwise unobservable state of affairs. Intuitionism is confounded. *Esse es percipi*, it says, though the dog which does not bark is as useful sometimes as the ones that do.

1B. Infallible Descriptions versus Fallible Descriptions and Abductions

Intuitionism is also faulty in this other way: It emphasizes description, requiring that explanation too should be only a kind of description, as explaining a lower-order sentence within a formalized system requires only that we specify its relation to some higher-order sentence. All of that might be set before an inspecting mind, as Descartes recommended in the *Rules*.[2] This and the other styles of intuitionist explanation described in Chapter 2 may remind us of the marvelous eyes in the pictures and busts of great philosophers, all of them a credit to our power for seeing the truth.

These wise men didn't need to speculate, because everything significant for reality was already set before their inspecting minds. Abductive explanation is speculative because many or most of the conditions for sensory data are not currently perceived, as none of them is ever inspectable. Does a tooth ache? Are the sums different each time we add the numbers? These are facts observed, facts provoking us to speculate about their conditions. We speculate about causes that might be sufficient to make these differences. We may even speculate about the conditions for phenomena when we have no current idea of a right answer, as we cannot determine just now why certain constants in nature should be as they are, e.g., the velocity of light. Abduction is, for all of these cases, an expression of our restlessness; we strain to locate ourselves within a comprehensible world.

We normally assume, under the intuitionist influence, but also because of the information available on the face of perception, that description is prior to explanation, and certainly prior to speculative, abductive explanations. This order is sometimes reversed. That happens when we review a previous description under the direction of a more discerning explanation. We look more carefully than before, searching for differences that were previously ignored. It also happens, sometimes, that the differences previously described and, *a fortiori*, perceived are made to lapse. This may happen when one theory is replaced by another, for then distinctions acknowledged by the first theory are obliterated by the one replacing it. We still see the occasional person having green eyes, though other distinctions observed by everyone demanding that witches be burnt are no longer observable to anyone. Intuitionism requires that descriptions should achieve a certain finality, as a clear and distinct idea is exactly seen and accurately reported. Hypothetical method allows that no description is exempt from revision.

1C. A Single, Infallible Inspection versus Repeated Fallible Observations

Intuitionists suppose that the truth of a claim may devolve exclusively upon our inspection of a single item within the given. Descartes is emblematic. He affirms "I am, I exist" on the basis of a single inspection, with discovery and confirmation occurring in the same moment. That the datum persisted, so that confirmation could be repeated, is incidental; the first report of Descrates' existence would not have been falsified had he been annihilated after the first instant of self-experience. Still, this example is odd, because of being a claim that something *is,* rather than a claim about *what* it is. There seem to be very few examples – I can think of none – where understanding advances more than a first step if it does not follow up the perception that something is with further claims about what it is. Descartes seems to have understood this qualm: He conflates the difference between *is* and *what*, wanting us to believe that all the truths about our nature are discovered in the moment when we confirm our existence, though our properties as thinkers are considerably more problematic than the discovery that we are. Still, the *cogito* is a paradigm for intuitionist method, as Descartes affirms existential and essential truths about a datum inspected in a single comprehending glance. There are, of course, other data for which intuitionists have claimed a single, exhaustive perception. Plato seems to have believed that *nous* apprehends the *is* and *what* of the Forms in a single, possibly sustained moment. It might also be said that we comprehend, in one sweeping inspection, all the logical geography of a word, or the axiomitized hypotheses and predictions of a science, though surely the likelihood of missing something important is increased as the subject is more complex.

This desire for a single, unchallengeable grasp of the thing inspected, expresses exactly the intuitionist belief that inspecting mind might possess its objects in a way that makes them permanently inalienable. This belief has two self-subverting consequences. First is the implication that nothing is worth knowing if it cannot be grasped in this conclusive way. Second is the discovery that many, most, or all of the things worth knowing elude this grasp because of showing less than all of themselves to inspection. Indeed, one motive for phenomenalism is the desire to reduce the range of things claimed for inspection to those grasped entirely, hence with finality.

Hypothetical method abjures every candidate for possession. So skeptical is it regarding this sort of finality as to require that every hypothesis be subject in principle to an infinity of tests, none of them definitive except the disconfirmations. This is the bias we should expect if sensory data are only the evidence of things about which we hypothesize, not the things themselves.

1D. The Role of Argument

Some intuitionists believe that argument is their principal achievement. Better a rigorous argument that makes a minor point, than a compelling idea undefended by an armada of clever arguments. This persuasion expresses the intuitionist taste for coherent structures, where all the articulations are seen to cohere. These are conditions for intuitionist certainty, as Descartes extols it. He marvels, in the *Rules*, at the self-evidence of each step within a deductive argument, and he regrets that we cannot comprehend all the steps of a long proof at once, enjoying thereby the self-evidence of a conclusion seen to be derived from its premises.[3] There is, of course, no evidence that Descartes treasured certainty for its own sake, or certainty about trivia.

There is no place for either of them in the requirements for abductive inference. Abduction mobilizes argument in support of explanation and description. Arguments for their own sake are arid and useless. We might as well settle for tautologies; they are, after all, perfect arguments. Abduction itself sometimes encourages this love of argument, as we forget the motive for explicating and testing a hypothesis, restricting ourselves instead to amplifying, formalizing, or defending it. Any one of these activities might absorb us altogether, diverting us from the matters represented, and the truth of our claims about them.

Those who prefer their arguments neat have forgotten the source and motive for our theorizing. It begins with an act of imagination. Discovering some anomaly within observed fact or theory, we retire into reflection, asking about the larger and currently unknown setting where this anomaly is remarked. Our hypothesis is a speculation about the circumstances that may prevail here. Our every subsequent step, including exposition and dialectic serves only to elaborate, confirm, or falsify this proposal. Argument is vital for justifying and testing a hypothesis, but argument without this impulse is void.

1E. The Attitude to Language

Intuitionists lapse easily into the vocabulary and grammar of their natural language as they describe content, or reflect upon the words and forms used to describe it. This is sometimes true even among the intuitionists who favor an "improved" language, for it may be ordinary language that is altered for the sake of clarity and logical form. Wittgenstein's remark, "The limits of my language are the limits of my world,"[4] helps to make this point. The only possible differentiations and orders of the world we inhabit are, he says, the ones rendered thinkable by the language used for talking about it. Where language is definitive of any experience we might have, it is a conceit, almost an impiety, to think that we might stand apart from language, changing it for some ulterior purpose.

Abduction renounces the idea that language might have some transcendental role in setting the horizons for every possible thought about the world. It denies, emphatically, that ordinary language might be the sacred and final authority about those differences which are thinkable. Instead, hypothesis promotes freedom and responsibility in the use of language, crediting us with the right to invent whatever words and grammar may be required for formulating or explicating our hypotheses. Certainly, we respect the laws of logic, and observe all the rules which facilitate expression and communication. But we are not in thrall to any rule except the principles of identity and non-contradiction, and their derivatives. We have made all the other rules, and we can change them, even when the wholesale substitution of a new language for the one currently in place is impractical.

The occasions for introducing new words, or even whole languages, are instructive. This happens when some part of mathematics is appropriated for scientific use. Its new grammar and interpretation rules may be quite different from those already accepted, but the new rules are learned by scientists who require them for explaining and describing some domain. Our use of them is legitimized by the success of our hypotheses, as they enable us to predict, mimic, control, or simply to represent and understand the pertinent phenomena. These are the theoretical terms that pass into ordinary speech, to be used uncritically by speakers who have little idea of their exact sense or the tests that secured their acceptance.

It is always possible that any set of theoretical terms may be superseded by the terms of a new and better hypothesis. What happens then to the old vocabulary as it endures in our dictionaries and speech habits?

Think of *nous*, *transcendental ego*, even *substance*. What do these words mean? What credit do they have, apart from the hypotheses in which they first appeared? We do use them, especially within philosophic discussions where the resort to traditional vocabulary is a respected practice. But these words do more than carry a useful nuance. They seem to designate entities or activities, so that ordinary language inherits both the words and the ontologies of discredited theories.

The relinquishing of old vocabularies is a cost we sometimes pay for new and successful hypotheses. Philosophy is slow to enter the cost because intuitionism is our habitual first strategy when addressing every issue. We reach for the words we know, not wanting to acknowledge that the theories from which the words derive may be too coarse-grained or false. This is nowhere more conspicuous than the philosophy of mind where the philosophic vocabulary of *belief, judgment, intentionality,* and *consciousness* is thought to define elemental differences. These are words that bend and restrict the claims of both ordinary language analysts and phenomenologists, as thinkers of both kinds start from the notion that mental lights are focused and directed within a self-enclosing amphitheater. Some ordinary language analysts fight the implications of these mentalistic words, arguing as behaviorists that the words need not be understood as typically they are. But whether endorsed or rejected, these words establish the conceptual setting in which philosophers persistently think about mind, even though there are other theories having different vocabularies, theories that would have us formulate our questions about mind in ways different from traditional ones. Rather than words endorsing the idea of conscious intentions and reflexivity, they favor a vocabulary that includes *information, schemas, association, matching,* and *problem-solving*. This is more than a dispute about alternative vocabularies, for the two sets of words are native to theories which represent mind and mental activity in radically different ways. The choice of vocabularies is, therefore, a choice between theories and their opposed claims about reality. Intuitionists prefer the words and theory they know best, though no philosopher would dare reflect upon the words of ancient physics in order to learn about motion. Intuitionism gambles that the parallel is imperfect, that we know our minds better than any science can, so that it is just as well if the traditional language of philosophical psychology ignores physiology and information theory.

Intuitionists who defend themselves by clinging to traditional language are only retreating into the storm cellar, not wanting to hear that our most familiar conceptualizations are founded within a mistaken, subjectivist idealism, and likely to be replaced by the language of a more comprehensive, physicalist theory of mind. There might sometime be an accommodation between old and new, with *belief, desire* and all the other familiar words reintroduced after their significations have been altered or extended. But if so, it will be the new theory, not the old intuitionist psychology, that prescribes the new meanings. Our appreciation for theory, and especially this one to be formulated, will have superseded the intuitionist adherence to a fundamental set of words expressing incontrovertible discoveries made within a self-intuiting mind.

There will, of course, be some intermediate stages. Suppose, for example, that no empirical theory is competent just now to replace the meanings of the old psychological vocabulary: *Self-consciousness* and *intentionality* are still the fixtures of our talk about mind. Suppose too that philosophy has satisfied itself that mind-body dualism is false in all its forms, and that mental activities can only be the behaviors of particular systems within brain and body. The result will be an intellectual community whose more general hypothesis, i.e., physicalism with regard to mind, is anomalous with the vocabulary signifying the finer-grain of mental life. *Intentionality* and *self-consciousness* will still mark the epicenters of our philosophic thinking, so that we are never free of their subjectivist implications though we repudiate the theory they express.

This is our current dilemma. Many of us do believe that mind-body dualism is false, or merely incoherent.[5] We speculate that there are physicalistic explanations for all of mental activity and development, though we do not have a vocabulary adequate for the wholesale reformulation of psychological notions. This is, we say, a transitional time when engineering and cognitive psychology are ahead of ordinary language. Yet, metaphysics is thought and written in ordinary language, so that the metaphysics of nature is hobbled by the enduring tendency to think about the world in terms of ordinary language. We shall sometimes have to think about mind while discounting the implications of the only words currently available to us, e.g., *intentional meaning*, finally inventing a vocabulary better suited to a better theory.

1F. Utility for Thought-directed Action

Intuitionism is useless as a method for directing action and practice. Inspecting mind discerns what is given or it imposes form upon content, thereby making experience intelligible and suitable for aesthetic contemplation. These are "transcendental" activities. They are not actions of the kind vital to theory. Theories will have to be confirmed. Speculating that river water is too cold for swimming, we may want to test it with a hand or foot. Even an abstracted concern for truth might be enough to provoke the experiment, but we shall have no choice if we are running from a bear or the law. These are actions carried on within the physical world. They test its character while achieving for us one or another accommodation within it.

Intuitionism cares nothing for these reality-testing behaviors, though it does sometimes want to appropriate and describe them in its own style, as we inspect the behaviors of our bodies when they are moved by thought and desire. I can, for example, regard my legs striding below me, all the while subject to my control while seeming to have a life of their own. Intuitionism wonders at the apparent independence of these motions while enjoying the control. It will not acknowledge that these behaviors are more than a sequence of appearances, that they are in fact probes of the things about us. We reach beyond ourselves to test or transform a world whose existence and character are independent of the fact that we think about and observe it. Intuitionism demurs. It has wanted to locate all of reality within us. It will not agree that we are merely participants within the world. Chided by common sense, encouraged to acknowledge the risks and opportunities in our circumstances, it draws the curtains of encircling consciousness, withdrawing into aesthetic inspection of the given.

1G. The Relation of Matters Known to the Inquirer

Intuition is necessarily singular and private, so that one inspecting mind can say nothing that would confirm the discoveries of any other. This is no less true whether the objects of inspection are Platonic Forms, the rules of ordinary language, or each thinker's own mind. Intuition alone could never establish that any of these inspectables are common to several minds. Intuitionists can only assume this commonality, as each of us checks his own discoveries, by comparing them to the reports of other thinkers. Do their words mean the same things as one's own? We cannot be sure.

Abduction never supposes that the objects signified by a hypothesis are peculiar to the mind of the one who proposes it. To the contrary, his hypothesis is meaningful because of signifying an eternal possibility, where possibles are independent both of theorizers and their hypotheses. There is the problem of coordination: How do I know that you and I are signifying the same possibility? Privacy and idiosyncratic usage is a problem. But it is less a problem than before, when all objects might be essentially private because of having no reality beyond the minds inspecting them. We solve the problem by coordinating our referents, as happens when the possibles are instantiated so that we have extra-mental, actual particulars for calibrating our different views of the world.

There might seem to be persistent problems in confirming that we do have common objects of speculation when the hypotheses at issue represent the internal states of a single person. But even here, the method of hypothesis is exempt from the isolating privacy of intuitionism. This is so because every state of affairs may have a diversity of effects; every hypothesis about this matter of fact may be confirmed by any of several kinds of observational evidence. The hypothesis about my toothache leaves me with special access to the evidence confirming it. But others can see the rotten tooth and swollen jaw. Where every state of affairs may have diverse effects, there is no hypothesis for which some one person might be, in principle, the only one able to testify for or against its truth.

1H. Justifying a Method

A method needs justification. We sometimes hope that a philosophic method might be self-certifying. Intuitionism promises to be a method of this sort, for it would have us say nothing that cannot be confirmed, either immediately by attention to the phenomena, or later as we reflect upon the rules or ideas mind uses as it differentiates and organizes the sensory given.

There are, however, two reasons for denying that our knowledge claims might be unconditionally true merely because we have reported the things inspected. *First* are the many theoretical claims confirmed circumstantially through a network of inferences, all of them fallible. There are numerous scientific claims of this sort, claims strong enough to support all of microphysics, though an intuitionist might repudiate all of them because theory overdescribes the confirming empirical evidence. *Second* are the many unacknowledged assumptions that intuitionists make as they promote the idea that mind might read philosophic truths off the face of the given. Is it sure that mind is a diaphanous medium where everything is visible and nothing is disguised? Are we convinced that all of reality reduces to the contents of this mind's sensorium, or to mind itself? This second consideration discredits the method altogether, as much for its idealism as for its merely dogmatic claim that every knowledge claim might be unconditioned and self-certifying. Having demanded that every judgment be irrefutable because certain, we have been willing to endorse a preposterous psychology and this crippled notion of reality. Finally rejecting the idea that knowledge claims should be certain, we abandon the method which promised that they would be.

Does hypothetical method have a more plausible justification? It does. We admit that a method's applications are conditioned, and that these conditions cannot be justified in the moment when the method is used to formulate or test a claim about some alleged matter of fact. There is nothing to equal the reflexive act of self-conscious mind as it certifies its own existence while inspecting some other thing. We also concede that the truth of hypotheses is not to be ascertained in the moment of formulating them, as "I am, I exist" is said to be confirmed. We loosen all of these requirements, because of wanting to advance from self-conscious mind into the world where body acts and lives. We do make mistakes; but we find and admit to them while proposing a different sort of justification for our method; i.e., that it provides understanding of ourselves and nature. How do we know that? By remarking our practical control, for we do accommodate ourselves to the world about us, securing and satisfying other people and ourselves within it. Our plans do work. Our maps do prove to be good representations of the possibilities instantiated here.

2. Why Intuitionism Survives

A pragmatism like mine is sometimes ridiculed for being crude. What else can we say of this vulgar emphasis on testability, with its origins in practice? The alternative is, presumably, a more refined aesthetic, with its promise that the good, the true, and the beautiful may be directly revealed to properly refined inspection. But then intuitionism barely conceals the self-satisfaction energizing its monadic reflection, and all the paraphernalia of its *a priori* assumptions. It foregoes abductive explanation, while proving itself worthless for directing action. This is the method of genteel reflection, but not at all the method whose use has been required to secure us as we affect this contemplative posture. Compare hypothesis. It supplies both explanations and the leading principles with which to accomplish our aims. Its own presuppositions, ontology, and psychology can be treated as hypotheses and tested. These are significant advantages. They justify the preference for hypothesis over intuition.

Why does intuitionism survive? Because perception is our insistent paradigm for understanding. Perception encourages the security we feel at having things we can see or touch. Inspection is reassuring in this same, almost palpable way. This is, furthermore, the easy route to categories and beliefs that are apparently viable. We have only to turn upon the rules or distinctions current in subject matters as close at hand as ordinary language or the rules and interests of one's culture, class, or gender. These subject matters, enforced by our way of knowing them, would seem to provide self-conviction and assured truths. These are rewards guaranteeing that intuition, not hypothesis, will always be the preferred method of most philosophic thinkers. That intuitionist conviction is bogus and its judgments superficial or false will not always deter us.

Science and practice manage to say many true things, without this passion for self-certifying answers. Perhaps philosophy too can forego them. Hypothesis requires a tolerance for error, and the confidence that we are safe and unembarrassed in a world whose character is not always apparent. It praises speculation, while committing us to an ontology of possibilities, only some of them instantiated. Yet all the while, it grounds our hypothetical reasoning in the urgency that we find our way in a world that is problematic or worse. Intuition has wanted to save us from error and anger by celebrating the delusion of a perfect autonomy. Abduction is, by comparison, a procedure for making do. We use it to achieve a more effective autonomy, acting within our circumstances so that we may secure and satisfy ourselves. Science is founded in the maps first made when plans are formulated. It extends these maps, moving past description to explanation, turning action in pursuit of self-interest into the experiments that test its hypotheses. Metaphysics makes use of this same method, applying it wherever possible in the same ways. There is no other method for discovering nature's categorial form and conditions.

3. Alternative Methods

Is there no third method, one superior to intuition and hypothesis too? There seem to be four alternatives, though each of them falls quickly to the one side or the other. Two are versions of intuitionism, the other two are hypothetical. Let us consider the four in this order: the analytic-synthetic method of Descartes and Locke, Kant's transcendental method, and two of Plato's methods.

Analysis-synthesis proceeds in the following way. It identifies certain elements, sometimes describing them as simples or axioms. It then constructs complexes from these elements, using imagined reconstruction or deduction. This is almost inevitably a version of intuitionism, as happens when the simples are clear and distinct ideas, or well-formed atomic sentences, both of them easily discerned. Equally, their relationships are inspectable, e.g., as reconstructions or deductions. These claims are explicit where Descartes describes the ideal case of an entire derivation seen at once, the resulting state of mind being certainty with self-evidence.[6] The intuitionism is also plain when Locke describes first the analysis of sensory experience as it culminates in the discovery of sensory elements, then the imagined recombination of these elements as it provides clarified surrogates for the normal objects of perception.[7] All three of the pertinent elements in both cases, namely the elements, rules of construction, and the complex formed by their application, are inspectable. Locke's "historical, plain method," like Descartes *more geometrico,* is an expression of the intuitionism we know already.

Kant's transcendental method is remarkable for being an example of hypothesis used in defense of intuition.[8] He uses hypothesis to locate the conditions making it possible for mind to have an inspectable experience. There are three points to consider. *First* is Kant's procedure. He argues from a characterization of experience to those conditions that must prevail if experience is to be truly characterizable in this way, i.e., it is unified. Notice that Kant's description of experience requires an explanatory hypothesis. Sensory data are atomic, he says, though experience as we find it is laced with relations. Something will have provided those relations; Kant's transcendental psychology is a hypothesis about what that something must be. *Second*, we see that the development of Kant's argument is typical of thought's progression as we think hypothetically. He begins with a question: How shall we explain the unity of experience? He answers with a hypothesis about the conditions for its unity, thereby inferring that unity would obtain if the hypothesis were correct. This is exactly the pattern we follow when seeing smoke coming from a window. Asking for an explanation, we hypothesize fire, then deduce that smoke is likely if there is a fire. *Third* is Kant's use of theoretical terms. He introduces the notions of "transcendental ego" and "forms of intuition" in order that he may specify the unifying conditions for experience. Why should we believe that these phrases signify real conditions for experience? Because, says the hypothesis, experience should be as we find it if these conditions do obtain. Never mind that Kant's hypothesis about mind's activity may be false, i.e., that we get the same experience if mind operates in some other way. It is only his use of the hypothetical method that is relevant here.

Finally, how shall we classify Plato's several methods? The direct apprehending of the Forms is, paradigmatically, intuitionism. His use of dialectic and myth is not.[9]

Dialectic requires that we should propose, and then criticize, a succession of claims about some topic. Each of our definitions exposes a little more of the issue, as we see more of the underlying picture in a children's game by lifting random pieces of the adhesive covering it. Dialectic is not so random; we learn to make a different or revised proposal on the basis of criticism directed at the ones previous. In the end, we should be able to propose a definition expressing all the virtues of all its antecedents, while telling very nearly what is essential to the subject at issue. Plato's dialectic is, in these respects, very much like Peirce's abduction. The search for definitions is a quest for those essential conditions that explain the otherwise disparate and seemingly unrelated expressions of the thing defined, e.g., justice or knowledge. There is also Plato's anticipation of Peirce's formula, i.e., we should ask about the empirical effects that would obtain if a proposed hypothesis were true. We have the intimation of this rule when Plato considers those behaviors that would count as just or unjust if one or another proposed definition were correct, e.g., as he rejects a definition which requires that we return a weapon to its demented owner. Dialectic is, in summary, the use of successive hypotheses under the controlling objective that we achieve a correct and comprehensive hypothesis about some matter at issue.

Plato resorts to myth as an intermediary step between dialectic and intuition. Dialectic exposes the complexity of an issue while pointing to a unitary vision which dialectic itself cannot supply, for we never do, or can, formulate the one unifying hypothesis that dialectic has promised. Instead, we are encouraged to find a unifying story by which to express the required idea. The allegory of the cave, the figure of the divided line, and the myth of Er are three instances where Plato expresses multidimensional and vastly complex ideas with great economy.

Myth has another advantage: It uses empirical language to signify matters of fact which are essentially unobservable. So, the allegory of the cave gives empirical expression to an ontological, epistemological, and moral progression, where only the first stages could be described literally by using empirical language. Myth is a powerful didactic tool for instructing the minds incapable of understanding anything not represented in figurative language. Yet, myth points beyond itself to a more complex reality than the one depicted by the mythico-empirical language. We discount that language at the moment when myth carries us beyond dialectic to the matters it prefigures. Intuition displaces myth as *nous* inspects the Forms. Everyone who is stalled short of that vision struggles with the mythic language, holding onto it even as he pushes away from it.

Myth too is an instance of hypothesis, for myth is a representation of things as they are, or may be. The only impediment to saying this is the mythic language: We forego the use of a technical vocabulary used literally for words having ordinary uses. The power of the metaphor depends upon using these words to tell a unified story construed at two levels: first, to say what the words ordinarily say; second, to represent a state of affairs which is structurally like the one represented by the ordinary sense of the words, but different ontologically. Nothing in this obscures the speculative, hypothetical use of myth, though we are reminded—and this should make us tremble – that the unitary hypotheses demanded of a systematic metaphysics may exceed our ability for telling a more literal story.

Should we conclude that intuition and hypothesis are the only two philosophic methods, each with its variant forms? That is apparently true, with one reservation. There are philosophers who use the two methods at once. The *Republic* shows Plato doing that: His book is a hypothesis about the conditions for the ideal state, with intuition to confirm the speculative claim that we know the Good. Philosophy does sometimes appear to be most powerful when it combines these two methods. Yet that very presumption to an elevated, comprehensive, and incorrigible view of things is our most subverting trait.

8

Facts Obscured by Values

Plato is so fundamental to philosophy that no one should be surprised to discover both intuition and hypothesis in him. More, Plato is, with Descartes, the example for all subsequent intuitionists, and also the author of the grandest hypothesis of all. There is nothing to equal the *Republic* for its combination of practical advice, psychology, ethics, social design, epistemology, ontology, and – crowning it all – his idea of the Good.[1] Every other speculative thinker measures himself, consciously or not, against the standard that Plato set, though no one dares to do as much.

The *Republic* is also, an inspiration and admonition in this other way. Like black holes postulated at the center of every galaxy, the energizers of their swirling motion, we inherit from Plato a center of gravity in the middle of our speculations. That vastly potent but invisible focus is the Good. Plato affirmed that value is the apogee of being, and the source for whatever is intelligible in all the rest of it. Too bad that Plato never managed to tell what the Good might be, apart from repeating that it is just the Good, or how it might have the effects he claims for it. Skeptical readers made two inferences: that the Good is not the cosmic source of every other thinkable difference, and that goodness or value does nevertheless have some important, if still unspecified, bearing on matters of fact. Why make this second inference? Partly because of the shadow cast by Plato's claim, partly because of suspecting that anything so important to our lives as value must also be decisive for matters of fact. Unable to confirm that this is so, we let value

223

retreat into the relative privacy of public life, then finally into the sanctuary of our private lives.

This retreat exactly parallels the recession of the Forms. Like the Good, the highest Form, they were to be cosmic exemplars for differences in being, so that every differentiation and relation could be traced to them. Philosophers demurred, finding it as difficult to believe in the other Forms as they had doubted the reality of the Good. The Forms too were reduced to socially sanctioned conceptual systems, or finally to each thinker's own projections of the differentiations and relations required for directing action or for making sensory data thinkable. Intelligibility, as much as value, was reduced to being a perspective on reality.

Remember now that the Good was to be the source of whatever is thinkable in all of being. What relation might there be in the correlation of private goods, to the thinkable orders projected by every thinker onto behavior or sensory data? Could it happen that each thinker's conceptual system is as much in thrall to his private good as Plato's Forms were to Plato's Good? This would imply that every thinker's hypotheses about the world are the expression of his values, not at all or only marginally the representations of things as they are, allegedly, in themselves. Isn't it more accurate, therefore, that hypotheses be described as sense-making, value-expressing interpretations? We have come full circle, catching ourselves at the end, as we did in the first pages of Chapter 1, having to justify the difference between hypotheses and interpretations.

How can we tell that a hypothesis representing some possible state of affairs has become an interpretation? We ask this question, Is the claim tested against reality, exposing it to disconfirmation? Or does the claim show its applicability to the world merely by prescribing the differentiations and orders credited to experience? If the former, this claim is a hypothesis; if the latter, it is an interpretation. What explains our persistence in using a conceptualization not tested against the world? The answer this time is only a surmise, for the condition we infer is the more or less acknowledged black hole at the center of our thinking: We use an interpretation, ignoring disconfirmations, if this sense-making framework is the expression of our values. Here are the Good and the Forms, both of them privatized, but one still dictating to the other.

Hypothetical method makes the problematic assumption that inquiry may be value-neutral, though doing this is naive, if we suppose that inquiry never could be morally or otherwise neutral. The obstacle dissolves if we make a simple distinction.

Every inquiry, from practice through science to metaphysics, is drenched in value. We are hungry but want to be fed; we care for the people whose illness we want to cure; competitors test their claims before we can test our own; we are vain and determined to justify ourselves. We are, however, clearheaded about our interest. Sand and stones won't feed us; quack medicine does not cure us. Hypotheses about the current state of the world are not an iota more likely to be true because of our interest in having them true. Thinking, we say, does not make it so, although we distinguish hypotheses representing matters of fact from the plans for changing them. Plans embody hypotheses about the terrain where the plans are to be enacted, and also hypotheses about those instrumental relations obtaining in the world. More, plans are directives, impelled by our values, for changing the world in ways that will secure and satisfy us.

The power of our valuings in shaping facts is, accordingly, minimized by these two differences: one between hypotheses and interpretations; another between the requirements for testing hypotheses and our interest in successful behavior. These are simple differences. Practice, itself, is the best evidence that we acknowledge these differences while acting upon them. Values may always distort our view of things. Error is always possible. But desire and interest can be discounted, and there are procedures for minimizing the risk of error, as we demand repeatable experiments made by scrupulous investigators.

Practice and science effectively defend themselves against these distractions. Metaphysics is more vulnerable than either of them, especially when competing metaphysical hypotheses are equally well confirmed by the same sensory data. Newton and Einstein predict different observables, but phenomenalism and physical object realism, or nominalism and realism with regard to universals predict the same empirical differences. We use additional criteria for deciding between these philosophic contraries, as we say that the true theory must be consistent, economical, systematic, plausible, applicable, and adequate. But these are values. Are we impaled again as these conceptual values determine our choice of "truths?"

Every regulative principle is a value in the limited respect that we value it as a directive or constraint upon inquiry. It does not follow that economy, for example, is valued in the way that seeking advantage for an individual or group interest is valued. Economy is justified by the repeated discovery that nature is simpler than our theories sometimes represent it as being. Their theoretical terms too often duplicate or overlap one another. The economy required of our theories is, we say, a demand justified by the discovered simplicity of nature. Using economy as a regulative principle within inquiry expresses this discovery. It also testifies that we are committed to the accurate representation of things. Economy is, therefore, no bias or interest of our own projected onto the acceptable representations of nature. The requirements for consistency, coherence, applicability, and adequacy are similarly founded in nature together with our determination that it be represented accurately.

Do fact and value nevertheless merge when hypotheses are tested in the interest of truth? Isn't truth a value? No, truth is the relation achieved when a hypothesis representing a possible state of affairs is satisfied by the actual state of affairs instantiating that possibility. We value having true hypotheses, but that does not make truth a value.

Our understanding of inquiry is enhanced, and our own prospects are improved, if we learn to reverse this introjection of the Platonic Good. Setting aside our values for a time, we discover within nature the values present there as consequential relations among actual states of affairs. These consequential values, as hot sun is good for corn, are ingredient within the facts. Only a preoccupation with ourselves has obscured these values to the advantage of our valuings. There are many viable accommodations that might be established between the values in and among things, and our concern for securing and satisfying ourselves.[2]

Metaphysics would have proved its worth if it made and confirmed no other claim about the world. But there is more. We are to formulate and test hypotheses about all of nature's categorial form and conditions, about all the aspects of our place in nature, and about the modes of being. There will always be errors, some that take hundreds of years to correct. That is awkward, but not disabling. It hasn't prevented us from learning many things about the world and ourselves, in practice, in science, and in metaphysics.

Notes

Introduction

1. David Weissman, *Intuition and Ideality* (Albany: State University of New York Press, 1987).

2. Ibid., 101–105.

3. Willard V. O. Quine, *Word and Object* (Cambridge: M.I.T. Press, 1967), p. 161.

4. Hans-Georg Gadamer, *Truth and Meaning* (New York: Crossroad, 1985), p. 401.

5. Ibid., 408.

6. Ibid., 415.

7. G. W. F. Hegel, *The Phenomenology of Mind*, trans. J. B. Baillie, (New York: Harper and Row, 1967), 514–15.

8. Ibid., 516.

9. Alfred North Whitehead, *Process and Reality* (New York: The Free Press, 1978), 5–6. Also see David Weissman, "The Spiral of Reflection," in *New Essays in Metaphysics*, ed. R. Neville (Albany: State University of New York Press, 1987), 297–300.

10. Whitehead, *Process and Reality*, 18.

11. Richard McKeon is a principal example. His views are reported in Walter Watson, *The Architectonics of Meaning* (Albany: State University of New York Press, 1985).

12. René Descartes, *Meditations,* in *René Descartes: The Essential Writings*, trans. J. Blom (New York: Harper and Row, 1977), 203.

13. Rudolf Carnap, "Empiricism, Semantics and Ontology," in *Semantics and the Philosophy of Language,* ed. L. Linsky (Urbana: University of Illinois Press, 1966), 218–21.

14. Plato, *Theatetus, The Collected Dialogues of Plato,* eds. E. Hamilton and H. Cairns (New York: Pantheon, 1964), 156E–157A, p. 861–62.

15. Ibid., 156D, p. 861.

16. C. S. Peirce, "The Fixation of Belief," *Collected Papers of Charles Sanders Peirce,* vol. 5, eds. C. Hartshorne and P. Weiss (Cambridge: Harvard University Press, 1965), pp. 223–247.

17. Weissman, *Intuition and Ideality,* 157–96.

18. David Weissman, *Eternal Possibilities,* (Carbondale: Southern Illinois University Press, 1977).

Chapter 1

1. Martin Heidegger, *Being and Time,* trans. J. Macquarrie and E. Robinson (New York: Harper and Row, 1962), 174.

2. Ibid., 98–99.

3. Ibid., 81–81.

4. C. S. Peirce, *Collected Papers of Charles Sanders Peirce,* vol. 5, 113–27.

5. David Weissman, *Dispositional Properties* (Carbondale: Southern Illinois University Press, 1965) 172 and 185–93; and "Dispositions as Geometrical-Structural Properties," *Review of Metaphysics,* 32 no. 2, (December 1978): 275–97.

6. David Hume, *A Treatise of Human Nature,* ed. L. A. Selby-Bigge and P. H. Nidditch (Oxford: Oxford University Press, 1978), 172.

7. John Stuart Mill, *On Liberty* (New York: Macmillan, 1987), 16.

8. John Stuart Mill, *Utilitarianism* (Indianapolis: Hackett, 1979), 4.

9. Immanuel Kant, *Critique of Pure Reason,* trans. N. Kemp Smith (New York: St. Martin's Press, 1965), 74–82.

10. Ludwig Wittgenstein, *Tractatus Logico-Philosophicus,* trans. D. F. Pears and B. F. McGuinness (New York: Humanities Press, 1963), para. 5.6, 195 para. 1, p. 7.

11. Ibid., para. 1.13, p. 7.

12. Ibid., para. 1.11, p. 7.

13. Weissman, *Eternal Possibilities,* 115–26, 145–49, and 154–61.

14. See, for example, Hans Reichenbach, *Philosophic Foundations of Quantum Mechanics* (Berkeley: University of California Press, 1944), 150–60; and Peter Gibbins, *Particles and Paradoxes* (Cambridge: Cambridge University Press, 1987), 137.

15. Weissman, *Eternal Possibilities,* 11–126.

16. Ibid., 110.

17. Kant, *Critique of Pure Reason,* 532–49.

Chapter 2

1. Plato, *Phaedo, The Collected Dialogues of Plato*, 66a–67b, p. 48–49.

2. Weissman, *Intuition and Ideality*, 164–65.

3. Descartes, *Meditations*, 196–97.

4. Ibid., 204.

5. Ibid., 200–201.

6. Edmund Husserl, *Cartesian Meditations*, trans. D. Cairns (The Hague: Martinus Nijhoff, 1970), 69.

7. Hume, *A Treatise of Human Nature*, 67.

8. Ibid., 251.

9. Husserl, *Cartesian Meditations*, 70–71.

10. Rudolf Carnap, *The Logical Structure of the World*, trans. R. A. George (Berkeley: University of California Press, 1967), 109.

11. Descartes, *Meditations*, 208, 206.

12. John Dewey, *Experience and Nature* (La Salle: Open Court, 1965), 138–71.

13. Ludwig Wittgenstein, *Philosophical Investigations*, trans. G. E. M. Anscombe (New York: Macmillan, 1966), paras. 1–21, pp. 1–10.

14. Hegel, *The Phenomenology of Mind*, 80.

15. Kant, *Critique of Pure Reason*, 180–87.

16. Carnap, "Empiricism, Semantics and Ontology," 218–21.

Chapter 3

1. Richard Rorty, *Philosophy and the Mirror of Nature* (Princeton: Princeton University Press, 1979), 389–94.

2. Whitehead, *Process and Reality*, 8.

3. Ibid., 16.

4. Ibid., 159.

5. Ibid., 157.

6. Ibid., 160.

7. Ibid., 18.

8. Hume, *A Treatise of Human Nature*, 1–274.

9. Ibid., 172.

10. Husserl, *Cartesian Meditations*, 77.

11. René Descartes, *Rules for the Direction of the Native Talents, René Descartes: The Essential Writings*, 37–41.

12. John Locke, *An Essay Concerning Human Understanding*, vol. 1, ed. A. C. Fraser (New York: Dover, 1959), 27.

13. Plato, *Republic, The Collected Dialogues of Plato*, 507c–511e, p. 744–47.

14. Whitehead, *Process and Reality*, 219–80.

15. Plato, *Republic*, 327a–354b, p. 576–605.

16. Willard V. O. Quine, "Two Dogmas of Empiricism," in *From a Logical Point of View* (New York: Harper and Row, 1961), 20–46.

17. Ibid., 43.

Chapter 4

1. Kant, *Critique of Pure Reason*, 65–91.

2. Ibid., 216–17.

3. Hume, *A Treatise of Human Nature*, 79.

4. Quentin Smith, "The Uncaused Beginning of the Universe," *Philosophy of Science*, 55 (March 1988): 39–57.

Chapter 5

1. Weissman, *Eternal Possibilities*, 109–111.

2. Ibid., 8, 109–110.

3. Willard V. O. Quine, "On What There Is," in *Semantics and the Philosophy of Language*, 191–92.

Chapter 6

1. Plato, *Apology, The Collected Works of Plato*, 24d, p. 10.

2. G. W. V. Leibniz, *Monadology, Monadology and Other Essays*, trans. P. and A. M. Schrecker (Indianapolis: Bobbs-Merrill, 1965), 149.

3. Wittgenstein, *Tractatus Logico-Philosophicus*, paras. 2.1–3, pp. 15–19.

4. Jerry Fodor, *The Language of Thought* (New York: Thomas Y. Crowell, 1975).

Chapter 7

1. Carnap, "Empiricism, Semantics and Ontology", 33.

2. Descartes, *Rules for the Direction of the Native Talents*, 37–41.

3. Ibid., 41–42.

4. Wittgenstein, *Tractatus Logico-Philosophicus*, para. 5.6, p. 115.

5. David Weissman, "Mental Structure," *Ratio*, 11, no. 1 (June 1969): 14–37.

6. Descartes, *Rules for the Direction of the Native Talents*, 42–43.

7. Locke, *An Essay Concerning Human Understanding*, vol. 2, 341–59.

8. Kant, *Critique of Pure Reason*, 22.

9. All of the dialogues illustrate Plato's use of dialectic. For the myths, see *Republic* 514a–516a, pp. 747–48 and 614b–21d, pp. 838–44.

Chapter 8

1. Plato, *Republic, The Collected Works of Plato*, 508c, p. 743.

2. See Paul W. Taylor, *Respect For Nature*, Princeton: Princeton University Press, 1986.

Index